A HISTORY OF
OF
STRATEGIC
BOMBING

By the same author:

The French Armies in the Seven Years' War
The French Forces in America, 1780–1783

With James L. Anderson:

The Gun in America: Origins of a National Dilemma

A HISTORY OF STRATEGIC BOMBING

LEE KENNETT

CHARLES SCRIBNER'S SONS
NEW YORK

For John

Copyright © 1982 Lee Kennett

Library of Congress Cataloging in Publication Data

Kennett, Lee B.
  A history of strategic bombing.

  Bibliography: p.
  Includes index.
  1. Bombing, Aerial—History.   2. World War, 1939–1945—Aerial
operations.   I. Title.
UG700.K46   1983   358.4′14′09   82-10673
ISBN 0-684-17781-1

1 3 5 7 9 11 13 15 17 19 F/C 20 18 16 14 12 10 8 6 4 2

Printed in the United States of America.

ACKNOWLEDGMENTS

A NUMBER OF PERSONS AND INSTITUTIONS helped to make this book possible. Most of the research was done in three great libraries: the Bibliothèque Nationale, the British Library, and the Library of Congress. Gen. Charles Christienne, head of the Service Historique de l'Armée de l'Air, offered his counsel and the bibliographical and photographic resources of his service. Professor Raimondo Luraghi of the University of Turin was of great assistance in providing information on aeronautical developments in Italy, while Dr. Jo. Chr. Allmayer-Beck, head of the Heeresgeschichtliches Museum, generously supplied data and photographs relating to Austria. The Stadtarchiv of Frankfurt am Main supplied photographs, as did the Library of Congress, the National Archives, the Defense Audiovisual Agency, and the National Air and Space Museum; to Claudia Oakes, associate curator at the museum, the author owes a special debt of gratitude. Professor Robin Higham of Kansas State University read the manuscript and made extremely valuable comments. Several colleagues at the University of Georgia gave generously of their time: Charles Wynes and John Haag read portions of the manuscript, Ronald Rader helped with texts in Russian, and James Buck translated Japanese materials. The final manuscript is a tribute to the clerical skills of Kathy Coley, Nancy Heaton, Ann Saye, and Janice Scarborough.

CONTENTS

vii

FOREWORD

"THE STRATEGIC AIR OFFENSIVE is a means of direct attack on the enemy state with the object of depriving it of the means or the will to continue the war." Some twenty years ago Sir Charles Webster and Noble Frankland offered this definition of strategic bombing, and it would be difficult to improve upon today. It clearly incorporates the sine qua non of the heavy bomber—its ability to pass over the obstacles offered by an enemy's armies and fleets and deliver a blow to its vitals. But it is not easy to take the definition further. Does a strategic bombing fleet contribute, albeit indirectly, to the struggle on land and sea? Does it open its own front in the war, or does it fight a war all its own? Just where are an enemy's vitals? Which is the more important target in that ambivalent phrase, "the means or the will"? Are attacks on the enemy's urban centers militarily sound? Are they morally justified? Or if they are militarily sound, are they justified ipso facto? Neither air power theorists nor air force generals have agreed on the answers to these questions, and the debates over them have been very much a part of the bomber's story.

If strategic bombing has been a controversial subject, it can also become an extremely technical one. Here I have tried to avoid adding needless complexities to what is after all a broad-stroke history intended for general readers. Finally, I have made a choice every historian must make when writing a book of this nature: I have chosen to place myself—and the reader—outside of the action, rather than in the middle of it. Some who read this book may regret that I did not take them through the darkened streets of London during the Blitz or send them over Germany inside a careening Lancaster bomber. But we can do more than simply know past events vicariously; we can understand them as well if we can see them and the men who participated in them in perspective, against the proper backdrop of time and place. In military history, then, the secret is to remain above the battle, yet not so far above it that the participants become faceless pawns. I leave it to the reader to determine if I have succeeded.

CHAPTER 1

A WEAPON
IS BORN

ON NOVEMBER 21, 1783, man turned a page in his history. On that day a crowd gathered at the outskirts of Paris to watch a physician and an army officer climb into the gondola of a hot-air balloon and become the first men to fly. To be sure, there had been some preliminary experiments earlier that year with the newly devised balloon: animals had been sent aloft and had returned no worse for wear, and men had already made a modest ascent in a carefully tethered balloon. But this was man's first free flight, and it was at once epochal and uneventful. The balloon rose gently to a height of about three thousand feet, drifted across the city, and then settled to earth again after being air-borne for about twenty-five minutes.

The first balloon flights caused a sensation throughout Europe. Ascensions multiplied, both in the hot-air Montgolfières and in the hydrogen-filled Charlières. The decade of the 1780s was in many ways a frivolous and jaded age, and it took the new "aerostatic machines" to its heart. Ascensions became as fashionable as costume balls, and so numerous that the Paris city authorities had to issue an ordinance governing their use—the world's first air traffic regulations. The distinctive form of the balloon lent itself to objects as diverse as chair backs and snuff boxes. Dr. Samuel Johnson regarded this "balloono-mania" as quite without justification. With the balloon man could now mount into the air, but that was all he could do: "The vehicles can

1

serve no use until we can guide them."[1] A full century would pass before the balloon became steerable, or, more properly, dirigible.

From the beginning, soldiers were intrigued by the balloon and what it might mean for the future of warfare. A French officer named Jean-Baptiste-Marie Meusnier proposed constructing an elongated balloon driven by propellers; his sketch, dating from 1785, looks remarkably like the zeppelins that made their appearance a century later. In England, military ballooning had a warm partisan in Maj. Gen. John Money. He was one of the first English aeronauts, making two ascensions in 1785. On one of his first flights an "improper current" blew him out over the English Channel, where his balloon went down and he spent seven hours treading water before a boat happened along to rescue him. Nothing daunted, Money continued his interest in balloons; in 1803 he published *A Short Treatise on the Use of Balloons,* in which he proposed that the British army adopt them as "observators." By that time the idea was no longer novel, for in 1794 the French revolutionary government had created a corps of balloonists, or *aérostiers,* who were to travel with the armies and serve as their eyes. The military balloons got some use, but authorities could not agree whether they were worth the considerable trouble involved in transporting and inflating them. After several years of trials the government decided to close down the service. The balloons were withdrawn and the *aérostiers* found themselves transferred to more conventional duties.

Here and there, reflective soldiers tried to see in the new devices something more than elevated observation posts. A writer in a German military review predicted that the first nation to occupy and control the air would be in a position to impose *Universal-monarchie,* which was the eighteenth century's way of saying global dominance. Some of the visions were ominous, revealing aerial weapons of awesome power. A Prussian lieutenant of engineers named J. C. G. Hayne was so impressed by the experiments in Paris that by January 1784 he had dashed off an entire book, the first lengthy work on military aeronautics. Hayne considered the balloon as a weapon and found it potentially a very powerful one. Balloons could undoubtedly be made to carry cannon, although Hayne was not quite sure how the guns would be accurately aimed or their recoil absorbed. Beyond a doubt, the balloon could be used to drop "grenades and other harmful things" on enemy troops and positions.[2] It could rain down fire and destruction on whole towns, with catastrophic results for the inhabitants. Some defenses might be possible: mortars could fire explosive charges at the balloons, while houses might fare better if they had armored roofs. But in the long run, Hayne felt this terrible danger would be removed another way. As the use of aerostatic machines for war became general and consequently a threat to all potential belligerents, the princes of his enlightened age would agree upon rules that would keep them from being instruments of terror and mass destruction.

Such enlightened self-interest and reasoned moderation in war were real enough when Hayne wrote, but they would soon disappear in the fierce wars of the French revolutionary era. The French revolutionaries were willing to go to unusual lengths to ensure the triumph of their cause, as they demonstrated during the Reign of Terror and in their use of that new invention the guillotine. And in that desperate year of 1793, when the Jacobin leadership had to face both foreign invasion and domestic insurrection, there was talk of using the balloon as a weapon of terror and mass destruction against the rebellious city of Toulon. The plan, if it can be called that, seems to have come from one of the inventive balloon pioneers—the Montgolfier brothers, Joseph Michel and Jacques Étienne—who proposed to transport over the city by aerostatic means some fourteen tons of explosives, which would then be dropped on the rebellious town and level it. How seriously this massive aerial bombardment was considered we do not know. In any event, Toulon soon succumbed to a conventional siege directed by a rising young officer named Napoleon Bonaparte.

The next time we hear of a terrifying air weapon, it is at the other end of Europe, and that episode too involved Napoleon. Sometime in the spring of 1812, when the emperor of the French was already marshaling his armies for the invasion of Russia, a German named Franz Leppig paid a visit to Czar Alexander I's diplomatic representative in Stuttgart. Leppig introduced himself as a "mechanic" and offered to construct for the Russian government a fleet of fifty dirigible balloons. The fleet could be built and ready for use within three months. Each airship would be capable of carrying forty men; more important, each craft would take aloft containers filled with gunpowder, and these could be rained down upon an enemy army "to bowl over entire squadrons."[3]

Alexander had a taste for the bizarre. He invited Leppig to Russia and set him to building his airships in a village outside Moscow. The czar's officials found three thousand yards of taffeta for the envelopes, or gas bags, and then rounded up a thousand Moscow prostitutes to sew them together. In accordance with Alexander's orders, Leppig worked in the deepest secrecy. He called himself Schmidt and told the workers, who were toiling away seventeen hours a day, that they were building agricultural machines. Despite these measures, news of the bizarre project leaked out; officers in Napoleon's entourage picked up and recorded in their diaries rumors of a gigantic balloon that would be sent to blow the Grand Army to pieces. By August 1812, when Napoleon's forces were already deep in Russia, Leppig had only just begun tests with a small version of his airship. If surviving pictures of it are accurate, the Leppig vessel resembled a fat, tailless fish. The envelope contained enough hydrogen to take the test model into the air, but the crude "wings" that were to propel it did not work satisfactorily. By this time, the French army was at the gates of Moscow, so Leppig and his balloons were hastily evacuated. The inventor and his creations took refuge in one town and then in another. Leppig continued his tests when he could, but without great success. A Russian official reported that the airship could rise only a few yards in the air and was incapable of making headway against the slightest breeze. Alexander grew impatient and had his artillery experts give their judgment on the project. They pronounced it hopeless. Leppig left Russia soon afterward, having spent 180,000 rubles of the czar's money. The governor of Moscow pronounced the whole scheme preposterous and called Leppig a charlatan. More recent judgments are not so harsh. The basic design of the craft was eminently sensible. Leppig's arrangement for attaching the elongated balloon to a rigid keel presaged by many decades the first semirigid airships. Where Leppig ran into trouble, as did many aerial "mechanics" who followed him, was in trying to govern the movements of the craft once it was airborne.

Even if man could not for the time being control the balloon's movement, he might still be able to use it as a weapon, provided nature cooperated with a favorable wind. This was the view put forward during the Mexican War of 1846–48 by a pioneer American aeronaut named John Wise. Wise suggested that tethered balloons bearing explosive charges could be sent aloft upwind of the Mexican-held Fort San Juan de Ulloa. The balloons would be reeled out until they were positioned over the fort and then would be made to rain their charges down on the Mexicans. This plan was never put into effect.

At the same time that the Mexican War was coming to an end, a cycle of violent revolutionary movements was sweeping over Europe. One of the major battlegrounds was Italy, where there was an uprising to throw off the yoke of the Austrian Hapsburgs. The Hapsburgs fought back and ultimately regained the upper hand. The fighting in Italy provided the first occasion during which a city was actually to be attacked with airborne bombs. The city was Venice, and the occasion was the siege that the Austrians mounted against it in the summer of 1849. The siege was not an easy one. Cholera and other diseases broke out among the Austrian troops, and in an effort to stem the contagion, the Austrians ordered the abandonment of several siege batteries in low-lying and swampy areas. The Austrian fleet had the port effectively blockaded, but its vessels drew too much water and therefore could not get close to the city. From the sea, as from the land, the besiegers were having difficulty bringing the city under the fire of their heavy guns. In June, Field Marshal Joseph Radetzky, commander of the Austrian forces in Italy, complained that the closest batteries were several thousand yards from the city. Radetzky had heard that the Austrian artillery had a new technique by which a city could be bombarded with projectiles borne by balloons. If there was such a weapon, now was the time to use it.

The technique Radetzky spoke of was the work of an Austrian lieutenant of artillery named Franz Uchatius, who had been conducting tests with it during the spring of 1849. The weapon consisted of a hot-air balloon carrying a bomb designed to explode on any sharp impact. The balloon was a small affair, eighteen feet in diameter and inexpensively made of linen and paper. The bomb was a pear-shaped container of cast iron filled with gunpowder. To use the Uchatius balloon bomb, the bombardier had first to study air currents and distances, take a position upwind of the target, and calculate the number of minutes it would take the balloon to drift over its objective. Then he would cut a requisite length of fuse, light it, and set the balloon free. The fuse ultimately reached and burned through the connection between balloon and bomb, releasing the latter. If the calcuations were accurate and the wind held, it was possible to release bombs over targets as far as four miles away.

Lieutenant Uchatius headed for Venice, carrying with him 14 of his balloons; an additional 110 were to follow shortly. Preliminary study told Uchatius that the balloons could not be sent over Venice from any land position. The devices would have to be released from shipboard, and for this purpose Uchatius installed himself and his apparatus on the paddle steamer *Vulkan*. On July 12, Uchatius released an unarmed test balloon from the deck of the *Vulkan* and then a fully armed one, which appeared to drop its bomb inside the city. Bad weather made it impossible to continue until July 15, when a second series went aloft. Then bad weather returned and obliged the Austrian fleet to weigh anchor and lift the blockade, thus ending the experiment. The exact number of balloons Uchatius released is not known, but the largest number given by any source is 200.

What was the practical effect of this first aerial bombardment of a city? The Austrian press spoke of its "frightful effects" and hinted that it would now be easy to reduce the Queen of the Adriatic to a pile of rubble. These reports were obviously quite far from the truth, for almost all the bombs seem to have dropped harmlessly into the water. An Italian writer claimed that only a single projectile had hit the city and that it exploded harmlessly on the Lido. The Venetians seem to have largely ignored the threat from the skies. (General Guglielmo Pepe, who left an account of his stay in the besieged city, barely mentioned the balloon bombs.) Most likely the defenders were preoccupied with more mundane problems, such as overcrowding, spoiled provisions, contaminated water, and an epidemic of cholera. Some versions of the bombardment say that the wind shifted, so that the balloons returned over the horrified Austrians; but an Austrian eyewitness does not mention this. He treated the whole matter as a minor experiment in which no one on the Austrian side placed any great hopes. But he added, "Many discoveries which we laugh at as childish and fantastic later vindicate themselves."[4]

After 1849 nothing further was heard of the Uchatius balloon bombs, although their inventor went on to become a general in the Austrian service. The military balloon resumed its traditional role of elevated observation post, following the armies in the Italian war of 1859, the American Civil War, and the Franco-Prussian War. This last conflict, more than any other, dramatized wartime ballooning when Paris was invested by the Prusso-German armies and obliged to communicate with the rest of the country by air. The frequent flights of these messenger balloons led the Prussian high command to request from the Krupp works a special gun that could be used to bring them down. The result was the *Ballonkanone* of 1870, perhaps the first antiaircraft cannon. It is curious, however, that neither the French nor the

Prussians used balloons as weapons during their bitterly fought war. The French dropped on their enemies nothing more dangerous than leaflets. There were schemes to unleash deadly "fulminating" balloons on the Prussians, but they came to nothing, perhaps because Paris itself would have been extremely vulnerable to such weapons if the Prussians had taken them up in turn.

After the Franco-Prussian War there was something of a resurgence of interest in ballooning. The 1880s saw the creation of balloon corps or "aerostatic sections"—usually attached to the corps of engineers—within the armies of most of the great powers. The late nineteenth century was a period of rapid overseas expansion, and colonial campaigns offered new and fertile fields for military ballooning. The British reported from South Africa that ascensions had a wonderful psychological effect on native populations, and the French sent a balloon detachment to Indochina in hopes that it would make a similar impression there. Here and there, inventors still labored to produce an effective air weapon, but their efforts yielded little beyond obscure and impractical devices such as the Rodeck "aerial torpedo" and Frederick A. Gower's "aerial batteries," which were refinements of Uchatius's idea. Gower urged his invention on the British War Office, insisting it would work wonders in the fighting then going on in the Sudan. One of the effects of his weapon was "to produce panic among masses of men," and Gower thought the Dervishes would be especially susceptible.[5]

Realistically, the prospects were not bright for any of these devices, concluded the German authority H. W. L. Moedebeck in a survey of military ballooning that he wrote in 1886. A century after its discovery, the balloon's offensive capacities were almost nil. At best it could be used against a city under siege, where the charges it hurled down would undermine the morale of the inhabitants, for "it undoubtedly produces a depressing effect to have things dropped on one from above."[6] The notion that aerial bombardment somehow placed a special emotional strain on those subjected to it was already well established; it would become more prominent when an effective air weapon appeared.

For the moment there was no air weapon, and Moedebeck and the other experts were not overly sanguine. But by the 1880s the reasonably informed European had no doubt that powerful air vessels would soon be cruising the skies at will. Popularizers of science saw them in the future and described them to their readers. And if science had not yet produced an airworthy ship, writers of science fiction and futuristic novels had launched several. Jules Verne introduced his readers to air power in *Clipper of the Clouds* (1873). Robur, the hero of the tale, dashed from continent to continent in a well-armed *aéronef*. But the *aéronef* was like Verne's fabulous submarine, the *Nautilus:* while it had a potential for combat, it was not solely intended for that purpose. In Albert Robida's *War in the Twentieth Century* (1883), the aerial war fleet appeared in all its power. Robida described a war that breaks out in April 1975 between Mozambique and Australia. The Australians begin the war with a surprise air attack, using a fleet of six hundred war balloons armored with gutta-percha and firing torpedo rockets that carried devastating two-gram charges of "superdynamite." H. G. Wells would later exploit this idea in his *War in the Air* (1908), which opened with a sudden, massive raid on New York by a German air fleet.

The popular literature of the late nineteenth century, because of its scientific and futuristic elements, had more than a casual relationship to the dawn of air power and, more particularly, to perceptions of that power. This sort of literature not only bred in its readers a faith in science and the inevitability of "progress," but it also created a kind of anticipation. When the armed airship did finally appear, it was already familiar to the popular mind. Not only was the weapon expected, but its role and functions had already been envisioned. The idea of the sudden, overwhelming air strike at the outset of a war appears first in the novels of Robida and Wells and then in the strategic thought of Giulio Douhet of the Italian air service. The general phenomenon of anticipation was at work with other weapons—the submarine, the tank, and disabling gases, for example. Indeed, the popular mind conceived of several weapons that military technology was not able to perfect, chief among them the fabled death ray. But somehow it was the realm of the air that lent itself most readily to prognostication and speculation. Here a certain "fantasy factor" operated, so that when airships and airplanes appeared, extravagant and impossible things would sometimes be expected of them.

The 1880s produced several breakthroughs in the direction of powered flight. In 1884 two captains in the French army, Charles Renard and Arthur Krebs, built a cigar-shaped balloon and suspended from it a sparlike structure to carry a crew, with a motor-driven propeller.

On August 9 of that year the *France,* as they called their ship, took off, successfully followed a course 4.2 miles long, and then returned to its starting point. The *France* had one major flaw, which severely limited its development. Its propeller was driven by an electric motor that required a half ton of batteries for a powered flight of under two hours. An alternative lay in the internal combustion engine, which was then being developed. Renard and Krebs were not able to marry the new power plant to the dirigible balloon, but others soon would. In 1886, Count Ferdinand von Zeppelin began to catalog in his diary the military uses of the dirigible he planned to build. In 1893, feeling close to his goal, he wrote the chief of staff of the German Army that his craft would be able to carry out reconnaissance, transport personnel and military supplies, and "bombard enemy fortifications and troop formations with projectiles."[7]

As the 1890s drew to a close there were further advances. Knowledgeable people sensed that when they crossed the threshold into the new century they would also be entering the air age. Ivan S. Bliokh, a Polish lawyer and writer, as well as one of the most perceptive men of the era, published in 1898 a vast treatise on warfare. To him the military implications of the coming conquest of the air were ominous. He foresaw that airships would very soon be dropping explosive charges, adding a new dimension to warfare: "It seems that we are very close to facing a danger to which our world cannot remain indifferent."[8]

Statesmen as well were beginning to show concern over the rapid growth of all kinds of armaments. During the same year that Bliokh wrote his treatise, Czar Nicholas II issued a call for an international conference to promote peace and regulate armaments and warfare. A large number of nations responded, and all of the great powers were represented at the international conference assembled at The Hague in 1899. In matters of land and naval warfare, the delegates found a great number of precedents and traditions to guide them, but when they turned their attention to war in the air, they found themselves in a field where there was neither law nor custom. The only precedents concerned observation balloons and the status of persons who manned them. When the French used the first balloons in battle, enemy generals vowed to hang the aerial observers as spies if they fell into their hands. During the Franco-Prussian War, Germany's Chancellor Otto von Bismarck threatened to do the same thing. After the war the issue was decided at a conference held in Brussels. An enemy balloonist could be summoned to descend and fired upon if he did not. If captured, he was classified as an "officer of observation" and treated as a prisoner of war. Beyond this there were no rules for war in the air.

In the circular that they issued in advance of the Hague conference, the Russians called for "prohibition of the discharge of any kind of projectile or explosive from balloons or by similar means."[9] The Russians meant the ban to be permanent, but they did not have their way. An American delegate, Capt. William R. Crozier, proposed instead that the prohibition be for a period of five years, reasoning that although the balloon as it existed in 1899 was a plaything of the winds and thus could only scatter its bombs indiscriminately, it was possible that the near future would see airships that could intervene precisely on the battlefield. If aerial bombardment could help decide the battle more quickly, it would produce shorter campaigns and wars and thus benefit humanity in general. The five-year ban was duly adopted.

It was not until 1907, three years after the ban expired, that the second Hague conference assembled. In the intervening years the technology of flight had made impressive strides. Wilbur and Orville Wright had taken a heavier-than-air machine aloft in 1903; but more important in the short term, Germany, France, and Italy were well on the road to perfecting dirigibles that could be used for military purposes. In 1903 the brothers Paul and Pierre Lebaudy produced a successful dirigible, which the French Army purchased two years later. Toward the end of 1905, the ship had successfully dropped projectiles, and the French government was sufficiently satisfied with the results of its tests to order a second Lebaudy airship in 1906.

At the 1907 Hague conference there were more calls for a permanent ban on aerial bombardment, but they were no more successful than before. In the end another temporary ban was proposed, but the French delegation opposed even this measure. The French argued that it was much more sensible to restrict bombing to legitimate military targets than to try to prohibit it altogether. They suggested that the Hague agreements on land warfare, which prohibited the bombardment of open or undefended cities, could simply be extended to cover aerial bombardments. Accordingly, article 25 of the Convention on Land Warfare was changed to read, "It is forbidden to attack or bombard by any means whatsoever, towns, villages, dwellings or buildings that are not defended."[10] This attempt to make one type of warfare conform to the rules of another was not entirely successful. For example, article 24 provided that the attackers should give the city a chance to surrender before opening their bombardment, but how could a parley possibly be carried on through the air? What if an open town contained a legitimate military objective, say an arsenal? In land warfare the army could simply march into the town and take possession of the facility; an air force could not. Some students of the laws of war believed that in this case the aircraft should follow the rule laid down for naval bombardment: an attacking fleet could bombard a military installation in an undefended city so long as it took due care to direct its fire at the legitimate target and no other. These rather imprecise regulations were the only ones to obtain a sizable number of ratifications; the ban on bombing was rejected by most of the great powers.

In the years following the second Hague conference the powers began to extend their arms race into the air. In October 1907, Kaiser Wilhelm II confided to his ministers that he was concerned about the semirigid airship *La Patrie,* recently acquired by the French Army. Reports of its performance indicated that it could penetrate 90 miles into German territory, operating at an altitude of about three thousand feet. While the airship was intended primarily for reconnaissance, the French had been experimenting with aerial bombing for some time, and their opposition to a ban on such bombing was disturbing to the Germans. The German artillery intensified its research into high-angle fire against moving objects, while the Krupp engineers set to work devising an aerial "torpedo" to use against intruders into German airspace.

When Germany enthusiastically adopted the zeppelin in 1908, there was considerable concern on the other side of the Rhine—especially when a zeppelin base opened at Metz, uncomfortably close to the French frontier and only a short flight from Paris. French ordnance facilities began the development of incendiary fléchettes to use against the zeppelin. As a further countermeasure, in September 1909 the French Army purchased five airplanes at one blow; within a year it placed orders for a hundred more. The Germans in turn began buying planes in 1910, so that the arms race spread to heavier-than-air craft. Nor was the rivalry in the air limited to the French and the Germans. Italy acquired its first dirigible in 1908 and its first airplane (a Wright) a year later. Its building program for 1910 called for nine dirigibles and ten planes. The British government and public followed these developments closely, partly because the country was far behind in this particular race and partly because the new weapons posed an unparalleled threat to its traditional position of isolation. In 1909, Sir Hiram Maxim pronounced Germany's growing force of zeppelins "a serious menace." They might strike at the very outset of a war, crippling the British home fleet while it rode at anchor and thus leading the way to a German invasion.[11]

The preoccupation with what could already be called the air menace showed itself quite clearly in the course of an international conference on aviation called by the French government in 1910. For some years jurists and aviators had discussed in rather academic fashion the question of airspace. Did the national boundaries extend vertically, so that all which lay above a nation was in its jurisdiction, or was the air, like the sea, open to all? The French jurist Paul Fauchille had suggested that national sovereignty might extend a certain distance upward, much as it extended over territorial waters. The aviator Ferdinand Ferber, who proclaimed himself a champion of "the freedom of the atmosphere," suggested that a commission of savants fix the height of the national territorial air zone; he himself felt that above fifteen hundred feet the skies should be open to all.

When Louis Blériot became the first to fly across the English Channel in 1909, the question could no longer be treated casually; accordingly, it came up at the Paris meeting. Almost immediately it became clear that freedom of the airways was not acceptable to many delegations. The British were most outspoken in laying claim to absolute control of their airspace; the French and German governments took more moderate positions. The conference adjourned without agreement, leaving the various nations to resolve the problem by statute or bilateral agreements. Great Britain asserted exclusive control of its airspace with the Aerial Navigation Act of 1911, made even more stringent in 1913. The French and German governments agreed that the military aircraft of the one could enter the airspace of the other only by invitation. The czar closed Russia to foreign flights with a decree that threatened foreign interlopers with prison terms.

In 1911 aerial warfare became a reality, for in that year fighting broke out between Italy and Turkey, and the Italians sent airplanes and dirigibles to the main seat of the war in Libya. By modern standards, the war offered a very limited test of air power: the Italians sent to Libya only two dirigibles and nine planes; the Turks had no air strength at all when the conflict began, and although they tried to obtain both planes and pilots, the war ended before they could get them into battle. But the fragile Blériots and Taubes that flew off the Libyan desert did inaugurate air operations with a number of "firsts" to their credit, including the first radio transmission from a ground station to an airplane. Guglielmo Marconi was there in person to conduct the experiment. Capt. Carlo Piazza flew the first mission in a brief reconnaissance over enemy lines on October 23, 1911; then, on November 1, Lt. Giulio Gavotti flew the first bombing mission, dropping one small projectile on Ain Zara and three more on the oasis of Taguira. This event did not go unnoticed. The next day the *Gazzetta del Popolo* proclaimed in its headline: AVIATOR LT. GAVOTTI THROWS BOMB ON ENEMY CAMP. TERRORIZED TURKS SCATTER UPON UNEXPECTED CELESTIAL ASSAULT. Elsewhere in Europe, newspapers also carried the story. Once begun, the bombing continued apace. On May 8, 1912, the Italian airmen carried out the first night bombing raid. Since the airplane had no lights on its instrument panel the pilot wore an electric lamp attached to his helmet.

It was March 1912 before the Italian dirigibles were able to begin operations. There were many difficulties, and the violent winds blew down their hangars more than once. Although the airships had the skies to themselves and Turkish antiaircraft artillery was almost non-existent, the Turkish infantry proved a surprisingly dangerous foe. The dirigibles found it difficult to go higher than a thousand yards, and at that altitude they were within the range of the Turkish soldiers' Mausers. The Turks were poor shots but enthusiastic ones. The very volume of fire almost guaranteed that a few bullets would pierce the envelope. The dirigibles' engines made such a clatter that crewmen could not hear the sound of the rifle fire. They had to monitor their gauges very carefully; a drop in hydrogen pressure was the first sign that they had been hit. The crews spent a good bit of time between missions patching bullet holes.

The bombing done by the Italian airplanes could hardly have been much more than a gesture, for the bombs themselves were very small and the planes could carry few of them. Old photographs show that the aviators often suspended a pair of bombs around their necks with a cord. The first projectiles thrown were Cipelli bombs, which were round, rather larger than an orange, and about two kilos in weight. The pilot-bombardier simply tossed the bomb over the side after having pulled the pin with his teeth. In theory, the dirigibles could do more serious bombing, since they could take aloft a sizable payload and use much larger bombs, usually adapted from artillery and mortar shells. In all, the airships flew 127 missions and released 330 bombs (about 10 of them incendiaries).

The results of the first aerial bombing operations must be deduced from highly contradictory sources. Italian general-staff reports rated the material damage as modest, but the psychological effect as significant. Bombardment from the air "dampened the enemy's ardor." Press communiqués showed that the new weapon had exceeded expectations in material damage as well as mental stress imposed on the Turks. Italian newspapers were generally enthusiastic; Prince Ludovico Potenziani told the Aero-Club d'Italia that their country had "conquered for herself the distinction" of being first to use the airplane and the dirigible in war.[12]

Outside of Italy there were conflicting judgments. An English reporter in the Turkish camp described air bombing as a terrible means of destruction that would revolutionize warfare, while a correspondent from the *Berliner Tageblatt* filed a story describing the offensive power of the airship and the airplane as almost nil. The latter view was shared by a French officer named Marzac who was in Libya as an observer. In his confidential report to the French Ministry of War, Marzac said he was present when an Italian dirigible released twenty-nine bombs on a Turkish camp containing eight thousand men. The bombs produced no casualties and no damage. Many of the projectiles sank into the sand without exploding; those that did detonate produced a small, harmless blast. Marzac added that the Turks were not in the least frightened by aerial bombardment.

The war in Libya ended in October 1912; by then another conflict was convulsing the smaller nations of southeastern Europe. The Balkan wars of 1912–13 were watched with considerable interest in the capitals of Europe, partly because the belligerents had obtained their war matériel from one or another of the great powers, who were anxious to see how their arms and equipment performed in war. None of the Balkan countries had an air force worthy of the name when war broke out, but most of them sought both planes and pilots. They recruited many of their pilots in western Europe and bought their planes on the secondhand market. A French aviator who flew for the Bulgarians found that most of the craft in the hastily assembled Bulgarian Air Force were incapable of flying. Here, as in Libya, some of the pilots dropped bombs, but usually only incidentally to their main mission of observation. French pilots generally refused to do any bombing, although their employers pressed them to do so. As one of the pilots explained, "We had agreed to fly with or without an observer, but not to become active belligerents and kill people against whom we had absolutely no resentment." The same pilot described the few bombs he saw dropped as "of a minimal effect, absolutely worthless against fortifications and scarcely dangerous for troops in dispersed order."[13] A British pilot named Headley, who dropped bombs for the Bulgarians, described their effect as chiefly psychological, an observation now familiar to us.

There was one other occasion for aerial bombardment before 1914, although it did not attract very much attention; this was in French Morocco, where French authority was being challenged by rebel bands. Early in 1912 the Ministry of War sent a six-plane escadrille there for use in reconnaissance and communications. The planes carried out these tasks well enough, but their pilots asked for machine guns to defend themselves if forced down and for bombs to use on targets they might encounter. The Ministry of War honored the latter request, contracting with a Danish inventor named Aasen, who was trying to sell aerial bombs he had perfected. The French authorities tested the small bombs and found them satisfactory. They ordered several hundred and sent a number to Morocco (the remainder would be dropped on the advancing German armies in 1914). French pilots in Morocco reported modest successes with their new weapon, although their bombing objectives were not those approved by the Hague convention. The aerial operations in Morocco were the first in colonial areas, and they gave a clear indication of the harsh character of this type of warfare, the purpose of which was to teach severe lessons, the only kind that seemed likely to impress a hardy, warlike people. French pilots bombed villages and markets and even tried to hit flocks. They used the incendiary fléchettes that had been developed to bring down zeppelins, for they found them useful in setting fire to grain fields.

While the airplane was still getting its first trials in war, it won a place for itself in the military establishments of Europe. In 1910 the air fleets of Germany, Austria-Hungary, Great Britain, France, and Russia contained some fifty airplanes in all; four years later, on the eve of World War I, the five powers had available for service a total of over seven hundred. In some countries appropriations for military aeronautics increased tenfold in that same period. By no stretch of the imagination could the airplane and the dirigible be said to have proved themselves in the obscure wars that preceded the world conflict of 1914–18. Why, then, did the military establishments hasten to add them in such numbers? Many military leaders were unsure exactly how they could use the new weapons; others probably accepted them against their better judgment. Giulio Douhet, who was the head of the Italian air service just before the war, claimed that the leadership of the Italian Army had absolutely no use for flying machines, but that it acquired a few as a sop to public opinion. It seems quite clear that the French Navy was interested in nothing more than a few balloons which, it thought, might be useful for detecting submarines; but it acquired airplanes as well, because members of the Chamber of Deputies felt it should have them and wrote them into the navy budget. A British newspaper launched a public subscription to present to the War Office—with great fanfare—a secondhand French dirigible that France did not want; the War Office then had to explain to indignant members of Parliament why it kept the deflated ship locked in a shed in Wormwood Scrubs.

In 1914 it was fashionable in pacifist circles to hint that the rapid growth of military aeronautics was essentially the work of aircraft manufacturers anxious to cut for themselves a larger slice of the armaments pie. Although recent studies argue that this may have been true, the larger truth is that military aeronautics was promoted by a broad spectrum of interests and from a wide range of motives. In almost every country, there were air-minded politicians and editors eager to lead crusades for aerial preparedness. There were soldiers intrigued by the possibilities of the new weapon and practical, patriotic industrialists like the brothers André and Édouard Michelin, who established an aerial bombing competition to find out if the bomber could be perfected. There was an international coterie of the wealthy and prominent—led by princes and grand dukes—who had taken to flying and become its propagandists. But masses of ordinary people were also fascinated by flight and wanted to give their country wings. When Count Zeppelin's pioneering airship was destroyed after a record-making flight in August 1908, the German people in a massive and spontaneous campaign gave the count 7 million marks with which to build another ship. When the Aero Club of Padua proposed early in 1912 a national subscription to buy the government a hundred airplanes, the outpouring was overwhelming. Italian schoolchildren donated 180,000 lire and Italians living abroad sent in 740,000 lire. The target was 2 million lire, but the total received exceeded 3.5 million—far more money than the aeronautical service needed or could use effectively.

What would the impact of these new weapons be in the event of a general European conflict? Serious students of the art of war were already at work seeking the answer to this question; their conclusions, tentative and theoretical, were hidden away in obscure technical journals. Within the flying fraternity there were prophets who spoke of an air war that would be at once apocalyptic and grandiose. In 1913 a French aviator named Pol Timonier shared his vision in a popular book with an arresting title: *How We Are Going to Torpedo Berlin with Our Squadron of Airplanes as Soon as the War Begins.* Timonier's scenario was as follows: twenty German dirigibles bearing upward of 132,000 pounds of explosives would strike at Paris and decimate its population "amidst indescribable horrors"; immediately afterward a vast swarm of French airplanes would retaliate, smothering Berlin under a deadly rain of 1,360 "torpedoes," winning the war then and there.[14] No one in 1913 could really know how accurate Timonier's scenario might be. As it turned out, he was partly right. Zeppelins did attack Paris, and by postwar computation the city was hit by some 154,000 pounds of explosives. Paris survived almost unscarred; as for Berlin, not a single bomb fell on the city during the four years of World War I.

CHAPTER 2

THE GREAT WAR

ON THE EVENING OF AUGUST 3, 1914, the German ambassador to France arrived at the Quai d'Orsay with a brief but momentous message from his government—a declaration of war. Armies were already marching in eastern Europe; Ambassador Wilhelm von Schoen's communication would set them in motion in the west as well. The message began with a list of provocative acts perpetrated by the French—and cited the bombardment of Nuremberg by a French plane the day before.

The "bombing" of Nuremberg long remained something of a mystery. The French always vigorously denied the charge and pointed out with inescapable logic that Nuremberg was deep inside Germany, so far from the French frontier that it was beyond the range of any aircraft then in French service. And since, on close examination, no one could find any hard evidence that the city was bombed, it was understandable for the Allies to assume that the whole episode was a piece of German prevarication. It is clear today that the diplomatic importance of the Nuremberg affair was nil. World War I would have broken out in any case, since by August 3 the German government had decided on war from motives of national policy. The Nuremberg bombing was a handy pretext, but another might have served as well.

Still, the Nuremberg affair is not without interest. First, it was not a conscious invention of the German general staff, which actually did receive reports of the bombing. These came from the Third Bavarian

Sole Survivor of the World's First Air Fleet. This balloon, named *Hercule,* was one of several used by the French Army at the end of the eighteenth century. The Austrians captured it in 1796, and it is currently on display at the Heeresgeschichtliches Museum in Vienna. *Courtesy the Heeresgeschichtliches Museum, Vienna*

The Bombing of Venice. This first aerial bombardment was carried out by Austrian forces in the summer of 1849. By most accounts the bombardment was a failure. *Courtesy the Heeresgeschichtliches Museum, Vienna*

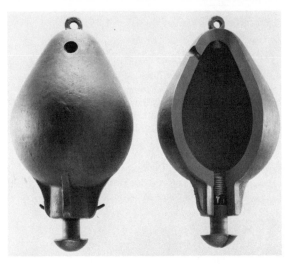

The First Aerial Bombs. These bombs were designed by the Austrian artillery officer Franz Uchatius and were used in the siege of Venice. They were of cast iron, in several sizes up to 40 pounds in weight, and designed to explode on impact. *Courtesy the Heeresgeschichtliches Museum, Vienna*

The Dirigible *La France*. This French airship of 1884 was an important breakthrough for military aeronautics; its chief handicap was its electric motor, which required a half ton of batteries. *Courtesy the Service Historique de l'Armée de l'Air*

Sixteen Men and a Dog. These were the passengers that Igor Sikorsky took aloft in his four-engined Ilya Murometz early in 1914. The extraordinary range and lifting capacity of this craft gave Russia a bomber for strategic operations at the outset of the war. *Courtesy the National Air and Space Museum, Smithsonian Institution*

Bombing, 1914 Style. At the beginning of World War I, aerial bombing was a matter of makeshiftness and personal initiative, as this German aviator demonstrates. *Courtesy the National Archives*

The First French Bombers. The Voisin pusher plane could carry several bombs and offered the bombardier an excellent view. This photograph was taken in 1915. *Courtesy the Service Historique de l'Armée de l'Air*

The Voisin Pusher. This design of 1914 was adopted by French bombing squadrons early in the war. It could carry several bombs and afforded the bombardier fine visibility. *Courtesy the Service Historique de l'Armée de l'Air*

Breguet 14 B2 Bombers. This plane became the standard day bomber of the French air service in 1917; it remained in use for another decade. *Courtesy the Service historique de l'Armée de l'Air*

The Bomber's Stock in Trade, 1915. By the second year of the war the French air service had developed a considerable panoply of bombs. The boxes on the bench contain hundreds of fléchettes, or steel darts. *Courtesy the Service Historique de l'Armée de l'Air*

Bombing Up. Transporting a 440-pound bomb on a French airfield during World War I. *Courtesy the Service Historique de l'Armée de l'Air*

The Bombs Grew Ever Larger. A German plane dropped this 660-pound bomb on the French town of Frouard early in 1918. *Courtesy the Service Historique de l'Armée de l'Air*

Maurice Farmann Bomber. This plane has been modified in order to carry a large bomb made from a 120mm shell. The bomb is visible behind the pilot. *Courtesy the Service Historique de l'Armée de l'Air*

Caudron C.23 BN2. This heavy bomber reached French squadrons just as World War I came to an end. *Courtesy the Service Historique de l'Armée de l'Air*

The Airship Was Vulnerable in War. Through combat and through accidents many of the great ships were lost during World War I. The wreckage of this zeppelin attracted great crowds in France. The photograph belonged to Billy Mitchell and may have been taken by him. *Courtesy the Library of Congress*

Army Corps, which relayed them in good faith. The reports derived from nothing more than simple rumor, which spread rapidly among a population already on edge. At the outbreak of the war there were alarums and excursions of this kind all over Europe. There was an erroneous report of a German zeppelin attack on England, which interrupted the Royal Flying Corps's (RFC) movement to France—but then, inhabitants of English Channel towns had for years been claiming to have seen zeppelins and twice the presence of zeppelins had been signaled in as unlikely a place as Cardiff. Late in July, German newspapers published garbled accounts of the shooting down of zeppelin Z-4 by the Russians; they later retracted the story.

The populations of Europe were particularly predisposed to accept stories of this kind, for in the years before the war, they had become sensitive to the menace of the airplane and, more particularly, to that of the airship. The reading, thinking element in the population knew something of the potential of air power, while the less well informed had read or at least heard the doomsday prophesies of the sensationalist press. At the outbreak of the war the Parisian daily *Figaro* warned inhabitants of the city that night zeppelin attacks were quite likely, although French pilots charged with intercepting them had sworn to ram the dirigibles if necessary. The *Times* of London consoled its readers with the thought that the larger the bombs dropped on the city, the fewer they would be in number.

No one placed great faith in the protection offered by the Hague agreements. The World Peace Foundation reported in 1914 that Great Britain was the only major belligerent that had ratified the ban on airborne projectiles: consequently the ban was inoperative and aerial bombardments were quite legal, "though they may offend the world's sense of humanity."[1] Almost all of the belligerents had ratified the Convention on Land Warfare, with its expanded clauses on the treatment of open cities. It was generally understood that within the war zone, the area in which armies contended and which was delineated by the range of their artillery, there would be little protection, save for churches, hospitals, and similar buildings if they were clearly marked. Outside the war zone, "open" towns and cities seemed to have some protection by virtue of the Hague agreements, but how durable this protection would be, no one could tell.

In the years leading up to 1914, the major powers had given little attention to the legal and moral implications of the weapons they were developing. Most of them were preoccupied with the technical aspects of bombing. The French, who issued a preliminary instruction on aerial bombardment in 1911, were busy testing a variety of bombsights. The German Army began work in 1912 to develop a family of specialized aerial projectiles, the so-called APK bombs—although before the outbreak of the war only one zeppelin seems to have dropped live charges in bombing experiments. A bombing policy presupposed a bombing capability, and only Germany came close to that capability in 1914, thanks to the zeppelin and the Schütte-Lanz airships. It is known, on the authority of Gen. Ernst von Hoeppner, head of the German air service in the second half of the war, that at the outset German authorities had decided to restrict bombing operations "strictly within the theatre of operations, that is, the area in which the armies were fighting."[2] He goes on to say that later this limitation had to be dropped because the French and British persisted in bombing defenseless towns well behind the war zone. Since in the first months of the war the Germans were collecting planes for the "Ostend Carrier Pigeon Detachment," a cover name for a force that could be used to bomb the port of Dover, Hoeppner's assertion should be read with circumspection.

The first zeppelin bombing attack took place over Liège on August 6, 1914. This was emphatically within the battle zone, since the city and its environs were the scene of intense fighting as the German Army tried to batter its way through to the French frontier. The zeppelin was apparently called in to help bombard forts that were holding up the German advance. Twenty-four days later, on the eve of the First Battle of the Marne, Paris became the first great city to undergo an air attack. The aggressor was not a zeppelin but a single birdlike Taube monoplane, which appeared over the Gare de l'Est section of the city shortly after noon on August 30. The pilot threw out five small bombs, apparently aimed at the railway station, since they fell into streets surrounding it. One exploded at 39, rue des Vinaigriers, killing a woman—the first of some five hundred Parisians to die as a result of German air and land bombardments. Yet there was something almost quixotic about the attack. Along with the bombs, the German pilot threw out a message attached to a streamer in the colors of the German Empire: "The German Army is at the gates of Paris. You have no choice but to surrender. Lieutenant von Hindelsen."[3]

There were Parisians living who could remember the terrible siege of 1870–71, so the fifty-odd tiny bombs that the Taubes dropped on the city in the last months of 1914 caused no panic, and only a momentary sense of outrage when one of the bombs damaged Notre Dame. For a few weeks that fall the "five o'clock Taube" became as much a part of the Parisian's afternoon as an aperitif. No one questioned the legality of the bombardment. For part of the time, Gen. Alexander von Kluck's army was almost at the gates of Paris, and forces sent out of the city helped turn the Germans back along the Marne. Paris was not an open city. It was ringed with fortifications, and its government was determined to defend it. The city even had air defenses, although at the outset these were only machine guns and searchlights on the Eiffel Tower. Had a Taube pilot fallen into French hands, most likely he would have been treated as any other prisoner of war. One Taube was brought down by a volley from French infantrymen, landing near some workmen digging trenches. When the workmen approached the plane, its pilot emptied his Mauser at them, wounding several. Thereupon, they beat him to death with their shovels. When Lieutenant von Hindelsen was shot down near Verdun early in 1915, he became just another prisoner of war, although French aviators dropped word of his fate to his unit.

Other belligerents did not accept the legitimacy of aerial bombardment so easily. When the dirigible that attacked the Latvian port of Liepāja in January 1915 was subsequently brought down by Russian fire, the Russian government announced its intention to put the captured crew on trial for "piracy," for having attacked an undefended town. The German government protested through neutral channels, and German newspapers called for the most severe reprisals—which never came to pass, because the Russian government relented. The British cabinet was forced to make a decision at about the same time; Baron Fisher, First Sea Lord, proposed shooting a captured German civilian for each British civilian killed in a zeppelin raid. When the cabinet refused to go along with his scheme, Fisher came close to resigning. (When the first zeppelin crew fell into British hands a little later, they were vastly relieved to know they would not be executed.) But a number of Englishmen continued to feel as strongly as Fisher about the zeppelin raids. Well into 1915, coroner's juries handling the deaths provoked by zeppelin bombs brought in verdicts of "willful murder" against Kaiser Wilhelm.

By the end of 1914 the Allies had made their own contribution to the spread of bombing with a series of raids into Germany. The first and most spectacular of these were mounted, oddly enough, by Britain's Royal Naval Air Service (RNAS). A shifting of ministerial responsibilities left the Admiralty charged with defending the air and sea approaches to the British Isles, the RFC having departed for France with the British Expeditionary Corps. Winston Churchill, First Lord of the Admiralty, regarded the German zeppelin and Schütte-Lanz airships as the greatest menace. These ships were most easy to find and destroy in their sheds, gigantic structures that a British pilot described as big as the Crystal Palace and just as vulnerable. On September 22 and again on October 8, RNAS planes flew out of Antwerp to attack the sheds at Cologne and Düsseldorf. They succeeded in destroying one airship and its shed, which disappeared in a gigantic ball of fire. In November and December, naval planes made similar raids on Friedrichshafen and Cuxhaven. On December 4, 1914, bombers of the French air service attacked Freiburg, located some fifty miles behind the German lines. The pilots tried to hit the railroad station, but their bombs scattered and killed a number of civilians. According to General Hoeppner, the British bombing attacks were a serious provocation, but the bombing of Freiburg made the French "the first power to introduce the horrors of the air war to a peaceable community."[4]

But it was Imperial Germany that first decided upon a sustained program of bombing—properly strategic in its scope and goals—outside the battle zone. This was not because the kaiser was inhuman, as Germany's enemies liked to believe; it was because in the zeppelin, Germany alone possessed the ideal weapon for such action, and the advantage could be made to count only if the fleet were used. Back in 1913, Helmuth von Moltke, chief of the German general staff, had hailed the zeppelin as a weapon "which far surpasses anything our enemies have and which they will not be able to rival in the forseeable future."[5] Von Moltke pushed development of the airship, so that at the outbreak of the war Germany had ten available for service and several others in the process of being built. These ships, although few in number, had two qualities for extended bombing operations that the airplane lacked: greater range and great load-lifting capacity. Some of the later zeppelin models could carry over 2 tons of bombs to the British Isles.

The temptation to use the airships was very strong among Germany's military leaders. The very existence of the airship fleet had had an intimidating effect on its neighbors before 1914, and with the advent of the war, "zeppelinitis" had if anything increased in the enemy camp. The impact would be even greater if the ships made attacks against targets deep inside France and England. Von Moltke thought the effect might be "extraordinary."[6] Another strong partisan of air attacks was Rear Adm. Paul Behncke, deputy chief of the naval staff. Gen. Paul von Hindenburg and Adm. Alfred von Tirpitz were won over as well.

It took a great deal of argument, however, to convince Wilhelm II. The Taube raids on Paris, minor though they were, prompted President Woodrow Wilson to send word to Berlin that such attacks were tarnishing Germany's image in the United States. Chancellor Theobald von Bethmann-Hollweg, a strong enemy of the proposed bombing, warned the kaiser that the diplomatic consequences could be serious. Beyond considerations of state policy, the kaiser found the idea of bombing England personally repugnant, particularly if the target should be the city of London. Wilhelm had many relatives and acquaintances in the city and seems to have had a particular horror of causing the death of one of his kinsmen in the British royal family. On January 7, 1915, after Freiburg suffered a punishing raid, he gave authorization for zeppelin attacks on England, excluding London. In February he extended the bombing zone to London, but ruled out attacks on residential areas and palaces. In May 1915, he gave a blanket authorization to bomb the portion of the British capital east of the Tower. In July, after the German city of Karlsruhe was hit by Allied bombers and the ducal palace badly damaged, the kaiser loosened the reins further. Zeppelin commanders were still under orders to aim their bombs at legitimate military targets only, but in seeking them out they could range over London at will.

Once the kaiser gave the authorization, the German high command lost no time in mounting its zeppelin offensive against England. The first raid on the English coast came on January 19, 1915. London, the ultimate target, first came under attack on the night of May 31–June 1. The story of this first air war against England has been told many times, and almost as well known are the strenuous efforts the British made to turn the intruders back—with guns, searchlights, smoke screens, sulfuric acid sprays, and, finally and most successfully, intercepting aircraft that fired incendiary bullets. There were in all fifty-one zeppelin raids, and although the last came in 1918, the German high command virtually ended the raids late in 1916, in the face of more effective resistance and consequently mounting losses.

The end of 1916 saw a shake-up in German aviation in general, including a critical review of air operations against England. The partisans of bombing had believed it would serve several purposes, but the results were discouraging. Admiral Behncke placed great faith in incendiary bombs, which he believed would set off vast fires in the warehouse and softgoods districts of London. But the city proved not to be very combustible, at least with the incendiary bombs that the Germans were then using; only once did the attacks set off a considerable blaze. Others said the port facilities in London and elsewhere would be high-yield targets. At the beginning of the war, it was believed (wrongly) that a large bomb exploding in a shallow harbor would generate shock waves that would crush the hulls of all nearby ships. Dockyards seemed particularly vulnerable; if they were destroyed, the flow of war matériel to France could be halted. But inviting as these targets were, hitting them was not an easy matter, in London or elsewhere. At best, bombing accuracy was not great, and a zeppelin commander who attacked at night, driven to high altitudes by antiaircraft fire and dazzled by searchlights, had a difficult time fixing on a military target, much less placing bombs on it. Lack of precision was not just a German problem: in a study made in 1915, the Allies found that their bombing planes had about one chance in four of striking a huge target like a zeppelin shed; against railway stations and junctions two bombs in a hundred would hit the objective.

Admiral Behncke believed that the raids might cause panic in the population "which may render it doubtful that the war can be continued."[7] Nothing that drastic happened, for the English did not give up; but there was ample evidence that British morale was suffering from the attacks. There was, for example, the testimonial that the aviation writer R. P. Hearne put in his book *Zeppelins and Super-Zeppelins:* "It is particularly humiliating to allow an enemy to come over your capital city and hurl bombs upon it. His aim may be very bad, the casualties may be few, but the moral effect is wholly undesirable. When the Zeppelins came to London they could have scored a galling technical triumph over us if they had showered us with confetti."[8]

It was undoubtedly what Hearne called "the principle of psychological influence" which led the German political and military authorities to open a new phase in the air war against England with new aircraft that became available in 1917.[9] These were the twin-engine Gotha and the *Riesenflugzeug*, or R-plane, a multiengine giant that could bring a ton of high explosives over London at a height of 14,000 feet. The new cycle of raids began on May 25, 1917, and ended almost exactly a year later, on May 20, 1918. There were twenty-seven of these raids in all, two-thirds of them conducted at night, with the city of London the target seventeen times. Initially, the bombers had a variety of assignments and tasks: they were to disrupt industry and communications, destroy supply dumps, and hinder cross-Channel traffic; but ultimately the flight orders simply read "to raid targets of military importance in Great Britain." By then, the planes were operating exclusively by night and from great heights, so there was no purpose in stipulating more specific objectives. The bomber crews were told that they were making war on "the morale of the English people," sapping their will to fight by showering them with high explosives. In that sort of operation the bombs counted no matter where they hit.[10]

In grim statistical terms, the new bombing planes were more efficient than the zeppelins had been. They took more lives with a smaller amount of explosives. But when the effects of all the attacks on England, by zeppelins and planes alike, are added up, the figures are surprisingly small. The Germans dropped on England less than 300 tons of bombs, killing fourteen hundred people and injuring forty-eight hundred more. These are the kinds of totals one would find reported for a single "quiet" day on the western front. Total property damage was put at slightly over £2 million—less than half what the Great War cost the British each day.

Yet the effect the Germans sought could not be expressed in statistics of this sort, and they were right in thinking that regardless of human and material losses, the raids would deliver a profound jolt to the British government and people. The British public had been shaken by the zeppelin attacks in the summer of 1916, but then had regained confidence with the slackening of the airship incursions. But during the following summer the Gothas and R-planes brought the menace back again in a spectacular display.

In the entire history of strategic bombing there was probably no episode so pregnant with consequences as the German air offensive against London in the late summer and early fall of 1917. On June 12 and again on July 7, 1917, flights of Gothas passed over London in broad daylight, strewing bombs as though the city had no air defenses at all. There were some panicky scenes in the streets of London that summer, and some words of rare violence in Parliament. At the end of September the raiders came on six successive nights; each evening as many as a third of a million Londoners were on the move, seeking shelter outside their homes and sometimes outside the city, spending sleepless nights listening to the pounding of the antiaircraft guns. The war cabinet became alarmed at rising absenteeism and falling production in the war industries in and about the capital. It blamed the newspapers for adding to the climate of fear, but the press could hardly conceal the massive dislocations the raids were producing in the daily life of the great metropolis. Foreign newspapers reported extensively on the aerial siege of London. Reading those reports in Italian newspapers, the Italian strategist Giulio Douhet found convincing proof that properly used, the bomber could paralyze an enemy's whole war effort.

Before the crisis subsided, the British government resolved on a series of radical measures, including the creation of an air force with strategic capability. This was not at all a new idea in Britain, as air power enthusiasts had called for an air force independent in status and function at the very beginning of the war. Lord Kitchener had argued for attacks on German industry in 1914, and the idea found support in both political and military circles. The policy had also found practical application in the activities of the RNAS. In its operations, it had directed its attention first to the zeppelin bases, then to submarine installations and marshaling yards, and ultimately to industrial targets in western Germany. Its Number 3 Wing, operating out of the French field at Luxeuil, had begun in the summer of 1916 a modest but methodical program of strategic bombardment; to carry out that program it had placed orders with British manufacturers for good bombers, the Sopwith 1 1/2 strutter and the Handley Page 0/400. The RNAS was destined to lose its bombers and ultimately its identity as well. In the spring of 1918, it was merged with the RFC to form the Royal Air Force (RAF).

Appointed as first chief of the new air staff was a somewhat reluctant Hugh Trenchard, fresh from command of the RFC in France, where the view prevailed that the function of the airplane was to assist ground troops. The almost precipitate creation of the RAF may have proceeded from sound military considerations, but there is no doubt that it was conceived in part to still both political and public clamor. The new force was charged with making good Prime Minister David Lloyd George's promise to the people of London: "We will give it all back to them and we will give it to them soon. We shall bomb Germany with compound interest."[11] Before 1917 ended, the first British effort at sustained retaliation was under way; by June 1918, Trenchard found himself with a new command, the Independent Air Force, created "for direct action against the heart of the German industrial system." There were even plans for a multinational inter-Allied air force with British, French, American, and Italian components. These conceptions were grandiose, and although their architects were full of confidence, they were not completely successful. The multinational force never came into existence, while Trenchard's Independent Air Force was just warming to its work when the armistice was signed. When the war ended, the Independent Air Force had dropped 660 tons of bombs; the Germans had been paid back, but not with the compound interest that Lloyd George promised.

Britain's eleventh-hour venture in strategic bombing did not find a great deal of favor with its chief ally. The French Army's air service had considerable experience of its own in strategic bombardment, but the lessons it had drawn from that experience were of a different order. The French high command was early attracted to the possibilities of aerial bombing. On September 27, 1914, Gen. Joseph Joffre signed an order creating Groupe de Bombardement no. 1 (GB 1), the first bombing unit created by any of the belligerents. It was formed of three escadrilles of Voisin pusher planes, which offered the bombardier a good view and could lift several of the 90mm artillery shells that served as makeshift bombs. GB 1 was in a sense the first strategic air arm as well, since it was not tied to a ground unit but took its orders directly from Joffre's chief of staff, who might send it on a mission within the battle zone or far behind it. At first, GB 1 served as an extension of the French artillery, hitting targets in the *arrière front*, no more than thirty miles from the front lines. Like the artillery, its forces proved most useful when used in mass. The first targets were enemy columns, depots, and heavy-artillery positions. But soon the Voisin bombers were seeking out targets within Germany, such as the Aviatik airplane factory in Freiburg and the Krupp works at Essen.

From the very beginning circumstances obliged the French to choose their targets carefully. First of all, much of the *arrière front* was French territory, either overrun by the Germans in 1914 or taken in 1871; in either case, the French hoped to reclaim the areas and were obliged to spare them as much as possible, for both practical and humanitarian reasons. Thus, a number of French-owned factories in

German-occupied territory were *réservés*—that is, off limits to French bombers. The general location of the front in northeastern France put a number of French towns within easy reach of the German air service, while German towns were correspondingly at greater range for French bombing planes. Berlin was out of range completely, while Paris was so close to the front—about sixty miles—that German planes crossing the lines at good altitude would be over the city before defending fighters could be alerted and climb up to intercept them.

For all these reasons, the French political and military leaders were anxious to avoid generalized bombardment of urban centers, a game in which they could only lose. The French high command had no interest in spectacular long-distance raids on German cities that did no serious damage to the enemy but invited retaliation. French headquarters steadily turned down the proposals of volunteers who offered to take a few pounds of explosives to Berlin in a specially equipped plane. The high command did from time to time order retaliation raids into Germany, but even these could not be made without the prior approval of the cabinet. But the French military leadership was not at all averse to raids in German territory that promised some tangible benefit or bore on the outcome of the ground battles without provoking a retaliatory raid on a French city; such was the case with the raid that GB 1 made on Ludwigshafen in May 1915, which was closely tied to the fighting on the ground. In April of that year, the Germans released several hundred tons of chlorine at the Allied lines, initiating gas warfare and catching their opponents by surprise. French intelligence traced the gas to the Badische Anilin und Soda Fabrik at Ludwigshafen, so the eighteen planes of GB 1 attacked the plant and a research laboratory at Oppau, doing some damage to both. (The Ludwigshafen plant was almost impossible to miss, since it covered more than a hundred acres.) Somewhat later French bombers made a similar raid on the vast Mauser works at Oberndorf, which produced 240,000 rifles a month.

Gradually a whole bombing policy grew up around what the French called *points sensibles* ("sensitive spots"), legitimate military targets whose destruction would block a critical supply line or production chain. In the plan of September 1916, blast furnaces in the Saar, Lorraine, and Luxembourg stood high on the list of priorities; they supplied about half of Germany's steel, they were near at hand, and finally, they were easy to spot, especially at night. This latter point was particularly important in 1916 and 1917, when, for lack of a good day bomber, the French squadrons switched to night operations. Another campaign was the so-called blockade of the Briey Basin, from which the Germans were drawing large quantities of iron ore. The mines themselves were difficult to bomb by their very nature; moreover, the ore went to different locations, so it was not feasible to bomb at the delivery end of the chain. The *points sensibles* seemed to be the junctions and stations in the basin's rail network, which moved the ore. They were concentrated around the city of Metz, and that is where French bombers set up their blockade. In a campaign that lasted more than two years, the French air service used 1,800 tons of bombs.

This approach to bombing accorded extremely well with the policy of the RNAS, whose operations in France came to be closely coordinated with those of French squadrons. When the RNAS departed the scene and was replaced by another force with other orders, the spirit of collaboration faded. Trenchard's Independent Air Force was not interested in joining in the Briey blockade. It was bent on retaliation. Even before the force was formed, British units had begun to hit German towns rather indiscriminately at the end of 1917. The Germans had warned that such attacks would lead to retaliation against the city of Paris; late in January German bombing planes hit the city for the first time in two and a half years. Sharp words passed between the two Allies, and Georges Clemenceau, the French premier, demanded a complete list of the British raids into Germany. In February the British agreed to restrict their bombing more carefully to factories and rail targets. French relations with the Independent Air Force could hardly have been cordial. It offended Gen. Ferdinand Foch by its very name; its operations, pursued in sovereign disregard for what was happening in the land battle, were anathema to Gen. Maurice Duval, head of the French air service. There was a general feeling among the French military that the British had come to draw the lightning, which would then strike their hosts.

The events on the western front dominated the headlines during the war and have tended to monopolize the attention of historians ever since. But there were other fronts, and they too offer lessons on the development of aerial bombardment. In May 1915, Italy entered the war on the Allied aide, and within hours of the opening of hostilities, two Austrian Taubes appeared over Venice to initiate the air war in that theater of operations. The Italians had the larger air force at the beginning of the war, and they had an excellent bombing plane in the Caproni trimotor, which entered service in 1915 (the Austrians had to rely on German assistance, including Gotha bombers). From 1916 on, the Italians generally had the upper hand. Even so, their air fleet remained a modest one; at the armistice they had 1,700 aircraft, while the British, French, and Germans had three times that number. The Italian air service had to divide its attention and its resources between the ground fighting in the north and the air and naval threat coming from the Adriatic. The Italians were able to identify a number of targets of strategic importance, such as the rail junction at Divaccia, near Trieste, and the mercury-refining facilities at Idria. But the Capronis were too few to mount steady and sustained bombing campaigns against them. Only toward the end of 1918 did the Italians have the means to create a special bombing force, or *massa di bombardamento,* of about fifty planes.

The Italians, like the French, had to exercise considerable care in selecting bombing targets. Many of the towns and cities behind the Austrian lines were Italian in population, and the Italian government had hopes of annexing them once the war was won. To strike beyond those areas was no easy task, in part because of distance and in part because of the Alps, which posed a formidable obstacle to the aircraft of the era. At the outset, the Italians hoped to make use of their dirigibles for long-distance bombing, for they had nine operational in 1915. They made thirty-two airship raids that year, but they soon discovered, as the Germans did, that the big ships were vulnerable. In 1916 the number of airship raids fell to sixteen, and the Italians lost three of their fleet, one of them under particularly tragic circumstances. On the night of May 4, the M-4 and a sister ship raided the Austrian base at Aisovizza, but on the return flight, the M-4 ran out of fuel. Dawn found it drifting helplessly over the Austrian positions at Gorizia. Two Austrian planes soon appeared, and their pilots made it clear by gestures that the Italians were to bring their ship to earth. The captain of the M-4 steadfastly refused. At length, the Austrians attacked the derelict airship and sent it down in an enormous streak of flame.

Much of the aerial bombardment on both sides was directed at the teeming port cities that rimmed the Adriatic. On the Italian side, much of the early bombing was done with paper. The Italians had dropped propaganda leaflets with some effect during the Libyan war, and now they began to address the Italian-speaking population of the Austro-Hungarian Empire. The leaflet campaign was distinguished by the participation of that flamboyant literary figure Gabriele D'Annunzio. In August 1915 he dropped war communiqués and poems to the inhabitants of Trieste. To the population of Zara, in Dalmatia, he sent down exhortations decorated with the Italian colors: "Believe in the joy of your second spring, when the Corinthian acanthus will flower again around your Latin columns."[12]

Both Austrians and Italians attacked military targets near, or inside, the cities on the Adriatic, but apparently without great accuracy. In October 1915, Italian bombers struck at military installations near Trieste; but to the Austrian authorities the bombs seemed to fall indiscriminately upon the city's population. Five days later, the Austrians retaliated by bombing Venice. One of the bombs struck a church and destroyed a Tiepolo fresco, bringing a protest from Pope Benedict XV. In January 1916, the Italians raided Ljubljana, headquarters of the Austrian Archduke Charles; in February the Austrians chose as target the ancient town of Ravenna. On that raid a bomb struck the Church of Saint Appolinaire, but the Austrian government issued a statement that claimed the damage to the church was a regrettable accident. Austrian bombers had been trying to hit the railway station nearby, but a high wind had blown the bombs off target. Subsequently, the Austrians were to claim their aviators were fired on by machine guns placed in church towers. The Italian authorities indignantly denied this charge and lodged another complaint of their own against the bombing of hospitals. In March 1917, Austrian bombs hit a military hospital that numbered among its patients a wounded soldier named Benito Mussolini. Six months later, Austrian bombers killed fifty people in a crowded hospital in Venice. Amidst charges and countercharges, the bombing of towns and cities spread and intensified; the Italians were the more vulnerable and they suffered most heavily. By the beginning of 1918, night raids on Padua and Treviso were so common that every evening there was an exodus into the countryside. Venice was the handiest target for the Austrians and received correspondingly heavy punishment. Early in 1918 the city underwent a prolonged night attack in which it received 300 bombs; by the war's end, it had been attacked forty-two times.

On the eastern front, bombing activity took on an entirely different complexion. There bombers with strategic capabilities made their first appearance, but the air war against the cities did not develop. Russia was technologically the most backward of the belligerents, yet paradoxically it was the only power possessing an efficient long-range bomber in 1914. The airplane was the Ilya Murometz (IM), the work of a brilliant young engineer named Igor Sikorsky. The IM had four engines and wings whose span was only a few inches less than that of the Flying Fortress of 1935. In an era when the lifting power of aircraft was so circumscribed that the RFC put a weight limit on its pilots, Sikorsky took the IM aloft accompanied by sixteen people and a dog. Translated into bombing capacity, this meant that the IM could carry over a ton of explosives several hundred miles, a feat not to be equaled until the Germans introduced their R-planes, which may have been inspired by Sikorsky's design.

There were four IM's in existence when the war broke out; it took the Russian authorities several months to decide how best to use them. In December 1914 the giant planes were formed into a special Flying Ship Squadron and sent to Yablonna, a base near Warsaw, with orders to carry out reconnaissance and bombing missions for the Russian armies. The IM's performed these tasks extremely well (only one was to be lost in combat). By 1915 the squadron contained fifty aircraft, twenty of them IM's (there were to be about seventy of these craft manufactured in all). In the first three years of the war, the bombers carried out 350 missions along a vast front stretching from the Black Sea to the Baltic. They flew photographic reconnaissance for the Russian Seventh Army and then gave bombing support to the Twelfth Army. On orders from the Russian high command, they attacked the German hydroplane base at Riga. They were capable of operating more than 150 miles behind the enemy lines, but the bulk of their activity was in what the Russians called the "operational" zone, the area behind the front, spanning 60 miles. The targets they struck in that zone were most frequently depots, marshaling yards, railway stations, and German troops held in reserve.

This pattern of bombardment was also the one that the Germans generally followed on the eastern front. Here they had available considerable means for long-distance bombing. First of all, the German airship fleet remained active there after it ceased to be used much in the west; then, too, it was the German practice to try out new weapons in the east before using them on the other front. This was the case with the R-planes; a detachment of them operated out of Vilna beginning in the summer of 1916, and an incomplete list of their missions indicates that they sought out the same categories of targets as the IM's.

Geography probably had a lot to do with the bombing patterns on the eastern front. Here distances were great and the transport facilities more limited; the railway network in eastern Europe generally was less dense than in the west, so the destruction of a single station, junction, or even a railway bridge or trestle could do great harm. Small wonder that rail targets figured frequently in bombing operations by both sides. At the same time, there were fewer cities, and the most important of these were not within bombing range. Berlin was outside the radius of the IM's, and not until 1918 did the German armies come within easy flying range of Petrograd (now Leningrad). The first bombs had hardly fallen on the city when the new Bolshevik government signed the Treaty of Brest-Litovsk, taking Russia out of the war.

Eight months later, the fighting came to an end on the western front. Europe would never be the same again, and neither would the art of war. The science of destruction had been advanced by the creation of a whole panoply of new weapons, not the least of them the airplane. Aerial bombardment, still a novelty in 1914, had become by 1918 a vast undertaking employing hundreds of specially designed aircraft. Early in the war bombing began to reach beyond the actual battlefields of the contending armies, and the distinction between combatant and noncombatant began to blur. To be sure, targets designated for the Gothas and the Handley Pages were legitimate military ones; but in practice it was impossible to pick such a target out of an urban complex and direct all of the bombs onto it. General Hoeppner wrote after the war, "Our opponents knew as well as we did that in an aerial bomb attack it was not just military targets that would be hit."[13] And there seems little doubt that as the war progressed there was less punctiliousness, less concern for the consequences when bombs strayed from their target. Toward the end of the war Lord Weir, the British air minister, told Trenchard that he need not be overly concerned at the inaccuracies involved in bombing German towns. Trenchard replied, "All the pilots drop their eggs well into the center of the town generally."[14]

Such comments by military personnel may seem reprehensible, but they at least understood the technical problems involved. The press, the public, and many politicians did not. When enemy bombs aimed at a barracks fell into residential areas all around it, these groups called the attack indiscriminate or terroristic and demanded reprisals.

There is no doubt that a number of bombing attacks on cities were essentially symbolic; they were undertaken mainly for political reasons—to embarrass the enemy and frighten him, and at the same time to provide stirring headlines for domestic consumption. It became a sort of game to demonstrate that the enemy's cities—particularly his capital—were vulnerable. Every belligerent capital in Europe was attacked from the air except Rome—no doubt because of the pope's presence. Even then the Austrians made it a point to fly near the city on their raids to Naples and other targets. As out of the way as Constantinople might seem, the French, British, and Russians all managed to bomb it. Petrograd escaped for a long time, but only because it was at extreme range. The Germans planned to attack it quite early by zeppelin (they needed a long winter night, mild winds, and moderate temperatures, but were never able to find these optimum conditions on the eastern front).

When Italy entered the war, Col. Giulio Douhet wanted to lead a squadron of Caproni bombers over Vienna and drop empty bombs on Schoenbrunn castle as a lesson in "power and chivalry."[15] The poet-aviator D'Annunzio tried unsuccessfully to make the flight in 1917, succeeding only in August 1918. He and his fellow airmen made a flight of 621 miles in all, strewing leaflets over Vienna. Berlin was the object of daring schemes, but it was maddeningly inaccessible, even though a British industrialist offered a reward of £1,000 to the first British aviator who dropped a bomb on the city. The giant Handley Page V/1500 bomber, capable of this feat, became operational in November 1918, and it is said that the first planes were on the point of leaving for Berlin when the armistice was signed.

In June 1916, a single Allied plane did make it over Berlin, a specially equipped Nieuport flown by Lt. Antoine Marchal of the French air service. Marchal's plan, approved by the French high command, was to fly across Europe from the western front to the Russian lines, passing over Berlin on the way—a flight of fourteen hours. Marchal made it over Berlin, where he tossed out leaflets announcing the French could also drop bombs, but that they did not make war on women and children. On the last leg of his flight, Marchal had to land because of a misfiring engine. He was changing spark plugs when a German patrol captured him about sixty miles from the Russian lines.

Flights like those of D'Annunzio and Marchal did little to alter the general impression that the air war was intensifying and degenerating into a decidedly unchivalrous affair. The German press communiqué following an Allied raid on Freiburg in April 1917 related that the enemy airmen had "selected" as targets the new municipal theater, the institutes, and the infirmaries. The Associated Press reported on May 30, 1918, "German airmen last night deliberately dropped bombs on hospitals in which there were scores of American and hundreds of French sick and wounded."[16] The savagery of the Germans in this instance seemed demonic; so, apparently, was their ability to find targets in the dark. It was widely believed on both sides that enemy bombers sought out prominent political and military figures for assassination by air. When German zeppelins struck Paris early in 1918, it was generally assumed that they had come after Lloyd George, who was staying at the Crillon Hotel. After French bombs struck the ducal palace at Karlsruhe, the German government sent word that it was establishing a prison camp for Allied officers just next door. This was not the limit of the enemy airmen's perfidy. In the last year of the war, there were persistent reports that German pilots were scattering poisoned candies; from Rumania came a story that German planes were dropping garlic laced with deadly bacilli.

Atrocity stories aside, the air war was becoming more intensive and was dealing out greater punishment to civilian populations. In part, this was the result of technological advances: the aerial bombs used in 1914 were so small they could be carried in the pocket; toward the end of the conflict, an R-plane managed to release over London a monster bomb thirteen feet long, weighing over a ton. Incendiary devices were steadily perfected. The Allies used them to destroy Bulgarian wheat fields, the French systematically set fire to the grain fields in German-occupied portions of their own country, and the Germans attempted with less success to ignite vast forests in Russia.

But it was the cities that were increasingly singled out for punishment. They were handy targets for reprisals, and in the first years of the war, it was not uncommon to bomb a town and throw out at the same time leaflets explaining that the attack was in reprisal for a specific transgression on the enemy's part. Inevitably, reprisals bred more reprisals. Early in 1917 the British cabinet warned the Germans of dire consequences if their submarines continued to attack hospital ships. Shortly afterward, there were two incidents of this kind, so the

Allies bombed Freiburg. One of the bombs struck a clinic, causing a great stir in the German press. German planes were consequently sent to pound the towns of Châlons and Épernay; this prompted the French to bomb Freiburg again and Trier as well. The last year of the war cost the city of Paris 244 lives, nearly half the deaths the city suffered during the entire war; in 1918, Paris had forty-four air raids, and from March until August it was also bombarded by a battery of giant cannon sixty miles away, known collectively as Big Bertha. (Actually, this famous cannon was not used in the bombardment of Paris.) London was to some degree spared, since after March 1918 the German high command committed its heavy bombers to the great land offensive in France. But German towns came to know aerial bombardment all too well. In 1918, Germany recorded 657 air raids, which produced twelve hundred casualties. Both figures had doubled since 1917.

There was worse to come. In September 1918 the German air service had available a new incendiary of unprecedented destructiveness. The Elektron bomb, as it was called, burned at between 2,000° and 3,000° Fahrenheit; it could not be extinguished by conventional methods. According to careful estimates, the new incendiaries could destroy a third of the city of Paris in a single raid. The Allies, too, were readying new and fearsome weapons. The huge Handley Page bombers would be able to range over Germany at will, and British ordnance was building for them a special one-ton bomb, which was never used (its casing is still on display in the basement of the Imperial War Museum). The cities of Germany were also to be the testing ground for a new conception in weaponry—aerial bombs filled with poison gas.

As the threat to their cities grew, authorities in each country made strenuous efforts at defense. Germany began the war with 18 heavy antiaircraft guns and ended it with 896. The French Défense contre Aéronefs (DCA) was a nonexistent service in 1914, but four years later it comprised forty-eight thousand officers and men. The telephone system offered a ready-made communications network for air defense (in 1914 German border police were able to telephone to Friedrichshafen that British planes were on the way), so the warning system developed around it. By 1915 the air defense of western Germany was being directed from Frankfurt; the French warning system was centralized in a school building in downtown Paris, where two switchboards and four *demoiselles téléphonistes* linked DCA headquarters with gun batteries, fighter fields, and fifty-odd observer posts. Within a short time, a whole panoply of antiaircraft weapons appeared. The Germans were using searchlights in air defense exercises as early as 1913. The British pushed the development of sound detectors, hoping to get an earlier warning of nighttime zeppelin raids; they even cut acoustical discs into the chalk cliffs along the Channel coast. The French produced a highly regarded mobile antiaircraft gun, their celebrated "75" mounted on a reinforced truck chassis. The British acquired a number of these eight-ton monsters for the defense of London, where they roared back and forth through darkened streets, seeking a clear shot at German raiders. The Italians contributed the barrage balloon; a double cordon of them guarded Venice to a height of ten thousand feet. Then there were the blackouts, the smoke generators, and the "decoy" towns whose lights twinkled alluringly in the midst of empty fields—in short, most of the measures employed when Europe went to war again twenty years later. But the early defense against the bomber was hampered by two considerations: night gave the attacker a telling advantage, and the defense could not match his mobility—it had to stand guard over a hundred towns, while he attacked just one.

At war's end, the bomber had emerged in the popular mind—with some justification—as the most dangerous weapon the conflict had spawned. This was a weapon from which no one was safe. It could penetrate frontiers at will and reach across entire nations. Indeed, there was no reason why it might not reach across oceans as well. In 1918 a goodly number of North Americans—and their leaders—were so mesmerized by the bomber that they believed they would be exposed to air attacks. As early as 1915, Canadian authorities worried that German-Americans in the United States might fly across the border and bomb government buildings in Ottawa. Improbable as the danger seems in retrospect, the authorities set up a network of observers. One day in 1918, an informant in New York State relayed word that three planeloads of Germans and explosives had crossed the border, headed for the Canadian capital. The authorities evacuated the Parliament building, darkened the city, and posted sharpshooters. No planes ever appeared.

What could happen to Ottawa could happen to New York, where an air raid scare in June 1918 was taken quite seriously. Late in 1917 a writer said in the [London] *Observer* that the Germans might try to bomb the city in 1918. Adm. Robert E. Peary, who was then involved with air defense matters, told the press that such a raid was a distinct possibility. According to the most frequently mentioned scenario, a large German submarine would bring a crated seaplane off the New York coast; there it would seize a freighter and use the freighter's cargo-handling equipment to uncrate and assemble the plane and lower it into the water. The craft would then take off for New York City with a cargo of high explosives.

The idea suddenly became more plausible in the late spring of 1918 when a German submarine actually appeared off New York and attacked a number of vessels. New Yorkers reported seeing flashing lights at sea. Then, on the docks, someone found a crippled pigeon bearing a mysterious message. Both were rushed to Naval Intelligence, where a spokesman said the pigeon "looked foreign."[17] Coney Island and Broadway dimmed their lights; antiaircraft guns appeared in Central Park. The city fathers set up an elaborate system of air-raid sirens throughout the city, but decided not to test them for fear they might provoke a panic. The officials of the American Banknote Company were not aware of this danger when they decided to test the sirens on their new building in the Bronx. The sirens struck up on the afternoon of July 1. Within minutes, police switchboards were jammed with calls. Hundreds of workers abandoned their machines; streams of people poured into precinct houses seeking shelter.

The Bronx soon returned to normal, and the incident faded from memory. The Germans never had large-scale plans to attack the city. But for a few anxious hours New York knew something of the fear that had seized London, Venice, and Freiburg. To the generation of 1918, air power seemed awesome and limitless. The primitive bombing planes of 1918 would send ominous echoes down the next two decades.

CHAPTER 3

THE
PROPHETS

THE ARMISTICE CAME NONE TOO SOON for the men in the trenches, and the sense of relief was almost as keen on the home front. Even in Germany, where the end brought defeat, it was not unwelcome. But in the 1920s there was one group that wished the war could have lasted longer; these were the men at work in various countries trying to figure out what the next war would be like, either because they were being paid by their government to do so or because they were soldiers with a professional curiosity. In either case, their task was not an easy one. The war had thrown open a Pandora's box of weaponry and then come to an end before men could learn how that weaponry could best be used. For example the Allies had planned to put ten thousand tanks in the field in 1919. Col. J. F. C. Fuller, apostle of armor in the years between the wars, could only speculate on what those tanks might have accomplished. Much the same was true of the bombing plane, although spokesmen for the RAF liked to say that operations in 1918 clearly demonstrated the strategic air offensive could work. James Molony Spaight, a British Air Ministry analyst who spent much of the interwar period studying and writing on bombing strategy, could not help reflecting, "In some respects it was unfortunate that the war ended when it did."[1]

Almost everyone conceded that military aviation had won its spurs and would figure prominently in future wars. Colonel Fuller was in agreement with B. H. Liddell Hart on this point. Gen. Hans von Seeckt, guiding spirit of the German Army in the 1920s, predicted waves of bombers opening hostilities in future wars. Marshal Ferdinand Foch, the most prestigious soldier of the postwar years, was categorical in his pronouncement: "One of the great factors in the next war will be aircraft." And Foch was thinking specifically of aerial bombardment; the effects of massive bombing attacks would be "almost incalculable."[2]

But Foch was speaking of a potential, one he felt could not be measured for the time being; for him, as for most of his contemporaries, the Great War had yielded only imperfect evidence of what air power might do in a major conflict. Then, to complicate the analyst's problems, the armistice was followed by nearly twenty years of peace, disturbed only by minor conflicts that taught no lessons in air strategy. In the 1920s the RAF saw action chiefly against obstreperous subjects within the British Empire—rebels like the "Mad Mullah" of Somaliland, who had neither air force nor air defenses and whose domains offered no bombing targets more tempting than *souks* and mud villages. The French air service fought much the same type of war against Moroccan rebels under Abd-el-Krim. It was not until the Spanish Civil War broke out in 1936 that the imperfect lessons of 1918 could be supplemented by any meaningful new data.

Where practice is lacking, theory thrives, and so, the 1920s and the early 1930s saw a good deal of speculative work. Some of this was done in official "think tanks," such as the U.S. Army Air Corps' Tactical School at Maxwell Field or the secret facility at Lipetsk, which the Soviet government put at the disposal of the German Army in exchange for technical advice. But theory does not thrive in secrecy, and fortunately for its development a new generation of aeronautical reviews provided the forum for discussions and debates over doctrine. The French *Revue de l'aéronautique militaire* set the pace when it appeared in 1921, but Italy's *Rivista Aeronautica,* launched four years later, quickly became the busiest marketplace for ideas on air power; from 1927 on, its pages were a forum for Giulio Douhet, his defenders, and his critics.

Then there were the spokesmen and theorists themselves—the celebrated, flamboyant ones like Douhet and Billy Mitchell, but also a constellation of lesser-known prophets. Theirs was the job of reading the evidence of the Great War, identifying the significant trends and lines of development and projecting them into the future. But it is important to note that these men were actually second-generation prophets, for along with the empirical evidence of the war they inherited a considerable, if somewhat disorganized, body of thought dating from before 1914. Part of their work involved examining the validity of some of these prewar notions in light of the experience of 1914–18. And since the strategic bombing doctrines that flowered the 1920s and 1930s have their roots in those early notions, it is with them that one should begin.

In the decade before 1914, serious students of warfare did a considerable amount of thinking about military aeronautics; after all, the airplane and the dirigible were already in existence, and their use in future wars seemed inevitable. Speculative works about air strategy and tactics began to appear in general treatises like Clément Ader's *Aviation militaire* (1909), but more often in obscure monographs and technical journals. Scattered and diverse as this "professional" literature was, it led the well-read expert to have certain expectations of the new weapons.

Although these first notions about how air weapons might be used were highly conjectural, the men who propounded them did not make them up out of thin air. The first prophets of air power reasoned by analogy, proceeding from certain aspects of war already familiar to them. Thus, they saw aviation in its reconnaissance role as a variant of the cavalry, the arm which had traditionally filled that function. Furthermore, it was logical and convenient to think of aircraft in a tactical role as extensions of the artillery, capable of dropping charges of explosives beyond the range of artillery. Well before 1914, there were predictions that military aeronautics would become the "fourth arm," taking its place in the army alongside infantry, cavalry, and artillery.

But another analogy suggested itself to some of the early theorists, and they pursued it until they arrived at a truly strategic conception of air power. Their point of departure was the premise that war in the air would resemble war on the seas. The parallels were, after all, numerous and compelling: both the airman and the sailor carried war into domains alien to man; they were able to fight there and, indeed, able to sustain themselves there, thanks only to the specialized craft that human genius had designed. It followed that in both cases the nature and form of warfare would be determined by what these craft could and could not do.

One of the qualities of both air- and seacraft was their extreme mobility; forces could be displaced and concentrated with a speed and an ease unknown in land warfare. In offensive operations, there was also more chance that movement might go undetected by the enemy until too late, so that descents could be made in superior force on an ill-prepared foe. After all, the entire enemy coast was vulnerable to a surface fleet, while an air fleet could strike any point inland as well. J. M. Spaight labeled this quality "penetrativeness."

The idea that the air weapon might be utilized for a sudden, decisive intervention at the opening of a conflict was widely current before 1914. Ferdinand Ferber considered that the first target would be the enemy air fleet: "When all the enemy airplanes have been destroyed or forced to land, then the escadrilles will imitate naval tactics, setting up their patrols over hangars and construction sites to see that the enemy does not occupy the air again."[3] There were a number of naval precedents for this sort of preemptive strike; the most recent, cited by Spaight and others, was the Japanese attack on the Russian naval forces in Port Arthur. None of the belligerents tried an aerial equivalent in 1914, of course; but the untested idea gained great currency in the 1930s, so that by September 1939 all the belligerents were braced for a first, massive blow at their air fleets.

With the enemy driven from the skies and command of the air established, other targets would present themselves. There was some awareness that bombing attacks might be used to disrupt the enemy's industry and sever his transport and communications lines—a form of warfare somewhat like a naval blockade in its effects. But that sort of warfare took much time, weakening the enemy gradually; the pre-1914 theorists thought in terms of short, sharp wars, so at this point many of them turned to another potential target, the city. Clément Ader was convinced that aircraft would attack urban centers, where they would become "veritable terrors."[4] Riley E. Scott, West Point graduate and winner of the Michelin bombing contest of 1912, wrote that "no great accuracy would be needed in the congested areas, and the loss of life from fire, high-explosive bombs and panic would be appalling."[5] The bombing of the cities seemed to promise a quick surrender, with an attack on the enemy's capital the most effective of all.

It was a dictum of Napoleonic warfare—still quoted in 1914—that when the enemy's capital came under bombardment, the war was considered over. Similarly, there was a theory that the modern, highly centralized state, with its complex economic and political structures, could not survive the destruction or even the substantial damaging of its capital. Lord Montagu of Beaulieu predicted in 1909 that a single massive air attack on London would disable the entire country. The destruction of Parliament, the ministries, and the post and telegraph offices—the central nervous system of the body politic—would produce in that body a massive and fatal paralysis. A Belgian officer named Poutrin, writing in the *Revue générale de l'aéronautique militaire* in June 1911, described how an equally stunning blow might be delivered to Paris.

If the first air attack surprised a nation's capital rather than its air installations, that nation might be knocked out of a war almost immediately, like a boxer felled before he could even assume a fighting stance. Just such an attack seems to have been considered by the French high command in the autumn of 1914. The Turkish government, neutral at the outbreak of the war, was leaning toward the Central Powers, and the Allies were anxious to keep the Turks from entering the war on the other side. A plan submitted by Captain de Goÿs of GB 1 called for the unit to be transferred to the eastern Mediterranean for a raid on Constantinople as soon as the Turkish government decided on war. The planes were to bomb military targets in and around the city and make noisy demonstrations in the skies above it. This might well stampede its volatile population and, given the turbulent nature of Turkish politics, lead to the overthrow of the government and the reversal of Turkey's foreign policy. The plan was given serious study at General Joffre's headquarters but was never implemented. So the aerial "knockout blow," as it was often called, remained in the realm of theoretical possibilities; like the lightning stroke at the enemy air force, it was often evoked in the literature of the 1920s and 1930s.

Clément Ader, who was in many ways the most perceptive of all the early writers on aerial warfare, foresaw that the threat to the cities would become an important consideration in state policy and that no country would feel the danger more than England: "She, more than any other, will be compelled by aviation to undergo a radical transformation."[6] Concern over the vulnerability of their great capital city would lead the English to abandon their traditional isolation and to seek mastery of the atmosphere just as they had sought dominance of the seas.

In addition to his remarkable prescience, Ader was noteworthy because of his idea that a nation could feel secure from an attack only if it could dominate the element through which that attack must come. The only answer to an enemy's air force is an air force of one's own. These forces would contend for mastery of the atmosphere in ways still unclear (although Ader and others speculated on the forms that aerial combat might take); but the war in the air would be as distinctive and as proper to its element as naval warfare was to the sea. It followed in Ader's mind that an air force could not simply be a "fourth arm." It should become the "third service," enjoying equality with the army and the navy and directed by its own minister. Douhet was reaching the same conclusion at about the same time. He wrote in 1910 that the Italian armed forces should be enlarged by the addition of a *fratello* ("little brother")—that is, an air force.

Before 1914 it was not easy to determine whether the obvious offensive potential of the airplane might be effectively countered or how this might be done. Early conceptions of air defense also borrowed heavily from naval warfare, introducing the aerial equivalent of picket ships and scouting vessels. Before the war, there were suggestions that Britain could best defend itself from zeppelin attack by means of a standing patrol of "hydroaeroplanes" guarding its air frontiers. Ader's solution to the security of Paris was a continuous shuttle of "sentinel" airplanes flying back and forth between two airfields well east of the city. In 1915 the Germans attempted this sort of "standing" defense along a section of the western front with an elaborate scheme they called the *Luftsperre*, or "air barrier," designed to seal off a section of the front. The problems with such a scheme proved insoluble. First of all, approaching enemy aircraft were difficult to spot, and the vigil was enormously complicated by the third dimension; to maintain aircraft on patrol at different altitudes and to replace them every hour or so when they needed to refuel required a tremendous number of airplanes. German military analyst Hans Ritter estimated that for a reasonably effective *Luftsperre* twelve miles long, 240 planes would have to be kept in the air, drawn from a pool of about 800 aircraft. In 1915 the Germans had about 1,000 machines available on the entire front. Ritter concluded, "An air barrier is generally an impossible thing."[7]

The alternative to defending a broad front in the air was to meet individual attacks as they developed. Unfortunately, the speed of attacking aircraft and the inevitable delays in detecting them and getting intercepting planes aloft—the "lag time"—meant it was impossible to organize an air defense for Paris and very difficult to do so for London before enemy bombers were over their target. Spaight laid down a general rule that air power could not be prevented by air power from penetrating an enemy's defense. Gen. Bernard Serrigny reasoned that a nation's vulnerability was essentially a "function of its distance from an enemy's bases of departure."[8]

This did not mean that the bombing plane always had the advantage over air defenses. Only in the first few months of the war—what the French called "the golden age of bombing"—could those planes go about their work without fear of serious hindrance. Soon fighter craft developed and made the bomber their prey. By September 1915, losses in French bombing units were approaching a crisis level; by 1917 the Germans abandoned long-distance day bombardment completely. There were several ways to meet the threat posed by the fighter: one was to increase the bomber's capacity to defend itself; another was formation flying, which allowed planes to put up a collective defense; and a third was to have the bombers escorted by fighting craft of one's own. But the most effective response for planes with long-distance missions was simply to carry out those missions at night. The enemy fighter, so formidable by day, did not even attempt night interceptions until the end of the war; even then, said William C. Sherman of the U.S. Army Air Service, they "advanced little beyond the crudities of the experimental stage."[9] For one of the early night-fighter pilots to sight an enemy bomber was no ordinary accomplishment; for him then to shoot the bomber down was a very extraordinary one. Sherman felt that night-fighter tactics might improve, but like most of the air strategists of the 1920s, he felt that the hours of darkness would belong to the bomber: "An inspection of the difficulties of the defensive . . . demonstrates that darkness increases many of them and decreases none. Nothing of human invention will ever entirely take the place of sunlight. Night attacks therefore will always be less liable to encounter opposition than those undertaken by day."[10]

For Sherman and for many of his contemporaries air defense meant defense by aircraft. Ground defenses, and antiaircraft guns in particular, he judged more a distraction to the bomber than a danger;

at most, antiaircraft fire would do no more than drive enemy planes to higher altitudes. This view was rooted in the experience of 1914–18. One of the great revelations of that war was the extraordinary difficulty of hitting aircraft, a difficulty that only grew as aircraft improved during the course of the war, increasing the speed and altitude at which they could operate. The antiaircraft guns of London, Venice, and Freiburg seemed to fire thousands of rounds with no appreciable effect; enemy bombers were able to fly unscathed through what seemed a torrent of projectiles. The ballistic problems were intimidating; for example, the 75mm shell—the type used by both French and British—took twelve seconds to reach an altitude of 16,500 feet. By that time, the aircraft at which it was fired would have traveled a third of a mile (assuming the plane was flying at 100 mph) and might have changed altitude and direction. The British Ministry of Munitions estimated that if the target were a plane 8,000 feet up, moving at 100 mph, the antiaircraft batteries would have to fire 162,000 rounds simultaneously in order to put a shell in every position that the plane might occupy. Small wonder that postwar estimates credited antiaircraft batteries with only one "kill" per 5,000–8,000 rounds. There was every reason to believe that aircraft would continue to improve in performance, flying ever faster and higher, becoming ever more elusive targets; yet, in the 1920s and the early 1930s, there were few compensating improvements in antiaircraft defense techniques, and few were visible on the horizon.

These difficulties of air defense seemed to confirm Spaight's notion of the distinctive "penetrativeness" of the airplane and, in general, enhanced the possibilities for its offensive use. If the bomber could thus "get through," to use Stanley Baldwin's phrase, what should it choose as its target? Here again, the war provided some answers, confirming some ideas of bombing policy and showing the weaknesses of others. In the first weeks of the war, aircraft often intervened directly against enemy troops and positions, sometimes with considerable success. But those were days when the war was still one of movement, when great bodies of infantry and cavalry could be caught on the march or bivouacked in the field. Soon the armies went to earth, and the front stabilized into a complex of trenches and "dug-in" gun emplacements designed to withstand bombardment. For airmen, the front now offered smaller and less vulnerable targets. For attacks to have any chance of success, they had to be delivered at low altitude, where plane and pilot were subjected to the dense and dangerous fire that had become characteristic of the front. Not surprisingly, bombing planes were drawn to targets elsewhere that were more accessible and less fiercely defended.

Direct intervention in the land battles was not totally abandoned, but generally the various air services did not regard it as a good investment. In the spring of 1918, when the Ludendorff offensive tore a great gap in the Allied line and the German Army broke out into the open field, French and British aircraft were sent to stem the German advance until new lines could be formed. The air attacks did slow the Germans down, but at great cost to the airmen. Some units suffered 25 percent casualties per day, and the life expectancy of an Allied pilot was eight days.

The impression left by such episodes was a durable one. Most air forces in the interwar period regarded direct intervention in the land battle as a mission to be undertaken only under exceptional circumstances, and that view was reflected in tactical manuals. To be sure, there was a school of thought which held that with specifically designed aircraft and suitable tactics the air arm could contribute directly and effectively in ground operations. Amedeo Mecozzi in Italy and Camille Rougeron in France pleaded the case for what they called assault aviation, but resistance was very strong. Most theorists were convinced that the next war would be like the last, characterized by continuous, stable fronts with intensive fire, supported by deep "operational" zones. This operational realm, with its varied and less fiercely defended targets, seemed a far better theater for bombing operations.

Attacks behind the front proper had the fundamental goal of preventing the enemy army from drawing on supplies and reinforcements; in a bombing policy with this purpose, targets in the operational zone tended to merge with industrial objectives further to the rear. Attacks on the transport system and especially the railways were common to both areas, while the enemy's supply of artillery shells might be interrupted by destroying a depot in the operational zone or by attacking the factory where the shells were produced. As the bomber pilot flew deeper into the enemy's territory, the targets below him changed subtly in nature. As he destroyed objectives further away from the front, there was less chance that the destruction would have a direct and immediate impact on that front—but more of a chance that it might have an eventual impact on all the fighting fronts and the war effort as well, and in ways more than purely military. Thus, almost imperceptibly, bombing would change from operational to strategic.

The evidence of the war seemed to indicate that great armies could be crippled and even destroyed simply by shutting off the flow of vital supplies. Capt. Hans Ritter speculated that Germany might well have won the Battle of Verdun if it had concentrated its bombing effort against the *voie sacrée*. This road was the only one by which the French could supply their army, and they could accomplish this only by running continuous truck convoys day and night. (In a ten-day period early in 1916, they transported 132 battalions of infantry and 22,000 tons of munitions and supplies.) Twentieth-century war machines proved so complex that they could be crippled by the shortage of a single commodity. The Germans worried constantly about their oil refinery at Pechelbronn; its absolutely critical production could have been stopped by a single well-placed French bomb. Although the French did bomb Pechelbronn several times, there was only minimal damage. As a general rule, the problem with the war against *points sensibles,* both in the operational zone and within the enemy's hinterland, was not so much a failure to identify the crucial targets as an inability to destroy them. There was a general tendency to overestimate the destructive effects of aerial bombs on unfortified structures, a tendency that continued to mislead air strategists during the interwar period.

Lacking any reliable data on the effects of truly massive aerial bombardment, postwar strategists were compelled to reason by analogy and extrapolation, a process that often led them to conclusions valid only on paper. Douhet, who was an artilleryman by training, "converted" an air attack into an artillery bombardment, where the destructive force was better known. He considered that 500 tons of aerial bombs would be the equivalent in destructiveness of ten thousand 305mm projectiles, since they would contain the same amount of high explosive. This quantity, he estimated, could be delivered in a single raid by a force of one thousand bombers. The French ace René Fonck calculated that a 4,400-pound bomb would destroy everything within a radius of 165 feet and a force of five hundred bombers each carrying such a projectile could level an area of 247 acres in a single night; in two or three weeks of mighty raids, they could destroy all of Paris. There are large discrepancies, however. Douhet says a city can be destroyed with 500 tons of high explosive, while Fonck estimates that 15,000–20,000 tons are needed. But there are other problems: all of the bombers must reach the city—many nights in succession, in Fonck's scenario—and distribute their bombs in such a way that each projectile complements the work of the others, forming a vast, continuous pattern of destruction. In order for the pattern to be flawless, each plane, each pilot, each bombardier, and each bomb had to function perfectly.

The inaccuracy of aerial bombing became obvious during the war, but it was the studies conducted after the conflict was over that indicated how serious the problem really was. Shortly after the war, the British Air Ministry conducted a bombing survey in the Rhine area where the Independent Air Force had been active; the survey revealed that air attacks on railway stations and junctions had not had any serious effect. Russia's Gen. N. N. Golovin reported the same result from the eastern front. When the French reoccupied the Briey Basin, they made a thorough study of the effects of their blockade. Of thirteen hundred bombs aimed at the Thionville railway station, only a hundred had struck the target, and a fourth of them failed to explode. The movement of iron ore through Thionville had continued uninterrupted. The Germans had not been encouraged either. They regarded the great arsenal at Woolwich, just east of London, as a prime bombing target; but during three and a half years of bombing raids, they managed to hit the sprawling complex—about two square miles of target—on only a single occasion.

Aerial bombing was thus a highly inaccurate undertaking and seemed likely to to remain so in the foreseeable future. Maj. Oliver Stewart, writing in 1925, said with disarming frankness that a bomber "can hit a town from ten thousand feet—if the town is big enough."[11] These words were not very reassuring, considering that the bombsight, the key element in accurate bombing, had been under continuous development for at least a dozen years. The instrument had grown significantly more complex since 1914, when French bombardiers used as a sighting device three nails driven into the fuselage of their Voisin pushers. By the mid-1920s the course-setting bombsight was coming into use; its chief advantage over the sights used in 1917–18 was that it freed the bombing plane from the necessity of approaching the target from upwind or downwind. In sheer accuracy, however, it offered little advantage over the sights used toward the end of the war. Major Oliver Stewart felt there would be no great improvements in the near future, and in fact, it was not until the late 1930s that another generation of more accurate bombsights appeared.

If, for the moment, it was not possible to hit objectives of limited size with a few accurately aimed bombs, the other solution was to direct at those objectives larger numbers of bombs not so accurately aimed. The French estimated that they could have effectively blockaded the Briey Basin even with the customary low rate of hits, although they would have needed to increase bombing tonnages a hundredfold. The practice of employing sizable numbers of bombers on a single raid was adopted by most belligerents and was further refined after the war. The practice in the French air service in the 1920s was to use the aerial equivalent of what the artillerymen called "zone fire." Fifty or more bombers would fly over the objective in succeeding formations, releasing their bombs so that they fell in a rectangular pattern 250–320 feet wide and 320 feet or more long. The target, lying within this rectangle, would of necessity be hit. As a French officer explained, "On account of the sources of error we have studied, it is necessary to use about 800 projectiles to produce the desired effect on a target."[12] This is an early example of a practice that came to be known as area bombing.

In the 1920s this technique had a severe limitation: it could only be used in day bombing. Night flying in near proximity to other planes was seldom attempted because of fear of collision. At night the bombers usually took off at regular intervals, going to their target Indian file and following a somewhat different route back. (The German Gothas had departed for England at five- or ten-minute intervals.) By the 1940s the difficulties of flying at night were being resolved, so that massive attacks were possible in World War II. Zone or area bombing also had the obvious disadvantage of inefficiency; the bombers had to transport and release several hundred bombs in order for a score of them to strike the target. The projectiles that missed a factory might explode harmlessly in a field, but there was also the possibility—a genuinely troubling one to some theorists of air power—that they would fall on the factory workers' homes.

Here we encounter that aspect of strategic bombardment which was at once the most promising and the most controversial: air attacks whose target was the enemy's civilian population or at least the morale of that population. One of the great discoveries of the war was the value of psychological factors. Despite all the sophisticated gadgetry of the war, it had been at bottom a contest of wills and of endurance. Germany's defeat offered eloquent proof, which the Germans themselves were the first to accept. The German Navy had scarcely seen action; not a single foot of German territory had been invaded. Yet, at the end of 1918, the whole country suffered a sort of collapse—a massive disintegration of confidence, of resolve, of belief in victory—which compelled the German government to sue for peace.

The Allies were witnesses to this astounding collapse, which some of their weapons and techniques helped induce. Much of the credit was claimed by Allied propaganda agencies, which spent half their time bolstering the morale of their own populations and the other half trying to undermine that of the Germans. Spokesmen for the Allied navies argued that privation and distress caused by their blockade had been major factors; but the experience of 1914–18 also confirmed the prewar notion that air attacks had significant psychological effects on those subjected to them. Sir Hugh Trenchard estimated that the psychological "yield" of the RAF's attacks on the Rhine towns was about twenty times the material damage inflicted. The RAF's postwar bombing survey in the Rhine verified what the British had noticed at Woolwich in 1917: when there was frequent bombing in the area, production fell. Workers who spent their nights in basements and subways listening for the sound of bombs either did not come to work or performed poorly if they did. Here was a bombing technique that could curb the enemy's war production without destroying its factories. It required neither great accuracy nor heavy commitment. After all, as P. R. C. Groves observed, a single airplane could keep an entire city awake. And if it triggered the air-raid warning system, it would produce the desired effect without dropping a single bomb. The town of Trier suffered seven air raids, but its air-raid warning system sent inhabitants scurrying to cover 107 times. The nearby town of Bous had seven raids and 300 alerts—and each alert emptied the factories for an hour and sometimes more.

Where the bombing of urban areas was done with any continuity, the stress on the population seemed to increase accordingly. During the height of the bombing attacks against London, thousands fled the eastern districts of the city, seeking safety in the fashionable West End. The official history of the RAF painted a grim picture of the exodus: "Night brought the unrelieved gloom of darkened streets and a brooding sense of danger."[13] In Italian cities frequently bombed by the Austrians hundreds of women and children went out into the surrounding countryside each evening to pass the night wherever they could find shelter.

What would happen if this sort of pressure were kept up, and perhaps even intensified with the bombing of crowded residential areas? How soon would the population reach the limit of its endurance, and what would it do when that limit was reached? Military leaders no doubt asked themselves those questions during the war. Capt. Rudolf Kleine, who led the Gotha attacks on London, proposed to the German high command an intensive campaign of "rolling" attacks night and day, to see if the population's "will to fight" could be broken.[14] His superiors were intrigued by the idea, but did not have the aircraft to undertake it.

After the war the notion of the apparent ability of bombers to shatter enemy morale continued to attract military theorists. Liddell Hart marveled at the profound psychological impression the Gothas had made on Londoners, out of all proportion to the material damage, which was slight. Spaight speculated that the bomber was like any new weapon: for a time after its introduction it has a powerful psychological effect. Firearms had enjoyed the same sort of status when they were first introduced. Inherent in this interpretation was the assumption that aerial bombardment would ultimately lose its intimidating effect. Group Capt. John Slessor, aide to Trenchard, preferred to think that the bomber was successful as a weapon against morale because it alone could attack the most vulnerable element in the population, masses of civilians who did not have the discipline and "sticking power" of the military. This was also the view of Douhet, who believed that the great cities contained "the most delicate and susceptible part of the enemy."[15]

Given the distinctive psychological impact of aerial bombing, the experts were led on to the still unanswered question, How would the civilian population react to serious and sustained attacks directed at its "morale"? Some foresaw that such attacks would trigger massive panics, and here and there in the bombing episodes of the war, there were indeed glimpses of what those panics might be like. A crowd stampeded into a London subway at the beginning of one raid, and a similar incident claimed sixty lives in the Paris metro. Others felt that the raids would generate deep anger. Douhet, who studied press reports of the 1917 attacks on London, concluded that the average

Londoner was as furious with his own government for its inability to protect him as he was with the Germans for attacking him. The anger would ultimately find outlets—perhaps in rioting and looting, as had occurred in isolated instances.

There seemed an ominous possibility that the masses, impelled by fury, terror, or a combination of those emotions, could turn against their own leaders. Frenzied mobs in the capital, seeking an end to the nightmare, might storm the centers of government. No less an authority than Marshal Foch told Groves that a massive air attack could have such "a crushing moral effect on a nation" that its government would find itself disarmed.[16] H. A. Jones, writing in the official history of the RAF, even suggested that the Germans could have provoked an emotional tidal wave in London, had they played their cards more astutely: "A German night-bombing campaign against London in February or early in March, 1918, might have had results leading to a popular clamour which the government might have found themselves unable to withstand."[17] This would be, in effect, a variant of the "knockout blow"; the bombers do not attack the centers of power directly, but instead, they set the masses in motion against those centers. In either case the outcome would be the same: the paralysis of the enemy, followed by his capitulation.

Even if it were an infallible means to victory, a bombing policy whose sole purpose was to demoralize the enemy's population would have been extremely difficult to defend in the period between the wars. Understandably enough in the aftermath of the slaughter of 1914–18, the public regarded any method of war designed to terrorize the civilian population as morally indefensible, and a number of air power theorists felt the same way. Some theorists preferred to link the concept of morale bombing with the more acceptable one of making war on the enemy's industries and other *points sensibles*. The actual purpose of strategic bombing became twofold: to deprive the enemy of both the material means and the will to continue the war. Even then, Billy Mitchell often spoke of the goals of strategic bombardment in curiously veiled terms; he mentions, for example, targets in the enemy's territory "which are further back than his troops are."[18] Others used the euphemism "direct action" for attacks directed at the enemy's capital. When John Slessor took up strategic bombing, he told his readers that "the moral issue should be borne in mind as a background to the consideration of the narrower—but probably not less important—aspect of the problem, the dislocation and restriction by air action of the supply of war material at the source."[19] By the "moral issue," Slessor meant morale, but although he mentioned it, he devoted his attention exclusively to the material effects of bombing.

Spaight came to grips with the ethical issue in several books. He was obviously troubled over the morality of attacks on the civilian population, and the twists and turns in his thinking are visible in his works. He presented the rationale for such attacks clearly and succinctly: "It is the sovereign people who will war today, and it is their nerve and morale that must be broken. The great cities are convenient assemblages of the sovereign people; therefore smash the cities and you smash the will to war."[20] Writing in 1924, Spaight was sure this bombing policy would work: "No amount of composure, no surplusage of bull-dog tenacity can save a people raided copiously, scientifically, systematically."[21] Six years later he was not so sure: "The difficulty is that you may not smash the will to war. You may only harden it, intensify it."[22] In 1924, Spaight could justify assaults on the cities, on the grounds that they would decide the war quickly and thus actually save lives; the slaughter, he said, would be "as nothing compared with that of the older war."[23] But, by 1930, attacks on urban populations were repugnant to Spaight. He called them "bad work for civilization" and he concentrated his efforts on preventing them.[24]

Spaight's dozen books on military aviation are repositories of intelligent analysis and intellectual honesty, but they offer no comprehensive theory of strategic air power. Their author knew he was dealing with a weapon that had scarcely been tested, and the future use of which depended upon a number of technological unknowns; hence, the tentative, conditional nature of his conclusions. At the same time, he was clearly repelled by the idea of training the weapon on urban masses, although in raw terms they offered the most rewarding target. What was needed was a theoretician who could move beyond both technological trammels and moral reservations, a prophet who could forge a bold, comprehensive strategy for the new weapon, drawn from "cold logic and mathematical calculation."[25] This prophet was Giulio Douhet.

Although Douhet is probably the most celebrated theorist of air power, he had surprisingly little firsthand contact with military aviation. He was posted to the Aviation Section of the Italian Army shortly before World War I and served as its director for a few months in 1913 and 1914. His tenure was a stormy one; he was transferred out of aviation after two investigations of his conduct (although the problem was not so much his advocacy of advanced ideas—as some of his admirers have hinted—but his dogmatic and imperious nature). He returned to the air service briefly in 1918 but retired from the army in the same year. In 1922, Mussolini named him "subsecretary of aeronautics," but Douhet soon abandoned that post as well. After 1923 he spent his time writing. It is more than likely that air power's most eloquent spokesman never learned to fly; in any event, his name does not appear on the lists of licensed pilots through 1918.

The details of Douhet's career are important because they help explain how his views on air power could be so sweeping and so categorical. They were developed in a vacuum of sorts, unfettered by practical considerations. Douhet's bombers always flew; his pilots always found their targets. Furthermore, Douhet's most productive years as a theorist, the 1920s, were also years of semi-isolation and bitterness, judging from his published letters. His views became more rigid, and their application, more thoroughgoing. In the 1921 edition of his *Command of the Air,* he proposed two air establishments, one independent and strategic, the other "auxiliary" to the land and sea forces; in his later work, the auxiliary air force was swept away. The offensive capabilities of the multiengined bomber grew in his perception until it became the supreme weapon for attack, and in the end, he would have abolished every other type of aircraft. From its status as "brother" and peer of the land and sea services, the air force rose to a sort of hegemony, having first call on the nation's resources because it alone could secure victory.

Like most other theorists of air power, Douhet spoke of the twin aims of strategic bombing as the destruction of both the enemy's matériel and his psychological means of resistance. If he never completely divorced the two, he did give strong indications that the campaign against morale was the more important. He had no compunctions about sending bombers against civilian populations, and on this subject he wrote with that relentless tough-mindedness so much in vogue in Fascist Italy. Making war on the masses was justified because it worked, and that was what counted: "Humanity and civilization may avert their eyes, but this is the way it will be, inevitably. And for that matter, the conception of belligerents and non-belligerents is outmoded. Today it is not armies but whole nations which make war; and all the citizens are belligerents and all are exposed to the hazards of war. The only salvation will be in caves, but those caves cannot hold entire cities, fleets, railways, bridges, industries, etc."[26]

The air war would be vicious and terrifying, and it would be won by the nation that endured stoically the enemy's blows and delivered more terrible ones itself. The quickest way to victory was through terror. If light bombing produced panic—and here Douhet was impressed above all by the reported effects of bombing on the population of London—then massive bombing would create mass hysteria. He placed great importance on the use of gas bombs, going so far as to say that his theories would not be valid if gas was not a successful weapon. He estimated that a modest air fleet of three hundred bombers, each carrying two tons of gas bombs, could kill fifty thousand people in each of ten different cities, and in eight missions the fleet would account for 4 million deaths in eighty different localities. This "terrifying offensive" would kill only one out of ten people in any given locality, but it would make life unbearable for the other nine and force the enemy population to its knees.[27]

This appalling vision did not go unchallenged. The publication of a second edition of *Command of the Air* in 1927 created a storm of controversy in the Regia Aeronautica (the 1921 edition seems to have been largely ignored). Douhet was deeply involved in these doctrinal battles—which he clearly relished—when death overtook him early in 1930. The supreme prophet of airborne Armageddon died peacefully in a rose garden on Saint Valentine's Day. At that time he could hardly have been known outside of Italy. *Command of the Air* did not appear in French, German, and Russian translations until the mid-1930s; American and British editions appeared in 1942 and 1943, respectively, although manuscript translations are known to have circulated earlier in the RAF and the U.S. Army Air Corps. Robin Higham, who studied the development of British air power concepts between the wars, concludes that the views of the Italian theorist counted for nothing in that development.

A half century after his death Giulio Douhet remains the best known theorist of air power and also the least understood. There is no satisfactory biography of the man, and studies of his thought have rarely gone beyond *Command of the Air,* a small sampling of his voluminous writings over two decades. Speculation and controversy still swirl about Douhet. Higham and other historians speak of the "myth" of his influence between the wars, and they can put forward some impressive evidence. Amedeo Mecozzi has questioned the originality of Douhet's thought, arguing that much seems to have been taken from the works of Ader and other early writers. There are those who see Douhet as a creature of Gianni Caproni, with whom he was closely associated for years. This interpretation finds special favor among Marxist historians.

We need not concern ourselves further with these quarrels. Whatever his reasons were for writing, Douhet stated the case for air power as no one else did—with all the stops out. Even if he offered nothing startlingly new, the views were advanced with ringing certitude and Latin fervor. Those who read *Command of the Air,* early or late, often found bold confirmation of ideas stirring in their own minds. But if the extreme case for air power attracted some, it repelled others. It frightened and provoked people all over Europe and strengthened them in their determination to see that the aerial Armageddon never took place.

CHAPTER 4

BANNING THE BOMBER

IF AIR POWER HAD ITS PROPHETS and its believers even before World War I, it also had its enemies, and they too became active before 1914. The last decade of the nineteenth century witnessed an acceleration of the armaments race, placing heavy financial burdens on governments and populations alike. In the 1890s the Russian government made the alarming discovery that it would have to replace the artillery pieces which it had fairly recently supplied to its army. These had been rendered obsolete by new and more efficient artillery adopted by Russia's neighbors. Alarmed at the cost, the Russians tried another solution; they proposed the International Peace Conference at The Hague. Other governments welcomed the chance to explore arms limitations, for they too were struggling with problems of rapid obsolescence and high replacement costs.

Neither the 1899 nor the 1907 Hague conference was able to bring the arms race to an end. If anything, investments in weaponry increased and so did protests. In many countries there was a vociferous element that preached another course entirely. Its leaders, often pacifist and internationalist in tone, denounced not only the armaments programs but also the militarism and chip-on-the-shoulder nationalism that promoted those programs. At first, these advocates of peaceful solutions and international understanding saw the airplane and the dirigible as allies, because they seemed likely to make national boundaries and barriers obsolete as they came and went at will through the open skies, promoting contacts and understanding between peoples and binding them together for mutual benefit. One of those who believed in this idyllic future for aviation was Bertha von Suttner, pacifist, reformer, and winner of the Nobel Peace Prize in 1905. Frau von Suttner lobbied vigorously at the first Hague conference in 1899. While there, she noted, "Inventors of airships and flying machines send me their plans and prospectuses."[1] By the conquest of the atmosphere, national boundaries, with their customs houses and fortifications, would soon disappear—or so said her correspondents.

But the airship and the "flying machine" began to show up regularly at army maneuvers and naval exercises and to make a place for themselves alongside the traditional weapons. At that point, the partisans of peace and international understanding began to feel doubtful about the role of the airplane. The German Social Democratic newspaper *Vorwärts* warned its readers on October 9, 1907, "It really seems that in addition to our lordly army and our not quite so lordly but very pretentious fleet, we must also have militarism in the air."

The Italo-Turkish War of 1911–12 brought the first use of the new air weapons as well as a round of protest against their use. The very first bombing attack against Ain Zara stirred up controversy when the Turks claimed the bomb had hit a hospital. The Italian government denied the charge but was concerned enough to try to find out discreetly if the Turks were telling the truth. They probably were not (the Italians had already shelled the objective by conventional means without any protests from the Turks); even so, the Ain Zara affair served to open a debate on the morality of aerial bombing.

Bertha von Suttner fiercely denounced what she called the "barbarization of the air," which would make war a totally different game: "We want to keep the old rules, where the pawns can take only one move and the knight can jump; where the queen is the most powerful piece and the king can "castle" to protect himself. But now we have new rules: each of us may have something drop on our squares from above, something that will blow the pieces off the gaming board."[2] In England two hundred prominent figures put their names to a memorial calling for the suppression of aerial weapons before they spread further; among the signers were Thomas Hardy, Lord Lister, A. Conan Doyle, H. G. Wells, and ten Anglican bishops. In Austria, Viktor Silberer, editor of the *Wiener Luftschiffer-Zeitung* and a ballooning enthusiast for thirty years, denounced "aerial militarism" as the

, of unscrupulous aircraft manufacturers, "especially the ɲch."[3]

When the nations of Europe rushed to arms in 1914, the martial ɲood and the confidence in rapid victory ended for a time all talk of banning or limiting the use of aerial weapons. But, as the conflict wore on, and as the bombing planes began to carry the war behind the battle lines and into the cities, other voices were raised against the spread of violence. First, there were the neutrals. In the autumn of 1914, Woodrow Wilson sought through his ambassador to Berlin to prevent the bombing of Allied cities. Pope Benedict XV made several overtures to the belligerents. Early in 1916, after the bombing of Ravenna, he appealed to both Italy and Austria to respect open cities; a spokesman for the pope said, "He wishes even more than that—that the use of aeroplane bombs in the Austro-Italian War could be entirely dispensed with."[4] In the last year of the war, the Spanish government made an unsuccessful effort to bring to a halt the bombing of all cities.

Even among the belligerents there was some resistance to widening the sphere of air operations. In England the wisdom of reprisal was much debated. Many professed they could not see the logic in punishing the inhabitants of a peaceful German town for the cruelties of a German U-boat commander. A conclave of the Church of England denounced reprisals, and the Archbishop of Canterbury spoke out against them. After the Allied reprisal raid against Freiburg in April 1917, members of both houses of Parliament registered strong objections, but these were swept away when the Germans intensified their attacks on English towns in May 1917. In Germany there were rumblings in Baden, whose towns were easy targets for Allied bombers. And in France, in March 1918, the government was bracing for a debate over its bombing policy. Then the Ludendorff offensive started, and everything else was forgotten.

At the end of the war, there were signals, although somewhat confusing ones, from the German government; members of the Reichstag raised the question of a mutual agreement to stop the bombing of urban targets, and the German government indicated on two separate occasions that it would examine seriously any proposals to that end which the Allies might make. In May 1918, there was even a bombing truce, although it was a partial and temporary one. The Archbishop of Cologne sent a request, transmitted by the Vatican, that the RAF refrain from bombing attacks in the interior of Germany on May 30 so that Germans could hold their traditional Corpus Christi processions safely. The British government honored the request. Unfortunately, on that same day, German long-range cannon fired a number of shells into Paris.

In October 1918, the German government took another step. It sought to return to its bombing policy of 1914, limiting aerial bombardment to the battle zone, in the obvious hope that the Allies would reciprocate. The Allies did not, but it should be noted that about the same time, the U.S. government was showing concern over the RAF's bombing offensive. Secretary of War Newton Baker sent word that the American air service would not participate in any plan which had as its objective "promiscuous bombing upon industry, commerce, or population."[5] What this might have meant for the air campaign of 1919, one can only guess; as it was, the war ended before American bombers could make anything more than a very modest contribution.

The end of the war brought the first, and in some ways the most successful, effort to reduce the aerial danger. Although the effort was completely one-sided, involving the forced aerial disarmament of Germany by the Allies, it is important because it demonstrated for the first time some of the practical difficulties in regulating air armaments. The aerial disarmament of Germany began with the armistice of November 1918. According to the armistice's terms, Germany was obliged to turn over sizable quantities of war material as a pledge of its good faith. Aircraft figured prominently in the list of seventeen hundred weapons to be surrendered; the Allies required that all aircraft of two types be included in that number: the Fokker D-VII fighters and the night bombers. A month later, the Allies complained that they had received only 25 bombers out of a total of 730 aircraft received (many of the Gothas and R-planes had been lost in missions over the western front).

When the Allies sat down to prepare their peace terms, they found that while they were in agreement on the disarmament of Germany, they differed very much on how, and to what degree, disarmament should be accomplished. When Lloyd George proposed setting a limit of two hundred thousand men for the German Army and air service combined, General Duval of the French air service questioned whether Germany should be allowed an air force at all. The other Allies made no objections to a blanket prohibition, so the text of the Treaty of Versailles came to read: "The armed forces of Germany must not include any military or naval air forces." A minor and temporary exception were the hundred seaplanes that the German government could continue to operate in order to aid in the search for the thousands of naval mines sown during the war. The American delegation asked whether the ban on the manufacture and importation of aircraft and their components applied only to military types or to commercial types as well. The British thought a ban on all production and importation for a period of two to five years might not be a bad thing, while the French favored a period of twenty or thirty years. In the end, the Americans and others argued successfully that a total ban was unduly punitive, and it was in force for only a few months.

What was also remarkable about these draconian provisions was the elaborate machinery that was set up to implement and enforce them. The Allies kept a careful count of Germany's aerial demilitarization, with the final tally showing that the German authorities destroyed or turned over to the Allies some sixteen thousand aircraft and sixteen dirigibles. The Germans had little chance to hold anything back. German airspace was open to Allied planes; in addition, the Inter-Allied Control Commission had the right to roam Germany, looking into arsenals, factories, and hangars. The inspection team that visited Poll Airfield near Cologne shortly after the armistice made what seemed a particularly ominous find—an unfinished bombing plane of truly gigantic proportions. Its wings, measuring half the length of a football field, were to carry ten motors; its landing wheels were seven feet, nine inches in diameter. Workmen said it was being built to raid New York.

These rights of inspection ultimately proved incompatible with Germany's notion of its own sovereignty, and indeed, it is hard to imagine any nation submitting to them unless, like Germany in 1918, it was submitting to force majeure. As emotions subsided and Germany was accepted back into the family of nations, the Allies made a series of concessions. In 1922 they permitted the production of commercial and civilian aircraft, in 1923 they relinquished to Germany complete control of its airspace, and in 1926 the Inter-Allied Control Commission withdrew. Germany was still committed to maintaining no military or naval air forces, but there was no longer any effective way to know if it were honoring its commitment.

The other problem in maintaining Germany's aerial disarmament was in distinguishing between military aircraft, which were prohibited, and commercial craft, which were not. Where the problem was most acute was in craft designed to carry sizable loads of passengers or merchandise. The basic hallmark of the bomber was also its ability to carry a heavy load, and in fact, the difference between bomber and transport was very small indeed. A plane built as a bomber could very easily be converted to haul passengers; Frederick Handley Page proved this at war's end when he placed rows of wicker seats in his 0/400 bombers and opened a passenger service between London and Paris. But convertibility worked two ways. Aircraft that the Germans had built as transports seemed to the Allied inspectors potential bombers, and they seized them forthwith, despite the vigorous protest of their German builders and owners. So frequent were the seizures and the disputes that in 1922 the Allied authorities drew up a set of guidelines, which they then imposed on the Germans. The Nine Rules, as they were called, classified as "military," and therefore illegal, any airplane with a speed of 170 kilometers (102 miles) an hour, a maximum ceiling of 4,000 meters (13,000 feet) or more, or "a useful load of more than 600 kgs. [1,320 lbs.] including pilot, mechanic and instruments."[6] So long as they were enforced, these rules effectively prevented Germany from building planes that could carry out aerial bombardment. Unfortunately, at the same time, they prevented Germany from building viable commercial aircraft. The Nine Rules, like so many other Allied regulations, ceased to be applied in the late 1920s.

The rather arbitrary disarming of Germany was only the first step in what many hoped would be a worldwide movement to reduce armaments. The impetus in the postwar world was strong, producing a significant agreement on limiting naval armaments at the Washington Naval Conference of 1921–22. The Aviation Subcomittee of the conference explored the possibility of limiting military aircraft (Billy Mitchell was one of the American representatives). Air power did not lend itself to the sorts of limitations that could be placed on battleships. To begin with, the subcommittee could find no basis for alloting so many planes to one country and so many to another. Furthermore, it was impossible to put restrictions on bombers, either in number or in performance, without also imposing restrictions on commercial aircraft that could be converted into bombers. This, said the subcommittee, would "shut the door" on aviation progress. These special problems were referred by the conference to the Commission of Jurists, which was to concern itself with "new agencies of warfare"—the airplane and the radio.

The Commission of Jurists met at The Hague from December 1922 until February 1923, when it issued a code of aerial warfare that came to be known as the Hague Draft Rules. The legal experts were from six countries: the United States, Great Britain, France, Italy, Japan, and the Netherlands; they were assisted in their deliberations by military and naval experts. At the outset the panel decided not to try to set limitations on the aircraft themselves (for example, number or type) but only the way they were used in war. Moreover, they decided that there was no purpose in resurrecting the rules of the earlier Hague conferences and that therefore they would start afresh.

The jurists did not conceal their feelings about aerial bombing as it had been practiced in the war: "The conscience of mankind revolts against this form of making war outside the actual theatre of military operations, and the feeling is universal that limitations ought to be imposed."[7] They also acknowledged that they had an extremely difficult task before them, and as it turned out, their views about what to do were very diverse. The Americans wanted to make a sharp distinction between bombing in, and outside of, the "combat area" with the latter being severely restricted. The Japanese and the Dutch, whose countries had a small area and dense populations, wanted the most thorough protection for cities and towns. The Italians wanted the airmen who bombed illegal targets brought to trial personally on charges of having committed acts of perfidy.

The Hague conferees ultimately agreed on a set of "Rules of Aerial Warfare," comprising sixty-two articles, of which five related to bombardment. The three most important were the following:

> Article 22.—Aerial bombardment for the purpose of terrorizing the civilian population, of destroying or damaging private property not of a military character, or of injuring non-combatants, is prohibited.
> Article 23.—Aerial bombardment for the purpose of enforcing compliance with requisitions in kind or payment of contributions in money is prohibited.
> Article 24.—(1) Aerial bombardment is legitimate only when directed at a military objective, that is to say, an object of which the destruction or injury would constitute a distinct military advantage to the belligerent.
> (2) Such bombardment is legitimate only when directed exclusively at the following objectives: military forces; military works; military establishments or depots; factories constituting important and well-known centres engaged in the manufacture of arms, ammunition, or distinctively military supplies; lines of communication or transportation used for military purposes.
> (3) The bombardment of cities, towns, villages, dwellings, or buildings not in the immediate neighbourhood of the operations of land

forces is prohibited. In cases where the objectives specified in paragraph (2) are so situated that they cannot be bombarded without the indiscriminate bombardment of the civilian population, the aircraft must abstain from bombardment.

(4) In the immediate neighbourhood of the operations of land forces, the bombardment of cities, towns, villages, dwellings, or buildings is legitimate provided that there exists a reasonable presumption that the military concentration is sufficiently important to justify such bombardment, having regard to the danger thus caused to the civilian population.

(5) A belligerent State is liable to pay compensation for injuries to person or to property caused by the violation by any of its officers or forces of the provisions of this article.[8]

Article 25 concerned the special identifying marks to be placed on hospitals, museums, and the like. Article 26 dealt with special "zones of protection" for historical monuments. (Both of these articles originated with the Italian delegation.)

The key provision is article 24, which Spaight immediately perceived would produce "difficulties." Spaight had served as air adviser to the British delegation at The Hague and dedicated his book *Air Power and War Rights* to the American jurist John Bassett Moore, who had chaired the Hague meeting, but in that same book he wrote:

> It is doubtful whether such rules for air bombardment as those drawn up by the jurists at the Hague in January–February, 1923, will save the world's great cities. The doctrine of the 'military objective,' useful within its own limits, will be no adequate protection. Any belligerent who chooses will be able to keep within the rules which embody that doctrine and yet use his air arms for a purpose quite distinct from the destruction of objects of military importance, namely, for the creation of a moral, political or psychological effect within the enemy country.[9]

In a future war the bombers would be drawn inexorably to cities and industrial centers; as in the last war, they would find convenient "military" targets to aim for in both places, even though they would not be able to hit them. Here Spaight quoted a French pilot of the Great War: "In the war reports there are always passages which make one smile, such as the dropping of ten bombs from a height of 2000 meters [6,600 feet] upon 'military establishments.'"[10]

Yet, Spaight could not accept the idea that aerial warfare might degenerate into what he called "strong cave-man stuff." He felt that in the next war most long-distance bombing would be done by night, and he hoped that an understanding could be reached whereby the night bombers could come and strike the vital centers, both political and economic, while the bulk of the population was not in them. The example that Spaight gave was the City of London. The day population of its 675 acres was over four hundred thousand people; at night that figure dropped to fourteen thousand. If arrangements could be made to lodge those fourteen thousand elsewhere, the City would become an area in which enemy bombers could do enormous material damage, but at the same time spare human life. "In brief," wrote Spaight, "I will give you property to destroy, if you will give me life to save."[11]

Spaight also found another reason for hope, one that perhaps only an Englishman could find. He dwelt at some length on the spirit of chivalry that had appeared in the various air services during the war. This might well be encouraged by requiring, for example, that an officer be in command of each airplane. With gentlemen at the controls, bombing squadrons would better resist the caveman approach to their work.

One of the American advisers at the Hague meeting was Capt. William C. Sherman, who was at the time an instructor in air tactics at the Command and General Staff School, Fort Leavenworth. Sherman held to the notion that considerations of fair play and humanity would mitigate the horrors of the next war in the air: "Among peoples in whom the spirit of sport has been strongly inculcated, it is peculiarly abhorrent to contemplate the waging of war on unarmed civilians of all ages and sexes."[12] In a more practical vein, he felt that the fear of reprisal would keep the air war from degenerating into indiscriminate attacks on the cities. These restraints seemed to him more likely to be effective than the Hague rules.

The skepticism that both Spaight and Sherman felt about the Hague rules was probably shared by a good many of the other technical delegates. As the Draft Rules became known, the reaction to them in military and aviation circles was sometimes emphatically hostile. C. G. Grey, editor of the *Aeroplane,* wrote in the issue of July 11, 1923, that the only practical result of the bombing code would be to "cramp the style" of the RAF at the beginning of a war: "If we go bang into the next war all hair and teeth and blood, as the saying goes, free from any fetters of rules and regulations, we may achieve quite useful results at the start." Such considerations as these probably impressed the governments of the interwar period. In any event, there was no rush to ratify the Hague rules. By 1939 they still were draft rules only and not legally binding on any of the belligerents; still, in the first months of the conflict they were voluntarily observed by those belligerents.

The idea of a code of bombing rules had to vie with another concept that enjoyed considerable popularity in the interwar period, that of an international air force. In its inception, the idea was probably traceable to the French. At the end of the war, the French government put forward what came to be called the Bourgeois Plan, which would have placed at the disposal of the League of Nations a multinational peacekeeping force. (France was probably the most influential member of the League in its early years and regarded it as an agency for preserving and policing the Versailles settlement.) The idea of an international air force attracted considerable attention in the late 1920s, with variants of the basic idea being put forward by a number of individuals and organizations. Essentially, the scheme would concentrate either the bulk or the totality of air power into a peacekeeping force under an international agency that would also regulate and monitor commercial aviation throughout the world. In his book *The World Crisis: The Aftermath,* Winston Churchill recommended giving the League a monopoly on air power, with each member supplying squadrons for League service. The French politician Edouard Herriot wanted to create a permanent international air force, while Adm. Robert Lawson of the Royal Navy proposed a "European Air Service" for police purposes. Even Douhet described a *gendarmeria aerea internazionale*, although he later dropped the idea.

Spaight embraced the idea and described to his readers how a fleet of bombers bearing the League of Nations initials in big red letters would bring a fictitious aggressor named Colossia to her knees. And Air Commodore L. E. O. Charlton, another prolific writer on aviation, put forth in fascinating detail a plan for an international strategic reserve. This air force would be composed of three thousand airplanes, the great bulk of them bombers. They were to be flown by men recruited between the ages of twenty-one and thirty, who signed up for ten years' service and, in doing so, gave up their national allegiance. As a point of delicacy they would not be required to participate in hostilities against their country of origin. The strategic reserve would be commanded by a marshal who took his orders from the League. The headquarters of the reserve was to be in Tunisia, but it would also have advance bases in France and Poland; it could use the airspace of any country at will above the altitude of 10,000 feet. Charlton, too, offered a scenario to explain how the reserve would work: an Italian dictator named Rodolfo Pizzicato began an aggressive war against Egypt, only to sue for peace twenty-four hours later, after reserve bombers had shattered Italy's naval bases and pushed its population to mass panic with a publicly announced plan to devastate the country's urban centers one by one.

Charlton was also a prominent participant in the sometimes noisy debate over air control in the British Empire, which frequently showed the bombing plane in a highly unfavorable light. Charlton went to serve with the RAF in Iraq in 1923. He soon discovered in a local hospital a number of victims of British bombs and learned that "an air bomb in Iraq was, more or less, the equivalent of a police truncheon at home."[13] After seeing a score of women and children killed and wounded and wounded camels run in circles until they dropped, Charlton sent his superior a strong letter of protest and left Iraq. About the same time, Evelyn Waugh reported from South Africa that British airmen there spent their time harassing a local tribe because it refused to pay a tax on its dogs. RAF spokesmen did their best to defend air control, which they painted as eminently humane when compared to the traditional methods employed by the British army: "Some casualties are bound to occur to tribesmen and their animals, and some damage to property, but the main purpose is to bring about submission with the minimum of destruction and loss of life. Aircraft skilfully used without causing serious loss can produce a maximum of discomfort and weariness for an indefinite time."[14]

Such assurances did little to silence the critics, and the debate boiled on, fueled by questions in Parliament and indignant letters to the *Times*. A similar agitation developed in France in 1925, when the government used airplanes against the followers of the Moroccan rebel Abd-el-Krim. Rumors spread that the French pilots were bombing mosques, and a clamor arose in the Chamber of Deputies. The affair took on international proportions when the press revealed that a band of American volunteers was flying with the French. At about the same time, the Spanish were trying out bombs against dissidents in their portion of Morocco. None of these episodes did much to enhance aerial bombing in the public eye.

By the early 1930s, storm clouds were gathering again over Europe itself; the experts were painting appalling pictures of what the next war in the air would be like, and political leaders were accepting those pictures as accurate. In November 1932, Prime Minister Stanley Baldwin solemnly warned the House of Commons that failure to abolish the bomber would mean the end of European civilization. When Baldwin spoke, he and his audience had their minds on the Conference for the Reduction and Limitation of Armaments, or Geneva Disarmament Conference, which was then beginning its deliberations. This would be the last international effort to ban the bomber before the storm broke. The governments and peoples of Europe seem to have sensed this, for the effort they made was an exceptional one.

The Geneva conference was billed as a "world" conference, and the representation was impressive; it included the United States and the Soviet Union, powers whose presence underlined the importance and the global scope of the disarmament problem. When the conference opened in February 1932, the delegations found before them a number of possible solutions. The Preparatory Commission had been working intermittently since 1926 to find ways to limit and regulate armaments; Subcommittee B, for example, had struggled with the almost insoluble problem of defining bombing planes and distinguishing them from transport craft.

There seems little doubt that when the conference opened, most of the delegations were genuinely interested in reducing and limiting arms, particularly in the air. But each nation wanted the swords to be beaten into plowshares in a certain way, and this was the rock on which the conference ultimately foundered. The French saw disarmament as a consequence of security, which necessarily came first. The British were willing to try a ban on weapons such as bombing planes or a prohibition of bombing itself, with one exception: they wanted to retain the use of bombers for the "air control" of their empire. The German delegation was not interested in disarmament itself—Germany being already disarmed, thanks to the Versailles Treaty—but in *Gleichberechtigung* ("equality of rights"); either other nations should disarm or Germany should be entitled to rearm. The German delegation was particularly anxious to wrest some victory here that it could offer to the German people, who in 1932 were increasingly drawn by the siren song of Adolf Hitler.

The French were the first to lay their cards on the table. They would accept equality of armament for the Germans if the conferees agreed to set up a powerful international police force under League of Nations control. All bombing planes would be transferred to the League, and their use by national governments prohibited. Civil aviation would also operate under international supervision. A number of small countries were ready to accept this program, but it ran into the firm opposition of a number of great powers, including the United States. Other nations offered recipes of their own; the British proposed in March 1933 an abolition of bombing except for police purposes in certain outlying regions. President Herbert Hoover proposed scrapping whole categories of arms, including all military aviation except naval observation planes.

Were the powers seriously considering abolishing their own air forces? Surprisingly, in many cases the answer was yes. Within each government there was something of a struggle, to be sure, but very often the army and navy leaders led the fight to get rid of the air force. Hoover was apparently sincere in his proposal to dismantle military aviation and was supported in that proposal by Gen. Douglas MacArthur, then chief of staff of the U.S. Army. MacArthur, who was trying to maintain a military establishment on the most meager of appropriations, decided the allotment for army aeronautics would be better used elsewhere.

In Great Britain, where interservice rivalries had been keen since the creation of the RAF, the "third service" was fighting for its life. For a time, the British government seriously contemplated abolishing all or part of its military aviation if that was what it took to get an international agreement which would protect Britain from aerial attacks. The other two services supported this policy, assuring the government that they would supply the nation's defense needs without the assistance of their upstart competitor. A Royal Navy spokesman added insult to injury when he endorsed a ban on bombers: "Only the Air Ministry want to retain these weapons for use against towns, a method of warfare which is revolting and un-English."[15] At the same time, in French government discussions the senior services were making similar charges against the Armée de l'Air.

But there was no agreement at Geneva. If the negotiators shared a common goal, they could not find a common path to it. Then, in late January 1933, Hitler became chancellor and took the tiller of German foreign policy. His view on air power, as on armaments generally, was to play for time and rush Germany's rearmament so that he could speak and act from a position of strength. In October 1933 the German delegation left Geneva; Hitler's government announced it was withdrawing from the League of Nations. From time to time, Hitler would make sibylline pronouncements about negotiations on air armaments: in 1934 he was willing to maintain an air force half the size of that of France; in 1935 he said the air war might be limited gradually, beginning with a ban on bombing outside the battle zone. But the French and the British found it impossible to translate these utterances into firm agreements, and it is probable that by 1935, Hitler was determined to make no commitment that would interfere with Germany's rearmament.

The rest of the delegations left Geneva in the spring of 1934. The French government announced that it would henceforth seek security through the "traditional" means. It would push its rearmament programs, and it would shore up its military alliances. The French would still show an interest in schemes being devised on the other side of the Channel to regulate the air war, but only if those schemes strengthened the security of France.

Long after the Geneva conference became history the British government persisted in its search for an answer to the air menace, a menace that it and the people it represented felt more keenly than anyone else. After the collapse of the Geneva conference the British pursued the idea of an "Air Locarno," an agreement by the major powers of Europe to abstain from aggressive air attacks and to turn their combined bomber forces on any transgressors. Hitler seemed interested briefly but then began to dwell on the difficulties; the French were interested too, but only if the British would sign a bilateral agreement spelling out how many RAF squadrons would come to the assistance of France if it were attacked.

After 1936 the British shifted their effort. Since bombers could not be abolished and bombing could not be outlawed by international agreement, perhaps at least it could be regulated and limited. This was a return to the philosophy of the Hague conference of 1922–23. Here again the War Office and the Admiralty were in favor of restricting aerial bombardment, while the Air Ministry was opposed. That ministry took a full year to draw up a plan for restricting warfare in the air. Then, in February 1938, Hitler made a speech before the Reichstag in which he threw cold water on any limitations scheme. The British chiefs of staff, the chief of the air staff excepted, could think of only one other step. Britain might declare publicly that in the event of another war it would observe the Hague Draft Rules. Others might be encouraged to follow its example. So ended a search for protection from the air menace that the historian Uri Bialer has portrayed as an obsession for those who ruled Britain in the thirties. But, even while they were searching, they were taking steps to create the most powerful strategic-bombing force Europe had ever seen.

CHAPTER 5

THE RISE OF
THE AIR FLEETS

IN THE YEARS FOLLOWING WORLD WAR I, France emerged as the greatest air power in Europe—indeed, in the world. In 1922 it and its allies in eastern Europe could muster 760 squadrons, about twice the air strength of all the rest of Europe combined. France's preeminence in the air was so great in the early 1920s that it became a concern for her neighbor across the Channel. At the time, there were policy disagreements between the two powers, and although the danger of war was a remote one, the British government found it had no way to counter a massive cross-Channel aerial assault. The RAF had been cut back drastically after the armistice, and much of its remaining strength was scattered throughout the British Empire. There were only five squadrons in England in 1922, so in August of that year the British cabinet ordered an increase in the RAF.

Yet there was no real aerial arms race in the 1920s. While the victors of 1918 maintained a certain strength, there was little impetus to modernize. The French kept the Breguet 14 bomber in production until 1927, a full decade after its introduction. The RAF did not get a new bomber until 1923, followed by a new fighter in 1924. Development of new aircraft was leisurely—up to seven years from the issuance of government specifications for a new bomber to its introduction in the squadrons. For one thing, air budgets were tight and funds for developmental work came only in driblets. But also, there seemed to be no hurry; in 1919 the British government adopted its "ten-year rule," which remained in force until 1932. Each year the cabinet renewed the rule, enjoining the armed services to make their plans and estimates on the assumption that there would be no major war for ten years.

Such a rule is perfectly understandable in the context of the times. In the 1920s the British and French could see no major aggressor except each other, and even this threat disappeared when relations between the two countries improved after 1923. Germany was manifestly unhappy over the outcome of the Great War, but it was disarmed and friendless, as were its former allies. The Soviet Union was a genuinely troubling presence, but for the time being, it presented no serious danger in the air. In their early zeal, the Soviets denounced the warplane as a tool of imperialism and talked of converting aircraft factories to the manufacture of furniture. But they decided to retain their air arm, appropriately renamed the Peasants' and Workers' Air Fleet. By 1923 the new regime was promoting aviation with slogans like "Proletarians, take to the air!" Aerial rearmament required more than enthusiasm, and the Soviets found it a slow, demanding enterprise.

For a decade, the Allies of 1918, and particularly the French, enjoyed military hegemony almost by default. The armaments and techniques dating from the Great War largely satisfied their needs. The chief enemies the British and French air forces had to contend with were Bedouins, Afghans, and Druses, all of whom could be intimidated with vintage aircraft and bombs left over from 1918. Not surprisingly, military air fleets fell behind commercial ones in incorporating improvements and innovations.

The picture changed radically in the thirties. The victors of 1918 and the peace they had imposed no longer seemed secure. The world economic crisis was accompanied by the emergence of totalitarian regimes with aggressive foreign policies. The military supremacy of the British and French came under challenge, nowhere quite so dramatically as in the air. In 1931 the Italian Air Force put on an impressive display of its power, and a number of observers concluded that the Fascist regime was approaching air parity with France. In the spring of 1935, Hitler delivered a profound shock to the British government when he told two of its envoys that his Luftwaffe was equal in strength to the RAF.

The thirties was a period of sometimes frantic activity as the air forces of Europe rushed to expand and modernize. Rearmament in the air was of course only part of rearmament in general. In each country the air service had to compete with sea and ground forces for a share of the defense budget. If the struggle was one common to all the air services, the result was not always the same. Britain's RAF was usually able to obtain a hefty third of the defense allocation, and in some years, its appropriation far exceeded that of the British army. At the other end of the scale was Poland's air service, the Lotnistvo Wojskowe, which received only 3–4 percent of defense appropriations for the years 1936–39.

Even when the funds were available, creating a bomber fleet was no easy task in the early thirties. An era of prolonged disarmament efforts and strong pacifist movements was not one receptive to developing such a patently offensive weapon as the bomber. The Soviets were proclaiming that the more bombers a country had, the more imperialistic it was. The very name *bomber* became an embarrassment. For a time in the thirties the French renamed their bomber force Heavy Defense Aviation, while the British referred to their bomber squadrons simply as Wessex Area. In America, Army Air Corps officials became uncomfortable whenever the press referred to the huge B-15 as a "superbomber." Design and development were considerably influenced by the international climate, and even by the ups and downs of the disarmament negotiations. The Germans curtailed work on their bomber needs in 1929 and 1930 in the belief that that type of aircraft would come under international regulation. The British delayed developing the heavy bomber partly because they believed for a time that they could convince the rest of Europe to adopt a weight limitation of three tons for bombing craft.

The quest for identity and purpose common to all the air services of the thirties ended differently for each of them. The RAF perhaps came closest to Douhet's ideal of an independent service committed to its own strategic offensive. The Luftwaffe and the Armée de l'Air were independent services also, but neither was oriented toward strategic operations divorced from the war on the ground. The U.S. Army Air Corps was an appendage of the army; nevertheless, it had a strong interest in strategic bombing. The Soviet air force, similarly dependent, did not share this strong interest. Italy's Regia Aeronautica had independence but no fixed views of its own function.

Why were there so many different responses to the challenge of air power? In each country key personalities no doubt played a role. Douhet's rigidity and thorniness of character probably helped assure that his ideas would not be adopted by the air service that he briefly headed. Hermann Goering's political standing and prestige certainly helped to secure the independence of the Luftwaffe, and there is also little doubt that it was Sir Hugh Trenchard who kept the RAF from losing its independent status in the interservice fighting of the early postwar period.

It is tempting to look beyond the interplay of personalities to see if there are any meaningful patterns and parallels in the air power "formulas" devised in the various countries. The American historian Bernard Brodie has suggested that every air force that had "the administrative and intellectual freedom" to do so was drawn to Douhetism.[1] But many air services—those of Continental powers with a traditionally preponderant land army—were bound to that army because of its "tremendous prestige and insistent demands."[2] The East German historian Olaf Groehler sees in strategic bombing a tool of imperialism, forged by a coalition of militarists and industrialists: Douhet and Caproni, Trenchard and Handley Page, Mitchell and William E. Boeing. The more powerful these *Luftkriegsextremisten* were in any given country, the more savagely destructive the bombing offensive they would devise.[3]

The proof of any theory is of course its applicability in specific cases; at this point, therefore, one should look at the combat doctrines and air fleets of the major powers as they emerged in the thirties.

If there is a single document in which the *raison d'être* of the RAF found expression, it is a memorandum that Sir Hugh Trenchard prepared in May 1928.[4] Trenchard did not have a flair with words either in speaking or in writing, but in this instance—perhaps with the help of his aides—he put his case for air power very clearly: "The aim of the air force," he began, "is to break down the enemy's means of resistance by attacks on objectives selected as most likely to achieve this end." He then proceeded to prove that this policy was militarily sound, the best way to use aircraft in war, and not "contrary either to international law or to the dictates of humanity." At the outset, the air force might contend with the enemy air fleet for air superiority, but this contest would be largely incidental to striking the key objectives, the enemy's "centers of production, transportation and communication." Trenchard went on to describe the proper targets: production facilities for everything "from boots to battleships," rail systems, docks and shipyards, wireless stations, and postal and telegraph systems.

Trenchard went to some pains to explain that this sort of bombardment was neither illegal nor inhumane. The indiscriminate bombing of a city for the purpose of terrorizing its inhabitants was improper, but striking at legitimate military targets within that city and causing "incidental destruction of civilian life and property" was altogether acceptable. Trenchard argued that it was legitimate to frighten away workers in war industries, since their work was part of the enemy war effort. This "moral" effect was a sort of bonus to be added to the material destruction achieved, but in Trenchard's view, it might be of greater importance. Civilians were primarily vulnerable to assault on their state of mind: "They are not disciplined and it cannot be expected of them that they will stick stolidly to their lathes and benches under the recurring threat of air bombardment." He spoke of generating "a state of panic" and cited examples of work stoppages in Germany in 1918. To buttress his argument he quoted the prediction of Marshal Foch about the critical nature of the bomber.

Trenchard retired from his post as chief of the air staff a year after he wrote the memorandum. The RAF entered the 1930s armed with his doctrines but not with an air fleet capable of carrying them out. In 1930 the fleet numbered about seven hundred planes, compared to eleven hundred in Mussolini's Regia Aeronautica and thirteen hundred in the French Air Force. The bombing craft of the early thirties were a kind of menagerie—Harts, Hinds, Wapitis, Wildebeests— bizarre in name and limited in performance. None of them had the ability to range over Europe with respectable bombloads, and in this sense they were inferior to the Handley Pages of 1918. Much of the explanation lies in the fact that the air war against a great power in Europe was only a theoretical possibility, while air control within the British Empire was a practical, everyday responsibility. Furthermore, in the troubled and disarmament-minded early thirties, it was probably wise not to dwell on devastating raids against a neighboring country's heartland. On the other hand, as policeman of the empire, the RAF could cast itself in a role somewhat more popular with both the British government and the public. A visiting Soviet aircraft designer saw the RAF's "image" displayed at the Hendon Air Show of 1936: "A big crowd of armed, dark-skinned people apparently personifying Arabs burst onto the airfield from some concealed hiding place. In white burnouses and headdresses they rushed at the stands, shouting and howling frightfully. But fighters appeared—strafed—bombs burst, machine guns rattled; the 'tribe' was wiped out to a single man."[5]

When Hitler came to power in 1933, the possibility of a major war increased and the future antagonist began to take on shape and substance. British air rearmament began seriously in 1934, with what was called Scheme A; once launched, it both accelerated and changed its objectives as the nation's military leaders reassessed their needs. By 1938 the schemes had run halfway through the alphabet with Scheme M, the purpose of which was to strengthen the fighter force. D. C. Watt has written that this and other measures to strengthen air defenses had to be achieved "in the teeth of the dominant British air force doctrine."[6] True to Trenchard's views on the preeminence of the offensive, the air staff would have liked two bombers for each fighter, although it was unsure what proportion of those bombers should be for day use or which objectives would be the best. Not until 1937 did the British air staff seriously begin to study target possibilities in Germany. The results of that study, incorporated into the "Western Air Plans," were not encouraging. There were few easy, vulnerable targets, particularly for the limited capabilities of Bomber Command. The rapid rise of the Luftwaffe further limited the possibilities for offensive action. Air strategists who had once spoken of aggressive bombing policies were now ready to limit their objectives sharply, striking none but obvious military targets in hopes that the Germans would do the same.

This drastic shrinking of expectations was a humiliating experience for an air force that had made the strategic offensive its credo for two decades; but, in the long run, the effect was salutary. In 1936 the RAF chose the heavy four-engine bomber as its future weapon, and in 1938 it intensified its efforts to develop such planes. The Stirling, Halifax, and Lancaster heavy bombers that those efforts ultimately yielded began to weigh in the balance in 1942, the critical year of World War II.

But, in 1939, Great Britain was to go to war with serious handicaps in the air. Radar and eight-gun fighters provided the "narrow margin" in the Battle of Britain, but Bomber Command suffered a series of failures in the first months of the war. Of its thirty-three operational squadrons, sixteen were equipped with aircraft incapable of mounting any sort of air offensive in the skies of Germany. The Bristol Blenheim, a civilian design hastily adapted to military use, was no longer the "wonder plane" it had been in 1936. And a third of Bomber Command's squadrons flew the Fairey Battle, described by one of its pilots as "that gentle old tin swallow." Slow and underarmed, the Battles had become virtually obsolescent by 1939. In the campaign of 1940, Luftwaffe pilots would swat them out of the air with appalling ease.

The British measured their own weakness by comparing it to the strength they saw in the Luftwaffe. But here there was a peculiar mirror effect. Sir Walter Raleigh had written of German air strategists during the Great War, "Their belief in frightfulness was a belief in fright. They judged others by themselves."[7] In the years leading up to World War II, the British Air Council made this same judgment of the Luftwaffe. It assumed that German air strategy was similar to its own and found in the German bombing squadrons an enormous strategic potential. At the outbreak of war in 1939, the British government stood braced for a massive aerial knockout blow that the Luftwaffe had neither the capability nor the intention of delivering.

Understanding the air force that Hitler and Goering created has been a continuing problem. British and American writers tend to draw the Luftwaffe larger than life, while German chroniclers are often severe in their judgments. The historian Karl-Heinz Völker once wrote a whole chapter on the *Schein und Sein* ("appearance and reality") of the Luftwaffe, in which he tried to dispel a number of persistent myths. One of the most enduring of these is that almost overnight the Nazis created an air force from nothing. Germany's masters inherited a fund of technical data and projections from the Technical Office of the Reichswehr, which had had for years a discreet but persistent interest in military aviation. The secret testing facilities that the Soviets provided at Lipetsk permitted experimentation with dive bombing years before Ernst Udet returned from the United States with his Curtiss Hawk dive-bomber.

During the late twenties the Germans carefully followed developments in neighboring countries and made plans for a future air force of their own. Initially, their interest was drawn to the multipurpose aircraft, but as early as 1927, they explored the possibilities of the long-range, four-engined bomber, a project concealed under the cover name *Gronabo*. An aerial rearmament scheme of 1932 called for building a 960-plane force by 1938, half of that force to consist of bombers. At first, the bombing plane fitted into the basically defensive strategy that was upheld for a considerable time after the Nazi takeover. In 1935, for example, the Wehrmacht maneuvers had as their "problem" a combined invasion by France and Czechoslovakia. The bomber was to assist the defending ground forces both directly and indirectly with missions in the tactical and "operational" zones.

Hitler and Goering did give considerable impetus to the development of bombers; they pressed the Junkers 52 transport into service as a *Behelfsbomber* (auxiliary bomber), but by 1936 they were able to introduce into the bombing squadrons the modern and efficient Heinkel 111. Hitler's purpose in so doing was as much political as military, and he may well have been inspired by a memorandum of 1933 on the *Risiko-Luftflotte,* prepared by Dr. Robert Knauss, a veteran of the air battles of 1918 who had become a Lufthansa official. Knauss argued that an air force with significant offensive power would give pause to any of German's neighbors (France especially) who might be tempted to intervene and block the continued rearmament of the Reich. For Hitler, as for his predecessors, the greatest air threat came from the French heavy bomber force. The French bombers, especially the Amiot 143, were heavily armed and more difficult to contend with than the German fighter force had anticipated. In 1932, German planners proposed a mass bombing attack at the outbreak of war to surprise and destroy the Amiots on the ground. The Wehrmacht would subsequently incorporate this surprise air strike into a number of its campaign plans.

After 1936, Hitler held enough cards to think in offensive terms, but none of the moves he contemplated seemed likely to produce a major conflagration. The *Feindbild* ("projected enemy") was France and its eastern alliance partners, notably Czechoslovakia. Until 1938 war with either Great Britain or the Soviet Union was not a major feature in German military planning. If war came, it would not be fought over a great distance, and if blitzkrieg tactics were successful, the campaign would not bog down into positional warfare but move to an early conclusion. For such conflicts a sizable force of medium bombers that could take a ton of bombs 300 miles beyond the frontiers of the Reich would be eminently satisfactory.

The Luftwaffe had its believers in the large strategic bomber, and they kept the idea alive through the thirties. The Luftwaffe also had under sporadic development the *Fernbomber* ("long-range bomber"), a four-engined plane with strategic capabilities. The *Fernbomber* never came to much—but not because of the death of its partisan, General Walther Wever, as is often said. Strategic bombing appeared as one of the Luftwaffe's missions in the *Luftkriegführung* ("operations manual"): "An attack on the enemy's sources of strength can influence the course of the war decisively. . . . But often it is only gradual in its effect and it carries with it the danger of exerting influence on the land and sea contests too late."[8] Creating a sizable force of strategic bombers might well have overtaxed Germany's productive capacity, as Völker points out; but perhaps more important, such a force had no place in the sort of war Germany planned to fight. By 1942, when the era of blitzkrieg was over, it was too late for Germany to restructure its air power.

The progress of German rearmament was followed nowhere as closely as in Paris. The French probably understood the threat from the air more clearly than the British, and certainly they reacted to it more quickly. In April 1933, little over two months after Hitler came to power, a report from the Direction Générale de la Guerre raised the alarming possibility of a massive preemptive air strike by an Italo-German air fleet. If the Nazis converted transport planes to bombers they and the Italians would have the capacity to bring 540 tons of bombs 120 miles into France. The Armée de l'Air could retaliate with only 235 tons. So perilous did this imbalance seem that the report urged all French aircraft to be armed with bombs, whatever their original function.

That same year, the French government began to rearm its air force according to Plan I, designed to add a thousand planes to the air fleet. This was followed by Plan II the next year and by a five-year plan in 1936; to these projects the government then added Plan III for air defense and Plan IV for increasing the fighter force. Despite all these efforts, by 1936 the Luftwaffe had probably grown stronger than the Armée de l'Air. Initially, the French relied heavily on their preponderance of bombers, which were a clear threat to Germany's cities if that power moved against any of France's allies in eastern Europe. A strengthening of the bomber force was thus the first stage in rearmament. There were two possibilities: either to develop new aircraft, ensuring a modern bomber force but with possibly costly delays, or to order models already tried and proven. In their haste, the French chose the latter course, and it proved disastrous. The Amiot 143s and Bloch 200s ordered in large number were designs dating from the late twenties—great angular machines with fixed undercarriages and unimpressive performance. (For example, the Bloch 200, the "Flying Flatiron," could not stay aloft if one of its two engines quit.) These orders were entrusted to an aircraft industry which had so atrophied between the wars that it could not complete delivery in four years. In the meantime, the Air Ministry launched an effort to modernize its fighter force and produce a second generation of bombers. When France declared war on September 3, 1939, its fighter squadrons had modern matériel and would receive even better aircraft in the near future. A new bomber was also on the way—the LéO 45, comparable in performance to the German medium bombers—but there were only five LéO's operational at the beginning of the war and fewer than a hundred in service when the storm broke in May 1940. The bulk of the French bomber force was still so outmoded that it was under orders to fly no war missions in the daylight.

The tactical manual for the French bomber force stipulated that it might operate in cooperation with the army or independently, as befitted its status as an independent service on equal footing with the army and navy. In point of fact, it was far from enjoying equal status (it calculated its share of the defense budget of 1935 as 12 percent) and had great difficulty asserting its independence from the army. In wartime the mobilization scheme placed the head of the Armée de l'Air under the generalissimo or supreme commander, who in the late thirties was Gen. Maurice Gamelin. Gen. Joseph Vuillemin, air force chief in that period, had to fight to retain even this arrangement. A plan put forward by the army in 1938 would have passed command of the Armée de l'Air to the generalissimo upon mobilization, with Vuillemin reduced to the role of adviser.

France too had its Douhetists, although surprisingly many of them were not in the Armée de l'Air; Paul Vauthier, Douhet's most outspoken disciple, was an artillery officer in the entourage of Marshal Henri Pétain, while his most incisive critic was the marine engineer Camille Rougeron. They and others carried on a lively debate about air power all through the thirties. But their theories had little application for the Armée de l'Air. When the French bomber force made its brief and tragic appearances in the whirlwind campaign of 1940, it was usually in sacrifice missions to save the deteriorating situation on the ground. On May 14, 1940, the critical day on which the German Army gained a toehold across the Meuse at Sedan, the lumbering Amiots joined the RAF's equally antiquated Fairey Battles in a futile attempt to bomb the German positions. German flak and fighters accounted for thirty-two of the sixty-seven Battles. Of the thirteen Amiots, five went down over Sedan and two crashed in French lines. The Germans held onto their pocket, as General Gamelin called it. Within a month, all of France fell into that pocket.

The month of June 1940, which brought defeat to the Armée de l'Air, saw Italy enter World War II. Next to the RAF, the Regia Aeronautica was the oldest independent air force in Europe, having been established in 1923, five years before the Armée de l'Air. After its creation the service became the showpiece of the Fascist regime. Italian planes and pilots garnered an impressive number of trophies and awards. In 1939 they held thirty-three of the eighty-four records in the categories fixed by the Fédération Aéronautique Internationale. And by 1939 no one could seriously debate air power without citing the works of the strategists Douhet and Mecozzi. The validity of Douhet's doctrines and the power of the Regia Aeronautica both found confirmation in the air maneuvers of August and September 1931, probably the most grandiose display of air power between the wars. For over a week, nearly a thousand planes fought mock battles. For an entire day, waves of planes delivered attacks against Milan. At the end of the day, the umpires ruled the city destroyed by high explosives, its population decimated by poison gas, and its government compelled to sue for peace.

The Regia Aeronautica did not formally adopt Douhet's ideas nor did it formally repudiate them. (The lessons learned in the 1931 maneuvers were never made public and the maneuvers were not repeated.) Beginning with the publication of a second edition of Douhet's *Command of the Air* in 1927, a raging doctrinal quarrel erupted in the pages of the *Rivista Aeronautica* and other journals. Along with matters of air strategy, personalities became involved, and ultimately so did the vital interests of highly placed military and political figures. Although Douhet died in 1930 the dispute was kept alive. (Colonel Mecozzi, who was perhaps Douhet's most persistent opponent, published a final blast against Douhetism in 1965.) The unfortunate result of this quarrel was that it prevented the Italian Air Force from arriving at "a basic air doctrine acceptable to all or even to a majority."[9]

For lack of any better foundation, the leaders of the Regia Aeronautica designed it on the assumption that it would be used in a limited war against an enemy with whom Italy shared a frontier, most likely France or Yugoslavia. This was probably a sound enough assumption in the 1920s, but not after Mussolini took Italy into the German orbit. Nevertheless, Italian aircraft continued to be designed on this premise. Bombers of limited range and carrying capacity could raid across the frontier without escort; fighters with even more limited range would defend Italy's airspace. Then, in 1940, the war spread across the Mediterranean, and Italy did not have the air strength to hit many vital targets. Raids on the Suez Canal were ineffectual, and those directed at the British petroleum facilities at Haifa were scarcely more successful.

The Achilles heel of this air force was its matériel. In November 1939 the Regia Aeronautica had only 450 combat-ready "modern" bombers and 129 first-class fighters. There would have been more planes available had Mussolini not sent some seven hundred to the Falangists in Spain. Moreover, Italy was selling warplanes in order to obtain badly needed foreign exchange. From 1937 to 1943, it shipped 1,554 aircraft to thirty-nine countries.

Italian aircraft, and especially Italian bombers, were all too often defective in design and mediocre in performance. Italian engineers could build superb racing engines of 2,500 horsepower, but they could not come up with a 1,000-horsepower in-line power plant suitable for mass production. Despite the lavishly equipped Guidonia Experimental Center and some brilliantly conceived designs, Italian bombers were generally adaptations—and not wholly successful ones—of commercial models. The Savoia-Marchetti SM 79, which made up three-fourths of the bombing force early in the war, was a typical case, "inferior in speed, range, armament and equipment to foreign bombers."[10] Like most Italian bombers, the SM 79 was a trimotor craft. This design made it difficult to protect the airplane from frontal attacks and deprived the bombardier of his position in the nose of the craft and of ready communication with the pilot. To add to this, Italian airmen went to war with a cumbersome and outmoded bombsight and had no bombs larger than 1,100 pounds.

It is clear that one reason for this state of affairs was the preoccupation with highly specialized competition craft that could break records and generate headlines. The same impulse led the regime to invest heavily in noisy displays. Air Marshal Italo Balbo, who was air minister from 1929 to 1933, was a master showman. He led an armada of sixty-one flying boats on a seventeen-hundred-mile circuit of the western Mediterranean in 1928 and took a smaller fleet of twenty-four to the Chicago World's Fair in 1933. Mussolini also flew, always to the accompaniment of press releases. Both men helped give the Regia Aeronautica the appearance of a kind of sportsmen's club, and both used it as a public relations medium. In the process, they neglected it as an instrument of war.

If Italy's air force was the most publicized in Europe, the Soviet Union's was probably the least well known. The country that had produced the first multiengined bomber did not abandon the idea of long-range bombing after 1918, perhaps in part because the new regime inherited a number of IM's and found them extremely useful in the period of the civil war. When the Soviet air force reequipped itself in the late 1920s, one of its most important units was the Heavy Bombing Brigade with trimotor aircraft whose appearance betrayed their German inspiration. In 1929 the Soviets brought out a twin-engined bomber of native inspiration, the TB-1, and one year later they successfully flew their four-engined ANT-6, or TB-3. It was "unveiled" two years later when nine of the giant planes participated in the 1932 May Day flyby. Thereafter, massed formations of the TB-3s figured prominently in parades and displays. By the time production stopped in 1937, about eight hundred of the giant planes were in existence. They were formed into brigades of fifty-odd machines, and in 1936 they formed a special heavy-bomber corps known as the Special Purpose Air Arm, or AON.

Although the Soviet Union probably possessed the most potent strategic bombing force in the world in the mid-1930s, its leaders showed little interest in strategic warfare as Trenchard and Douhet understood the term. Soviet air strategists certainly were not ignorant of what was happening in the West. They wrote knowledgeably about the Briey air blockade and the lessons to be learned from it. In 1935, Douhet's *Command of the Air* appeared in Russian with an introduction by V. V. Khripin, a leading air strategist soon afterward appointed to command the AON. Khripin was particularly interested in heavy bombers, as was A. N. Lapchinskii, professor of air tactics at Frunze Military Academy. They were the most prominent figures in a wide-ranging discussion of heavy-bomber strategy carried on in the military press of the late twenties and thirties. Western observers reported that it was more an exposition of views than a true debate. It seems to have been understood that the Soviet air force would remain organically a part of the Red Army. There were no clarion calls for "independence" such as Billy Mitchell was making in the United States.

In the Soviet Union, as in Nazi Germany, no strong contrast was made between a "static" war on the ground and a "dynamic" air war.

The blitzkrieg had its Russian parallel in Marshal Tukhashevskii's concept of "deep battle," which seemed to offer to the air arm opportunities unknown in positional warfare. Khripin and Lapchinskii both distinguished three different spheres of action for offensive aviation. The first was essentially tactical, involving participation and support in the land battle. The second was "operational," offering an indirect role in battle by striking behind the enemy front. The third, which Khripin called "strategic" and Lapchinskii "independent," were operations such as the German bombing of London and the French air blockade of Briey.

Direct participation in the land battle very much interested Soviet strategists. They were familiar with the work of Mecozzi and Rougeron, and in the thirties their practical and theoretical work in the field put them ahead of everyone except the Luftwaffe. "Operational" bombing was at least equally attractive, for it was in this type of operation that the IM's had proved their value in the Great War: "Wartime practice showed that bombing attacks on objectives in the operational rear constituted the main mission of heavy aviation."[11] Both Khripin and Lapchinskii cite as prime targets the depots, reserves, and transport facilities in the "deep rear." According to Lapchinskii, there was no limit in depth to operations of this sort, and no matter how far removed they were from the ground action, they were still made in relation to that action. The third type of offensive operations, in which the air arm essentially fights its own war, held no charms for Soviet theorists, who emphatically rejected the Douhetist notion that the bomber alone would win the war. Some said the theory might work against primitive peoples easily terrorized—no doubt a reference to the "air control" practices of the Western colonial powers—but Lapchinskii put the Soviet point of view unequivocally: "We do not see how in reality this point of view could be carried out anywhere."[12]

The fortunes of Soviet "heavy aviation" declined in the late thirties. In part, this was because the TB-3s with their top speed of less than 200 miles an hour had grown obsolete and a satisfactory replacement was slow to appear. But, more than anything else, the heavy bombers suffered from the loss of their partisans and their chiefs. The Great Purge swept away Khripin and Lapchinskii, for reasons which remain obscure. Both men had formerly been in the Czarist air service and maintained intellectual contacts with Western strategists or at least with their works—and in the atmosphere of the purge era, either transgression could lead a man to Lubianka prison and the firing squad. There is also a theory that both men incurred Stalin's anger because of the poor performance of the Soviet bombers sent to the Spanish Loyalists. None of the theories has been satisfactorily proved.

The heavy-bomber force survived, although it underwent another organizational change in 1940, becoming the DBA-GK, or Long-Range Bomber Arm of the Supreme Command. In June 1941 it consisted of eight hundred bombers, only a small proportion of the seven thousand or more aircraft available for operations against Germany. Deployed well to the rear, the heavy-bomber units were largely spared in the devastating attacks that the Luftwaffe delivered against air installations at the beginning of Operation Barbarossa (some estimates put the Soviet losses at over fifteen hundred planes for the single day of June 22). With much of Soviet tactical aviation capability destroyed, the bombers of the DBA-GK took up the tactical role, striking at river crossings, rail junctions, and advancing panzer columns. In that catastrophic summer, Stalin ordered the bombing of Berlin "at all costs." The hastily formed Special-Purpose Heavy-Bomber Regiment struck Berlin twice with a handful of planes, suffering heavy losses each time.[13] Having permitted himself this gesture, the Soviet leader directed his bombers back to targets closer at hand. On those targets they would expend most of their energies for the rest of the war.

There was a clearly observable basic continuity in Soviet bomber doctrine from the First World War to the Second; and there is a similar thread of consistency running through American strategic thought, traceable all the way back to 1917 when Gen. H. H. ("Hap") Arnold recalled that "despite Billy Mitchell's eagerness to blow up Germany, we hadn't a single bomber."[14] The bombing squadrons of the American air service made only the most modest contribution to victory, at least in statistical terms. They dropped a total of 138 tons of bombs, a figure so unimpressive that in the records it was converted to 275,000 pounds.

The experience of the Great War was nonetheless valuable for the development of American military aviation; it provided the point of departure for air strategists and particularly for the men who formulated bomber doctrine between the wars. American exposure to the principle of strategic bombardment occurred in 1917 and 1918 and it "took." Actually, the exposure was a multiple one, so that it is impossible to tell which of the contacts might have been the crucial one.

Billy Mitchell was a frequent visitor to the headquarters of Sir Hugh Trenchard, and he became a frank admirer both of the man and of his notions of aerial warfare. At the same time, other American air officers worked with the RNAS and so became familiar with the ideas of Viscount Tiverton and Spencer Grey on the value of precise strikes on critical industrial objectives. In addition, in 1917, an American military delegation known as the Bolling mission visited Italy, where it heard Gianni Caproni describe the views on strategic bombing that he shared with his good friend Giulio Douhet.

The American officers who brought these ideas back with them had to nurture them in a decidedly hostile climate. The U.S. Army Air Service (Air Corps after 1926) was an organic part of the army, which considered its role exclusively one of assistance to the land forces and had no intentions of allowing it to embark on campaigns of its own. Beyond this, such a supremely offensive weapon as the strategic bomber had no attraction for a generation of Americans who hoped to stay out of foreign wars and would defend themselves only if directly attacked. Even so, the believers in air power, led by Billy Mitchell, waged a long and often noisy campaign for an independent air force with strategic capabilities. The struggle cost Mitchell his career and it did not produce independence for the air arm; still, by the early thirties it provided the fragile basis for a strategic air potential. First of all, the army agreed to the creation of a "headquarters air force," a concentration of offensive elements into a compact mass for possible strategic development. Then, the Air Corps found an acceptable "defensive" role for the strategic bomber it sought. In 1931 an agreement between American military and naval high commands assigned to the army all land-based weapons for coastal defense. If the weapons had sufficient range, land-based aircraft could detect hostile warships long before they came in sight of the coasts, and what is more, they could sink them. Mitchell had proved this in his own spectacular way. Long-range bombers could be rapidly deployed on either coast and could rush their support to any threatened positions in the Pacific or the Caribbean.

And finally, in 1935, the Air Corps found the bomber it had been looking for. In 1933 it had sought heavy-bomber designs from American builders. They responded with a monster, the slow and ponderous XB15, but also with several other designs, including the XB17, which first took the air in July 1935; within six months the Air Corps decided to place orders for sixty-five of the new aircraft, which it described as "the best bombardment aircraft in existence" prudently adding "particularly for coastal defense."[15] When war broke out in Europe in 1939 the GHQ Air Force had only thirteen B-17s, but a second bomber, the B-24, was off the drawing board and in the air. At the time of Pearl Harbor, design work had been completed for the B-29, third and last of the "heavies" which would see the U.S. Army Air Forces through World War II.

While the American strategic-bombing force was passing through its gestation period, strategists were refining the doctrine that would govern its use. Understandably, they carried on their discussions well out of earshot of the army general staff. Much of the theoretical work seems to have been done in the Air Corps Tactical School, which moved to Maxwell Field in 1931. In the preceding decade, the manuals prepared by the school espoused area bombing of the enemy's interior by night and put considerable stress on the morale or "terrorizing" effect of such raids. But, in the thirties, the emphasis changed. This may be in part because of studies made by Donald Wilson and other instructors at the school, which showed how the economic life of sections of the United States could be disrupted by the destruction of certain key facilities; this led Wilson to decide that "the real target is industry itself, not national morale."[16]

The evolution of the doctrine of precision bombing may owe something to the dislike of the imprecise or indiscriminate bombing voiced at various times by American leaders and the American public. It has even been argued—and not altogether implausibly—that precision bombing represented an old and well-anchored tradition in America's military past, that of marksmanship. The precision-bombing strategy was challenging, to say the least. First of all, precision bombing would almost certainly be daylight bombing, which meant that the bomber would need speed, armament, or both for its own defense. Second, the bombsight would have to promise greater accuracy than any previously known. Neither the B-17 Flying Fortress bomber nor the Norden bombsight, first tested in 1931, offered any guarantees, but they both seemed promising, so that the concept was pursued.

Such apparently was the genesis of that idea sometimes called the "pickle barrel" doctrine of precision bombing. Created and shaped in the dusty classrooms of an Alabama airbase, it would seek a mighty affirmation ten years later in the skies over Germany.

CHAPTER 6

ON THE EVE

SOMEWHERE IN THE ARCHIVES OF THE FRENCH AIR FORCE is the report of an officer sent to inspect forward air observation posts shortly after mobilization in 1939. In one post the observer on duty had almost none of the equipment he needed in order to make accurate sightings. He could not record the exact time an airplane passed over because his watch did not have a minute hand. Asked to explain the distinguishing characteristics of the Messerschmitt 109, he said he recognized it by the way its engine smoked. Countless episodes of this nature could be found in 1939; drawn together, they tell a story of makeshift and unpreparedness in every aspect of the coming war in the air. In each country, historians tend to write about the shortcomings of their air service as if it were alone in its lack of preparation. In fact, the phenomenon was a general one, and its basic causes were common to all the major belligerents.

Many of these causes are already familiar and apply to the land and sea services as well: years of complacent thinking and austerity budgets, followed by a mood of crisis and a deluge of money pumped into hastily devised rearmament programs that would nevertheless "peak" after 1939. But the air arm had a particularly hard time of it for an additional reason. To a greater degree than the other services, it had been mobilized for a struggle that the great powers waged all through the thirties to influence, to deter, and to intimidate their neighbors by presenting an enhanced image of their military strength. No weapon lent itself to this sort of campaign more readily than the airplane. As an arm in rapid evolution with a potential not yet fixed, it offered an ideal means to impress a probable enemy. As J. M. Spaight observed, the warplane's mystery was half its power. The most extravagant claims might be made for it, and no one could really deny them. Here was a weapon to conjure with, and no one understood this better than Adolf Hitler. His first bombing force, his *Risiko-Luftflotte,* was little more than an imposing façade; the Junkers 52s that figured on its registers remained for the most part in the everyday transport service of Lufthansa, which made them available as auxiliary bombers. Later, when Hitler was extorting concessions from President Emil Hacha of Czechoslovakia, he told him—among other things—that unless Germany got its way, the Luftwaffe would wipe Prague from the face of the earth. Hitler may not have believed the Luftwaffe could actually do this, but then he was only interested in making Hacha believe it. But the Führer too was susceptible to this sort of pressure. In 1938 he and Goering were anxious to learn more about the range of British bombers and what sort of danger they might pose to the towns of western Germany. And the British, of course, were doing what they could to make their squadrons of Blenheims and Battles appear more formidable than they really were.

Not surprisingly, each power tried to display its air weapons to best advantage. Every competition, every air show became a vehicle for propaganda. The Luftwaffe demonstrated aircraft that were delicate and specially engineered thoroughbreds capable of extraordinary performance and then announced that they were production-line warplanes. The British seriously considered going after speed records with a racing version of their Spitfire. The French showed up at an international meet in 1939 with several samples of a new twin-engined bomber. The planes had had their serial numbers altered to give the impression there were several hundred in existence rather than the dozen the Armée de l'Air actually possessed.

Unsubtle as their ploy was, the French were following what seemed a sensible rule: If an offensive weapon like the bomber is to serve as deterrent or instrument of intimidation, then it must be demonstrated to exist, and in impressive numbers. If necessary its ability to "reach" a potential enemy could be advertised with a carefully prepared long-distance flight—or "raid" as it was called in French—with appropriate press coverage. But numbers were essential. A force of six hundred twin-engined bombers weighed more heavily in the balance than half that number of four-engined craft. (Goering once told Field Marshal Albert Kesselring that he was building twin-engined bombers rather than four-engine ones because Hitler would ask him how many bombers he had, not how many engines they carried.) This consideration, nonsensical as it may seem from the purely military perspective, nevertheless figured prominently in the creation of the air fleets of the thirties.

Not only did the air force need to look redoubtable to a prospective foe, but it also had to project a reassuring image to the public, particularly in the late thirties, when apocalyptic visions of the coming air war were common. The thousands who watched the carefully staged aerial derring-do at the Hendon Air Show or at one of the Regia Aeronautica's "air days" came away suitably impressed; and the American public was similarly reassured when B-17s flew far out into the Atlantic and successfully "intercepted" an Italian liner seven hundred miles or so from North America.

There was also an image to be maintained within the halls of government if the air force were to hold its own with the older services. Here the best course was to stress the capabilities of air power and to say little about its limitations. When the British Air Staff began in the late thirties to look closely at what damage Bomber Command could do within Germany, its studies showed the possibilities to be very limited. A historian who has recently studied the records concluded, "Much of this seems to have been kept from the politicians by a service anxious not to undercut its own role."[1] But then it is just as likely that while Royal Navy leaders spoke confidently in council about their ability to handle the German submarine menace, in private they were scratching their heads.

Each air service also tended to stress the destructive capacities of its probable foe; to do otherwise would be playing into the hands of the enemies of air power itself, prominent among them the leaders of the land and sea services. The British Air Staff grossly overestimated the casualties the Luftwaffe would be able to inflict on London, although that is not to say they did so intentionally. General Albert Denain, French air minister in the early thirties, painted for the French Senate a harrowing picture of what the air fleets of Italy and Germany might do in a combined attack. Plausible or not, this prospect helped win appropriations for the Armée de l'Air, for the answer to the air menace from abroad was a powerful air fleet of one's own. After the Regia Aeronautica concluded its 1931 maneuvers, it showered Italian towns with leaflets. The mock attacks on the towns could have been real ones, and the moral drawn was clear: "Let us not forget that the enemy air offensive will be paralyzed and defeated only if we are powerful in the air and if we have a strong national air force."[2]

An air force designed to dissuade or to intimidate performs that essential function simply by existing. Only if it fails in its function will it actually be used. And a "shop window" force—as someone once described the RAF of the thirties—will of necessity be much concerned with how it looks, sometimes to the detriment of how it performs. Many airmen of World War II looked back on their prewar flying experience as a sterile routine that did not prepare them adequately for combat. Navigation, to take a single example, was insufficiently taught in most air forces, as though wars were expected to be fought over familiar terrain and on cloudless days only. Flying at night and in bad weather posed formidable challenges to most military pilots of 1939. RAF pilots did not as a general rule fly over water, and they could even be reprimanded for taking a short cut across an estuary. Luftwaffe pilots were also unaccustomed to navigation over bodies of water. When they began to cross the North Sea and probe the British coastline in 1938, they sometimes missed their intended landfall by fifty miles. Sometimes these errors led to embarrassment, as when a flight of Italian bombers sent to aid Spain's Gen. Francisco Franco ended up in French North Africa.

The men who led the air forces of Europe could certainly have done more to prepare those forces for the demands of war; but, in fairness to them, it must be said that they could only go so far in anticipating what the next war would be like. By 1938 the lessons of the Great War were twenty years old and of doubtful validity in many cases. Would the rules of combat at twenty-five thousand feet be the same as they had been at ten thousand? What effect would the higher speed of aircraft have on air battles? The French decided that fighter engagements would become so complex that a squadron commander in a special "command" plane would have to supervise the battle from a distance, directing the movements of his fighters by radio.

Bombing squadrons also were eager to know what air combat would be like. Would the bombers' all-metal construction make them less vulnerable to fighter attacks, or would the generation of new fighters carrying eight machine guns or 20mm cannon take heavy toll? Each bomber design of 1939 represented a series of compromises, of critical decisions by designers obliged to choose between conflicting theories. There were many schools of thought on what the bomber should be, none of them confirmed by the test of war. Some argued the advantages of the multipurpose aircraft. This idea was called *odnotipnost* by the Russians and *Mehrzweckflugzeug* by the Germans; the French made several attempts to build a bombardment-combat-reconnaissance (BCR) plane. Others felt the bomber should be a highly specialized aircraft, distinguished above all by its ability to carry heavy loads over long distances. This avenue of thinking often led to gigantism, as in the B-15 and the Italian Caproni 90 P.B. One school of thinkers, including Douhet, believed the bomber should rely for protection on heavy armament. French bombers of the thirties were built on this principle; they bristled with machine guns so placed that every angle of attack was covered. The other school, and the more popular one in the late thirties, favored the *Schnellbomber,* the superior speed of which would see it to its target and back. Designers of fast bombers strove for aerodynamically clean forms, so they created internal bays for bomb storage, thus ending the easy convertibility of transport plane to bomber.

By flying higher and faster, bombers only complicated their own job of hitting and destroying their objective: there needed to be advances in bombardment too. Bombs with greater destructiveness and better ballistic prospects would be forthcoming, as well as improved aiming devices. The tachometric bombsight was under development in the thirties, but in 1939, bombing accuracy left much to be desired. The 1938 edition of the French bombing manual advised the bombardier of a Bloch 200 that if he aimed at a rectangle 825 feet by 660 feet—a factory-sized target—from an altitude of 10,000 feet he could expect to score a hit with about one bomb out of nine. The Luftwaffe could do no better. Its best bombing crews, working in optimum weather conditions from a height of 13,200 feet could put about 2 percent of their bombs into a target roughly the size of a football field. These mediocre results in horizontal bombing encouraged the Germans to explore the *Schrägangriff,* a bombing run incorporating a shallow dive at about thirty degrees. Accuracy picked up appreciably with this technique. The basic fact remains that while the British,

French, and German air forces went to war pledged to hit "military targets only," most of their bombs would fall on whoever or whatever had the misfortune to be in the vicinity of those targets.

The most pressing problem in the late thirties was air defense. This was particularly true for the British and French governments. Faced with a powerful Luftwaffe and the fading deterrent effect of their aging bombers, they reordered their priorities to renovate fighter squadrons and bolster long-neglected antiaircraft defenses. In the short term, the problem was nightmarish. In September 1938, when the Sudeten crisis brought Europe to the very edge of the precipice, the Allies calculated that they would be assailed by a force of twelve hundred German bombers. Fighter Command then had ninety-three eight-gun fighters capable of catching them, while the Armée de l'Air had perhaps twenty of the modern cannon-equipped Morane-Saulnier 406s.

The high speed of the *Schnellbomber* not only relegated a whole generation of fighter craft to the scrap heap but also overwhelmed the traditional warning systems. It took such systems from twenty to fifty minutes to effect fighter interception of an attacking force of bombers. In such a space of time, bombers moving at 3.6 miles a minute could cross the Rhine toward Paris (or come in from the Channel to London), strike their target, and be well on the way home. From 1935 on, the great powers were pushing research in a dozen different directions in their quest for a better detection system. In laboratories all over Europe, scientists were experimenting with infrared rays, ultrasensitive acoustical devices, and the cathode tube—the last of which would lead them to radar.

As a rule, antiaircraft weapons suffered from great neglect in the interwar period. A historian of ground defenses described their state in 1939 as one of "catastrophic backwardness."[3] Antiaircraft batteries had not done a very effective job of protecting European cities in the Great War, and after it was over, the ground defense systems were entrusted to any service that would take them. If the army took on this obligation, it tended to give it low priority, insisting that the fighter planes of the air force were a better line of defense. If the air force inherited ground defense, it too tended to neglect it in favor of aircraft. In Italy the service was confided to a Blackshirt militia, while in Britain it passed to the territorial army. Although the Luftwaffe took over responsibility for ground defense against air attack, it showed little interest in defending German cities until it was too late. In keeping with the dictum that an air force was the best defense against an air force, Goering announced in 1935 that his air fleet would be strong enough "to repel attack at any time."[4] Much of the antiaircraft material of 1939 dated from 1918. Trials in the thirties demonstrated that the vintage searchlights could not find high-flying aircraft, and target predictors were overwhelmed by the higher speeds. In some cases, neither guns nor lights could be traversed fast enough to keep up with the fast-moving bombers. A hasty renovation was under way but would come too late to help belligerents such as France or Poland. The heavy flak gun of 1939, which most cities relied upon for their defense from bombers, ranged in bore size from 75mm to 94mm and was designed for use at maximum ranges of 23,000–26,000 feet; thus, most bombers of 1939 could fly above the flak barrage. The Germans had the best cannon initially in their 88mm, designed for air defenses in the mid-1930s and subsequently adapted to ground use as well. The Soviets introduced new models in 1930 and 1939, while the French embarked on a crash program to produce 90mm cannon of a model devised back in 1922 but never put into production by the army.

With the slender resources at hand, most of the belligerents concentrated their efforts on the protection of their largest cities. In 1938 the British government assigned 181 guns to the protection of London, slightly more than half of those they had available to defend the entire country. At the outbreak of the war, Paris was guarded by 90mm guns on loan from the French Navy, the only such guns available. At the beginning of hostilities, Moscow was protected by an air defense perimeter with a radius of some twelve miles. It contained six zones, each with twenty-five batteries. Germany seemed to have a broader protective system with its *Luftverteidigungszone West,* a flak belt that Goering created along the western frontier, with great fanfare, in 1938. But like the Siegfried Line of which it was the aerial counterpart, it was more imposing in press releases than in reality.

The greatest danger to the cities would come at night, when the modest effectiveness of the antiaircraft gun would decline even further. The only other defense was the night fighter, a plane that appeared in the Great War. But this weapon too had evolved little in two decades. The basic techniques were still those devised in 1914–18. Fighters could work in conjunction with searchlights, trying to attack every plane that the light fixed in their beams; or they could use what the French called *chasse obscure,* in which the fighter pilot tried to find and attack his quarry in the dark. The Luftwaffe began trials with night fighters in 1936, and at about the same time, the French intensified their own researches. The French Air Force had two specialized night-fighter units at the beginning of the war, but these had little success.

If all these handicaps and shortcomings in air defense are combined and then compared with the capabilities of the *Schnellbomber,* it is easy to see how the British Air Staff could advise the government that a German air offensive against England might produce sixty thousand casualties in the first week and that little or nothing could be done to prevent this. The British government was particularly alarmed by the threat from the air, but no government could be indifferent to it. In each country, the authorities had to decide how much they could tell their populations and how they could prepare them for the dangers ahead.

Ordinary citizens had certainly not been kept in ignorance of the bomber and what it could do. Prognostications of what the next war would be like could be found in literature of every kind and level, most of it saying that the coming conflict would be of unparalleled butchery and that the bomber would have a more than modest role in making it so devastating. Experts like Liddell Hart and J. F. C. Fuller provided forecasts for the military reader, and H. G. Wells passed on his vision to the more literary set. Writers with less talent but no less imagination wrote about the coming Armageddon in popular magazines and Sunday supplements. A Frenchman who lived through the era recalled:

> For years the Parisian had a literature which promised him that when war came he would receive the delicate attentions of chemical and ballistic marvels straight out of Dante, with bombs thirty feet long which would spread cholera morbus at the same time they pulverized an entire *arrondissement.* . . . Obviously most of the inhabitants along the Seine felt that the only war worthy of their attention was the war in the air. To their minds Hitler's air fleet would have no more urgent mission than the destruction of the Nouvelles Galeries department store and the Pont des Arts.[5]

Even for the most worldly-wise, it must have been hard to affect this sort of irony in the thirties. How could one not be impressed by the finding of Joerg Joergensen, a Swedish professor whose field of specialization was "the effect of a future war upon the spiritual and mental attitudes of the civilian populations and the fighting forces"? Contributing to an international symposium organized by the Interparliamentary Union, Joergensen dwelt on the massive air raids that would open the next conflict: "This phase of the war will produce the greatest panic and be characterized by the utmost barbarity. All moral principles, all education and discipline will be forgotten. Each individual person in the attacked area will have only one idea—to save himself and his family at all costs. The instinct of self-preservation will involuntarily oust all other emotions, and human existence will degenerate into wild chaos."[6]

Liddell Hart believed that the chaos, the disorganization, and the dumb shock might resemble the situation in Japan immediately following the earthquake of 1923. The panic produced by Orson Welles's "War of the Worlds" broadcast in 1938 seemed to others an indication of the hysteria a sudden air attack would generate. Some theorized that the vibrations of the bombs would overtax the human nervous system, and others believed the most deadly effect would be produced by "silent" attacks in which the bombers glided over the city with their engines off. But, to many writers, the worst weapon was the one that had never been used on cities—gas. A fleet of bombers equipped with aerial spray apparatus similar to that used for insecticides might glide over a city in the dead of night, releasing a "dew of death."

No new weapons of terror made their appearance in the conflicts that dominated the headlines of the late thirties, but those already known seemed somehow more menacing. The photograph of a Chinese baby crying amidst the debris of a bomb-shattered city is arresting even today, while the attack on the Spanish town of Guernica generated a seismic wave of horror. The air aspects of the Spanish Civil War come in for close scrutiny for the hints they provide about the effectiveness of bombing. John Langdon-Davies, who witnessed the attacks on Barcelona early in 1938, felt that the excitable nature and incorrigible curiosity of the Spaniards would be their undoing: "They would not take shelter. They preferred instead to blacken every balcony so as to get a good view of the bursting shrapnel."[7] Another observer, this one a British expert on civil defense, confirmed this impression: "There has been no stampede in mass of the whole of a nerve-wracked population. No wild and unreasoned panic. No terrible and uncontrolled hysteria and certainly no thought of beseeching the government to seek an immediate and unconditional peace."[8] Camille Rougeron concluded from the episodes in Spain that, in the event of all-out warfare, the civilian population would hold up very well.

But it is clear that these reassuring findings represent only the minority view, at least in the eyes of the European public as a whole, which was caught up in visions of the apocalypse. Fiction was a logical medium for enlarging on this theme, and the era of the thirties saw numerous examples of the *Weltuntergangsroman,* in which the Western world, or parts of it, collapsed to the accompaniment of bursting bombs. One example of this genre was *War in the Air,* by "Major Hilders." The author was actually Dr. Robert Knauss, the pilot and Lufthansa official who put forward the *Risiko-Luftflotte* idea. The book appeared in Germany in 1932 and was subsequently translated into several languages. It created a considerable stir in France, and the Russian edition contained an introduction by Lapchinskii.

War in the Air told the story of a brief, intense conflict between Britain and France. The key battles were fought in the air, and the central episode was the destruction of Paris by the British bombing fleet of mammoth "G planes," which released on the city 734 tons of high explosives, 20 tons of mustard gas, and 4,280 incendiary bombs. These toppled the Eiffel Tower and turned the city into "a stoney desert." As for those Parisians who survived the initial blast: "The ant-like swarm of humanity disappears into cellars where it awaits further explosions with all its thousands of limbs atremble. Many go raving mad, pregnant women give birth. Whosoever is rash enough to thrust a head out of a cellar, reels back the next instant, coughing and vomiting."[9] As soon as it can take to the streets, this multitude storms the buses leaving the city, clinging to the overloaded vehicles "thick as grapes." Prowling mobs tear to pieces anyone they find in the uniform of the Armée de l'Air. Looting breaks out, and in the poorer districts, crowds begin to erect barricades at the urging of Communist agitators. A second bombing attack completes the work of the first. A red flag flies over Paris, where the insurgents follow orders radioed from Moscow. Caught between ruin and revolution, the French government sues for peace.

It was partly to counteract the effect of such appalling visions as this that many governments launched programs aimed at educating the public—but also at preparing it for the realities of air warfare, which were grim enough. This work had already been started in most countries by organizations—usually private ones—founded soon after the war. In Poland there was a society for "chemical defense" dating from the early twenties. In 1928, Frenchmen concerned about chemical warfare founded the League Against Chemical Warfare and for the Protection of the Civilian Population. Many of these organizations combined an interest in civil defense with a desire to have chemical warfare banned by international agreement.

The first government to concern itself directly with civil defense was the Soviet regime, which seems to have been preoccupied with the dangers of chemical warfare as early as 1920. In 1924 it sponsored the Society of Friends of Chemical Defense and the Chemical Industry, which grew and combined with other groups to form Osoaviakhim (an acronym for Society for the Promotion of Aviation and Chemical Defense), whose province included both aviation and air defense. In the thirties, Osoaviakhim trained some 28 million Russians in civil defense. The British government created the Air Raids Precaution (ARP) Committee in 1924, but its approach was totally different. For ten years the committee led a sort of shadow existence, for fear its work might alarm the public. Not until 1934 did it begin to publish civil-defense materials.

The thirties saw a considerable expansion of governmental activity in "passive defense," as it was called in many countries. At the same time, there appeared a new generation of air-defense organizations, such as the Union Nationale pour la Défense Aérienne in France and the Reichsluftschutzbund in Germany. These usually had official endorsement and quite often an air force general as president; not surprisingly, they preached both air defense and air power. A major development was the enactment of civil-defense legislation, such as the German law of June 26, 1935, and the British statute of 1937. Finally, civil-defense exercises became a feature of urban life. As early as 1935, air-raid drills took place in London, Vienna, Leningrad, Zurich, Berlin, Naples, Prague, and Tokyo.

These efforts were not always well received. When the French authorities ordered trial blackouts in certain towns, antiwar protesters built bonfires in the streets. The British ARP Committee engaged in a running feud with a body calling itself the Cambridge Scientists' Anti-War Group. The scientists felt that many of the committee's recommendations were unsound, so they published their own manual in 1937. They even detected a sinister purpose behind the official campaign: "It is reasonable to conclude . . . that the government under cover of protecting the public is planning a large-scale regimentation of the population and the sweeping away of civil liberty, protected as it is by law, as a preparatory step towards government by autocratic power which they foresee some future eventuality may compel."[10]

In most cases, the government tried to combat the more apocalyptic and irresponsible stories. Poison gas probably caused the greatest fear, perhaps because it had already been used on the battlefields of the Great War. (Biological or germ warfare was a threat that did not have the same immediacy.) In their publications both British and French governments assured their populations that despite rumors to the contrary, chemists had discovered no new and superdeadly gases since the armistice. (Neither government knew of the Tabun and Sarin nerve gases discovered in Germany in the mid-1930s.) Although they did not say so publicly, both governments knew from experiments that substances like mustard gas sprayed from aircraft did not present much of a danger to urban populations.

Many civil-defense publications of the thirties dwelt at length on a disaster that occurred in Hamburg in 1928, because it in some ways mimicked the effect of a poison gas attack on a large city and at the same time showed those effects to be surprisingly limited. The accident was a explosion in a chemical works that released into the industrial quarter of Hamburg eleven tons of phosgene, the most deadly gas employed in World War I. The phosgene cloud passed through part of the town and into the countryside, where it dissipated. The casualties were eleven dead and two hundred hospitalized.

The effect of high-explosive bombs on cities was to some degree already known, thanks to calculations made after the bombardments of 1914–18 and confirmed by the fragmentary evidence compiled during the Spanish Civil War. Casualties ran about fifty per ton of explosives, one-third of these being fatalities. And there was some evidence that the extrapolations often made from these figures were unjustified. That is to say, if a single one-ton bomb killed or wounded fifty Londoners, then a thousand such bombs would not necessarily kill or wound fifty thousand. Here again an industrial accident in Germany was instructive, and it seemed to point to a principle of diminishing returns as the tonnage increased. On September 21, 1921, at an Oppau chemical works, 4,500 tons of ammonium sulfonitrate exploded. The mammoth blast created a crater 250 feet in diameter and about fifty feet deep. The sound was heard nearly two hundred miles away, and property damage was massive in the town of Oppau, which bordered the plant; scarcely a window pane survived in the whole area. Yet, the majority of the 2,000 workers in the plant escaped serious injury. In Oppau proper, only fifty inhabitants lost their lives.

Other than high explosives and gas, the great danger was fire. Here the experience of World War I was only of limited validity. In general, the incendiary bombs had been failures when used against the cities, but the early incendiaries were inefficient and were not used intensively. Sensationalist writers exploited this issue too. They described fires so intense that girders melted in buildings and the streets ran with rivers of molten steel. Once again the authorities were reassuring, but in the late thirties the danger of firebombing was the subject of some serious study. A British scientist with the National Physical Laboratory at Teddington called the fire risk "practically an unknown factor."[11] *Branddirektor* Hans Rumpf was a German specialist who studied the San Francisco earthquake of 1906, the Hamburg fire of 1846, and other urban conflagrations. He concluded that great fires were possible in big cities with modern architecture if they were subjected to intensive attack. Rumpf would see in his own country a terrible confirmation of his conclusion.

The "passive defense" publications of the thirties are an exotic subliterature that a social historian should someday explore. The "what to do" air-raid manuals are a good example: a jolly, reassuring British writer declared that the only time a Londoner need fear a gas attack was after a heavy meal. A French manual given to soldiers being separated from the service told them, "One morning thousands of airplanes will appear over Paris, over Lille, Lyons or Marseilles, and in twenty-four hours all their inhabitants may be asphyxiated and most of the houses in flames."[12] An Italian manual of 1939 dwelt at length on methods of combating germ warfare and passed on the reassuring information that Italy was building bombing planes so rapid that no fighter plane could ever catch them. The air-warden *Service Manual* of the New York Police Department posed this fascinating problem for trainees: "A gas bomb hits the corner of X and W streets. A police patrol car is passing at the time and is heavily splashed. The driver and assistant are hit by some of the liquid. The police box at the side of the road is heavily contaminated. The odor of geraniums is very strong in the air. What do you do?" [13]

The citizen's need for protection from enemy bombers spawned a new industry that advertised its wares in such publications as *La défense aérienne* and *Fire Protection and Air Raids Precaution Review*. An Italian firm supplied gas masks for dogs, while a Czech concern offered a gasproof perambulator with its own air pump. There was fireproof clothing and even ARP underwear. Wartime apparel for women would include gas masks; protective boots, gloves, and goggles; and steel helmets. These items were recommended by a German civil-defense authority who also called for dresses cut like uniforms that would offer "mechanical protection for the breast and climatic protection for the abdomen." He argued that such clothing "is not only becoming but also includes the advantage of giving some psychological support to the person who wears it." [14] Other specialists designed bombproof and gasproof structures. There was the Consul individual shelter "for your key personnel," and Col. Alessandro Romani's cone-like structure that contained some 160 cubic yards of reinforced concrete and could protect sixteen people. In Germany the Winkel Tower, in four sizes, was advertised, while a Swiss inventor introduced the Schindler stronghold. Russian engineers drew plans for whole cities redesigned to resist air attacks. Colonel Paul Vauthier proposed rehousing the population in "tower cities" along the lines of Le Corbusier's designs. In wartime, the first five floors of the towers would be cleared in case of contamination by gas, while the top three floors, also evacuated, would absorb bomb hits. A pair of Paris architects put forward the most fantastic scheme of all: a tower almost seven thousand feet high equipped with three hundred guns.

For all these lifesaving devices and schemes, the nations of Europe went to war in 1939 with scant protection for their great cities. The British government, always the most sensitive to air attack, was gravely concerned about the fate of its city dwellers; though the Soviet government had championed civil defense for two decades, Marshal Kliment Voroshilov pronounced it unsatisfactory. In most other countries preparations were even less advanced. For one thing, the practical problems of protecting large urban populations—as people understood those problems in 1939—seemed so immense as to defy solution. An international commission of experts that met in Rome in 1939 under

Red Cross auspices succeeded only in underscoring the difficulties. A German expert at the conference estimated that it would cost over 800 million gold francs to provide shelters for the population of a large city—a cost so staggering as to be prohibitive. Even the hermetically sealed ambulances that the Red Cross recommended for gas warfare were an added burden to a heavily encumbered defense budget.

It was difficult to build or adapt shelters that would give protection against the three dangers of explosives, fire, and gas. The experts felt that adequate protection against gas would be extremely difficult to achieve for large urban populations. The discipline and the constant vigilance required seemed beyond the capacities of civilians. Most of the makeshift shelters available to the population in the event of air attacks—basements and subway stations, for example—would become death traps as the heavy and low-lying poison gases seeped into them. Governments could do little more than supply their populations with gas masks, and in the late thirties these were being manufactured by the millions. Government planners were generally distrustful of mass shelters. Joseph Goebbels feared they would be breeding places for microbes and political decadence, while British planners feared mass panic. P. R. C. Groves offered a particularly ghastly scenario for what would happen if there were a power failure while the population was sheltered in the subway system. The sudden and complete darkness would produce mindless panic, and then the howling, struggling mass of humanity would suffocate from lack of ventilation. In psychological journals other experts speculated on the mental damage the bomber could do; there was much talk of mass neurosis, conversion hysteria, and exotic conditions like "bunker fever" and "deep-shelter mentality."

If the great cities could not be rendered safe, at least the losses could be cut by evacuating a part of the population. During the Great War, sizable numbers of people had left the heavily bombarded cities, often on their own initiative and also at governmental direction. Most governments drew up contingency plans for evacuating various portions of their populations, particularly the children. The larger French cities had such plans, endorsed by Gen. Maurice Gamelin; the Polish capital was to shed 150,000 of its inhabitants. These and most other schemes were not fully executed when war came. In Britain, by contrast, the declaration of war triggered an exodus of 3 million people from the city of London alone.

War brought another, more discreet exodus. This was the rather general shift of military command posts outside the capitals so that they would not be paralyzed by the initial "knockout" blow the enemy was expected to deliver. The RAF's Fighter Command had chosen headquarters at Bentley Priory, north of London, while Bomber Command was still awaiting completion of wartime headquarters at High Wycombe, which featured an underground operations room. On mobilization, the headquarters of the Armée de l'Air shifted to "Point Z," the chateau of Saint-Jean-les-deux-Jumeaux, while General Gamelin, supreme commander of the Allied forces, went to earth in the south casemate of the chateau of Vincennes. The Luftwaffe's essential services shifted to the Wildpark and the Oberkommando des Heeres repaired to Zossen, where its bombproofs were concealed under peaceful cottages. But, by and large, political authority remained in the capital. The national leaders may have had little choice but to remain with their people as a gesture of confidence and solidarity. In their bombproofs and their bunkers they would share the city's fate.

CHAPTER 7

TOWARD
TOTAL WAR

NOT LONG AFTER GREAT BRITAIN WENT TO WAR AGAINST GERMANY, a British medical journal published an article about a bizarre pattern of behavior observed in a certain number of Londoners. Having absorbed the belief that their city would be visited with fire and destruction from the first hour of the war, they were having difficulty adjusting to the fact that nothing had happened either to them or to their city. To be sure, in those first days of September there were some tense moments for Londoners: almost as soon as Prime Minister Neville Chamberlain finished his radio address announcing the war, the sirens began to sound throughout the city—a French aircraft coming in from the Channel had triggered the air-defense system. Not long afterward, the radar screens showed other mysterious blips, and Fighter Command sent up squadron after squadron as the menace grew. There were no German aircraft in this Battle of Barking Creek, as it was called. The blips were actually made by British planes, and the fighter squadrons were sent up to intercept one another.

In France, which went to war a few hours after Britain, there were similar incidents: sirens routed Parisians from their beds and sent them to their cellars on the night of September 4–5. The following night, a British plane blundered into the city's air-defense perimeter, provoking a second false alarm. Berlin had its first air-raid alert on September 1, the day Germany went to war against Poland. The city had a second false alarm at four in the morning on September 5. On the third, fighter squadrons all over Germany kept planes and pilots on *Sitzungsbereitschaft,* or "reinforced alert": the pilots remained seated in their Messerschmitts with motors kept warm, waiting only for the signal to take off and intercept the Blenheims and the Whitleys of the RAF.

The war that broke out that September had two distinct levels. In the east it was unfolding with terrific intensity as the Wehrmacht unveiled the blitzkrieg against the luckless Poles. In the west, however, the strange calm of the "Phoney War" endured for eight months. Opposing armies simply observed each other, while in the air, activity was so minimal that the British Air Ministry's daily bulletin for October 31 reported with tongue in cheek, "The subsiding of the waters of the Rhine seems to be the only movement to report from the Western Front." Adolf Hitler was chiefly responsible for this state of affairs. It suited his purposes for the war to remain dormant in the west while his forces expended most of their effort in a whirlwind campaign against Poland. The Führer took a number of steps to ensure that the air war would not flare up in the west. He readily agreed to Franklin Roosevelt's plea of September 1 that the belligerents refrain from bombing civilian populations and unfortified cities. He ordered sharp limitations on the Luftwaffe's activities on the western front, and in his War Directive No. 2 of September 3, he forbade bombing attacks on British soil and ruled them out against France as well, except for reprisal raids. In general, the Luftwaffe was to make sure that the opening of the air war was not brought about by German actions.

The British and French also went to considerable lengths to avoid provoking an all-out conflict in the air. They too accepted Roosevelt's appeal and steadfastly refused to launch any air offensive to help the beleaguered Poles. Allied aircraft flying missions "over the line" were not permitted to carry bombs, for fear they might be dropped accidentally. The British and French governments did, however, make contingency plans. In October 1939 they agreed upon the German cities they would attack in reprisal if German bombers raided their towns. The British chose Berlin, the tantalizing but elusive target of the last war. The French high command sent Premier Edouard Daladier a list of German cities and asked him to make his choice. Across the top of the list the premier scrawled the name of the German city that had particularly unpleasant memories for him—Munich.

Meanwhile, the war unfolding in the east revealed the activity of the Luftwaffe to be intense but nonetheless directed at legitimate military targets. In the first two days, the German air force spent most of its time trying to destroy the modest strength the Poles had in the air, and then German bombers switched targets from Polish airfields to roads, bridges, and rail lines, as they sought to disrupt the Polish Army's mobilization. Allied observers in Poland pronounced the German air operations for the first two weeks of the war well within the spirit of the 1923 Draft Rules. There was no evidence of terror attacks on cities; in cases where civilians were hit, accidents or "spillover" seemed to be the cause. At the beginning of the war, Hitler had sent the Poles word through the intermediary of the Dutch government that the Luftwaffe would attack military targets only, and the Germans seemed to be keeping their word.

The order prescribing "military targets only" had indeed been passed to the German air force, but this did not prevent Hermann Goering from preparing a display of German aerial might designed to overcome the Poles and shatter their morale. Operation Seaside, set for the first day of the war, was to be a massive raid on Warsaw. The targets would be military ones in, and around, the city, but a huge audience would see the Luftwaffe darken the skies with its planes, a spectacle intended to intimidate the people of Warsaw and give pause to those in power in London and Paris. But on the morning of September 1, visibility over Warsaw was so poor that Goering had to issue a cancellation order. Later that morning, a hundred German fighters and bombers appeared over the Polish capital, where they ran into fierce opposition from Polish fighters and ground defenses; obviously, the bombers failed to do much material or psychological damage.

It was not until September 13 that the Luftwaffe could give Warsaw its full attention; bad weather returned thereafter, so it was not until September 17 that the city's martyrdom began in earnest. Virtually surrounded now by the German Army, it came under heavy air and land bombardment. In truth, the city was not the "Fortress Warsaw" that German dispatches spoke of. The Polish government had left the capital, and in the power vacuum that resulted, Gen. Juliusz Rommel and the city administration began to improvise resistance among the population and the one hundred thousand soldiers who found themselves in the city. But the essential point was that the people of Warsaw chose to fight and rejected several calls to lay down their arms. Hitler was to say later that he had tried five times to get the city to surrender (including having the Luftwaffe drop leaflets demanding capitulation).

The defenders wanted to send noncombatants out of the city under a flag of truce. Negotiations to that end failed, apparently because of mutual distrust and misunderstandings. For example, a column of refugees trying to leave the city was fired on by German troops who had not yet received the order to let them pass. Thereafter, the Germans redoubled the air and ground bombardments, driven by the Führer's order to reduce the city before the end of the month. While the Luftwaffe's bombers were trying to adhere to the injunction "military targets only," they were having great problems with accuracy. Even the dive-bombing Stukas had trouble; they flew repeated missions against the city's bridges, but without destroying them. German airmen who participated in the raid of September 13, when 183 planes were over the city at the same time, spoke of bad timing, near collision, and virtual chaos over the target. Toward the end, when the city was hidden under a pall of smoke, German bombers crisscrossed over it while their crews threw out incendiaries by the shovelful, stoking the mighty furnace ten thousand feet below.

Under the incessant pounding, Warsaw's vital services began to fail. Telephones ceased to function over much of the city, followed by the failure of electric power generally. On September 29, with hundreds of fires raging throughout Warsaw, water pressure began to drop in the mains. The end had come. Two days later, Polish negotiators went out to arrange the surrender. Warsaw had been struck by about five thousand tons of German bombs, one-fourth of the total amount the Luftwaffe used in the Polish campaign. About three thousand Polish soldiers fell victim to air and land bombardments, and about eight times that number of civilians.

When Field Marshal Kesselring was in the dock at Nuremberg six years later, he defended the bombardment of the city in the following terms: "In the German view, Warsaw was a fortress, and moreover it had strong air defenses. Thus, it fell under the stipulations of the Hague Convention for land warfare, which can analogously be applied to air warfare."[1] He also claimed that German bomber crews had done everything humanly possible to strike only military objectives.

But the reduction of the city was not just a military operation; it was also a media event. Hitler had staged the operation partly for the harvest of fright and dread it would yield, and his expectations were met fully. The showman and the extortionist in the Führer led him to give the spectacle the widest possible dissemination in such vehicles as the harrowing propaganda film *Baptism by Fire.* The film showed a Germany as terrible and inexorable in its might as Hitler imagined it. People in London or Paris, seeing what fate might befall them, would pressure their governments to make an accommodation with Germany. So while the Luftwaffe viewed the bombardment of Warsaw as a legitimate military operation, the Ministry of Propaganda turned it into an apocalypse of Wagnerian grandeur. The Allies were bound to react, but not necessarily in the ways Hitler and Goebbels imagined. On October 16, 1939, after reviewing German operations in Poland, the British Air Ministry decided it could no longer be bound by the Draft Rules it had pledged to observe or by its acceptance of Roosevelt's appeal. Henceforth, British air policy would be governed by expediency.

There was no doubt that the generation of 1939 was stunned and horrified by the spectacle of Warsaw in flames. It seemed to fulfill perfectly the most dire predictions that Douhet and other military Cassandras had been making for years. Had contemporaries been less obsessed with the *Götterdämmerung* image, they might have read in the bombardment of Warsaw something quite different. In the space of four weeks, the city absorbed ten times the tonnage of bombs dropped on Great Britain in the four years of World War I. At the end of those four weeks, the city was badly punished, but far from obliterated—although some "experts" had written that 5,000 tons was sufficient to raze a city the size of Paris. Finally, despite the intensity of the bombardment, the inhabitants of Warsaw did not go into a blind panic. To be sure, the population was uneasy and a prey to rumor; but a recent study has shown that what they feared most from the Luftwaffe was that it might parachute spies and saboteurs into the city or drop "poisoned objects"—a curious revival of the "poisoned candy" stories of World War I.[2] But there were no stampedes, no looting, no assaults on the centers of authority—in short, none of the scenes of frenzy and terror so often described in the literature of the thirties. The people of Warsaw lost their battle, but not their dignity.

At the other end of Europe, a strange, muted air war had begun on the night of September 3, when British Whitley bombers flew over several German cities and unleashed on them clouds of leaflets. The British government had hopes of appealing directly to the German people; the leaflets were messages to them from Prime Minister

Neville Chamberlain. Even if that ploy proved unsuccessful, leaflet dropping served notice that German cities were vulnerable at night, yet was not an action sufficiently provocative to escalate the war to dangerous proportion. By the spring of 1940, the RAF had dropped 50 million leaflets over Germany, Austria, Poland, and Czechoslovakia. There is no evidence that this mass of paper had any effect on the course of World War II, but the leaflet work gave Bomber Command invaluable experience in learning its way around in the night skies of central Europe. (Neither the French nor the Germans were so enthusiastic about dropping leaflets, but their reconaissance flights sometimes carried them.)

The leaflet campaign caused some embarrassment to Hermann Goering. Charged with the air defense of the Reich, he could do very little to stop these intrusions. Ground defenses were ineffective, and for the moment, the Luftwaffe had no night fighters. The Reichsmarschall could only affect a good-natured tolerance: "If they want to fly about over Germany from time to time at high altitude and throw out their laughable propaganda papers, then that's all right with me. But if they should substitute bombs for propaganda, then retaliation will come in the wink of an eye."[3]

Opportunities for offensive operations were very limited, since for the time being, both sides were avoiding any objectives that carried the risk of hitting civilians and their property. Virtually the only "safe" targets in this respect were enemy warships. Goering wanted to open the war with a spectacular bombing operation against the British home fleet, or at least a strike against the aircraft carrier *Hermes,* then riding at anchor at Sheerness. But Hitler refused: Germany was not going to initiate the air war. It was the RAF that did that on September 4 with surprise raids on German naval units at Wilhelmshaven and Brunnsbüttel. The Luftwaffe replied with a raid on elements of the British fleet off Great Fisher Bank on September 26, and another on October 16 into the Firth of Forth, where H.M.S. *Hood* was reported at anchor. The *Hood* was there, but docked, or nearly so. The pilots of the Junkers 88s passed it up for fear they might put a bomb on the shore; they bombed smaller vessels, with indifferent results.

By December 19 the Royal Navy could report fifteen separate air attacks on its ships. The Luftwaffe had damaged a cruiser and a destroyer, neither of them seriously. The RAF did not do much better. By the spring of 1940, it had made 861 sorties against enemy warships, causing slight damage to the *Emden* and the *Scheer*. The cost was high—forty-one bombers lost. It was in these raids that Bomber Command began to realize just how vulnerable its bombers were to German air defenses. In forays across the North Sea on December 14 and again on December 18, small formations of Wellington bombers ran into intense fighter opposition. (German radar, which was just becoming operational along the North Sea coast, gave advance warning of their approach.) Underarmed and without self-sealing gas tanks, the Wellingtons suffered 50 percent losses on each raid. In the meantime, confirmation came from France that the Fairey Battles were even more vulnerable. Ten squadrons were stationed in eastern France as an "advance air striking force" threatening German industry. But after September 30 it was difficult to pretend that the threat was a serious one. On that day a reconnaissance patrol of five Battles was set upon by a score of German fighters. Within minutes four Battles were shot out of the sky; the fifth made it back to base *in extremis*.

Bomber Command thus had good reason to think its squadrons would suffer sizable losses if committed over enemy territory in daylight raids. Yet British agreements with the French called for the RAF to undertake day bombing, while the Armée de l'Air would restrict bombing operations to nighttime until its new bombers were ready for service. Beyond that, Bomber Command felt that when the storm broke, its logical targets were the same Ruhr industrial centers the Independent Air Force had attacked in 1918—although it was also attracted to a somewhat more refined "oil plan," in which the destruction of carefully selected targets would make the German war machine literally run out of fuel in a short time. The French high command opposed both ideas. Extending bombing operations to German towns—what the British called "taking the gloves off"—would invite attacks on French towns, which were more vulnerable than German ones. Moreover, in General Gamelin's view, the function of bombing squadrons was to help tilt the balance in the land battle. The French too had held on to the ideas of 1918.

These quarrels had not been resolved when the German armies burst across the frontiers on May 10, 1940. For those who had followed the Polish campaign, the development of the German air attack was familiar. The first massive strike made early on the morning of May 10 was at Allied airfields; it was largely unsuccessful, probably because of early morning mist. Thereafter, the German bomber squadrons turned increasingly to transport and communications targets, and when the bombers attacked urban centers, it was clearly those targets they were seeking. The most disturbing attack of the day was the one made on the German town of Freiburg, which produced scores of casualties among the townspeople and led to violent denunciations in the German press. What most concerned the Allies was that they knew their aircraft had not attacked the city, and they feared the Germans had engineered the incident in order to justify all-out attacks on British and French towns. What actually happened was that German bombers with orders to hit targets in Dijon lost their way and bombed Freiburg by mistake. The German government was unable to keep the news from leaking out, so it did the next best thing and blamed the Allies.

Four days later, another city made the headlines—Rotterdam. The German forces that invaded the Low Countries were under orders to overrun the region quickly, and to that end, they used a number of unconventional means, including paratroops, airborne units, and even soldiers dressed in Dutch uniforms. By May 14 they had made good progress but had run into serious resistance in Rotterdam, where the northern part of the city was stubbornly held by Dutch forces. The German general directing the attack felt that a "short but devastating air raid" might break the enemy's resistance and bring it to surrender.[4] The request for air assistance went through channels until it reached Kampfgeschwader 54, which prepared its hundred-odd Heinkel 111s for the attack. In the meantime, the Germans decided to continue their parley with the Dutch defenders so the air bombardment was canceled—but this message too went through channels, and did not reach Kampfgeschwader 54 in time. The German authorities in Rotterdam fired pink flares to warn the bombers away, but one wave of fifty Heinkels did not see the signal and dropped its bombs on target. The explosions were followed by raging fires and much of the city was gutted. Allied wire services were soon reporting that thousands of people had lost their lives in an attack on a city that had already surrendered. The actual casualties were about a thousand killed, but some seventy-eight thousand people were left homeless. To the British government, the attack on Rotterdam meant an end to the period of restraint in air warfare. The gloves were off.

On May 15 the British war cabinet made the perilous decision to cross the Rubicon—in this case, the Rhine—and Bomber Command prepared an attack for that night against oil and railway targets in the Ruhr. British leaders thought the attack east of the Rhine might well bring the Luftwaffe over British towns, and a warning to that effect went out to air-defense units. That night ninety-nine British bombers took off for Germany—the beginning of a strategic air offensive that would last for five years.

The May 15 raid into the Ruhr did not provoke a particularly violent reaction from the Germans; most important, no Heinkels crossed the Channel on reprisal missions. For the time being, the Luftwaffe continued to give its full attention to the Battle of France. Nevertheless, the attack had made an impression. It was certainly in Hitler's mind when he issued his Directive No. 13 nine days later. The German air force was to concentrate its efforts on influencing the land battles and interrupting Allied traffic in the Channel. But there was more: "Independently of the operations in France, the Luftwaffe is to undertake a full-scale offensive against the British homeland as soon as sufficient forces are available. It is to institute a crushing reprisal raid as response to the English attacks on the Ruhr area."[5]

Bomber Command's raids into Germany did bring a prompt and angry reaction from the French high command. With the Germans across the Meuse in force and a portion of his line disintegrating, General Gamelin insisted that the air forces of both countries use all their energies to help stem the flow of panzers into France. Gamelin did not have his way completely, nor did Gen. Maxime Weygand, who took over from him on May 19. Bomber Command served two masters in those hectic days of May and early June. The bombing squadrons struck Germany (the only proper target for them, according to their leaders) whenever they could; they attacked airfields, crossroads, and rail centers behind the enemy armies when they had to. This "operational" bombing in support of the land forces made at best a mediocre contribution. The bombers were flying at night, seeking fairly precise targets; the missions, hastily planned, were very imperfectly executed. The RAF was then experimenting with photographs of the target taken with the aid of flares, and these revealed more than once that not only was the specific objective nowhere in view, but the Hampdens and Wellingtons were releasing their bombs over the wrong town. On the other hand, it is easy to understand the exasperation of the French generals; with their front torn open and their armies reeling, it seemed hardly the time to sprinkle explosives over the Ruhr Valley.

By the end of May, the German armies had liquidated the Dunkirk pocket, and in the first days of June, they broke across the Somme, the last barrier that might have held them. On June 3 the Luftwaffe executed Operation Paula, a massive raid in, and around, Paris. The attack had been planned for some time, and French intelligence knew it was coming, thanks to its interception of German orders, but faulty transmission kept French fighter units from being notified until German bombs began to rain down on their airfields. Several hundred German bombers swung around the city, hitting thirteen airfields, a score of factories, including the Citroën works on the Seine; one bomb—fortunately a dud—dropped through the roof of the French Air Ministry and landed in the middle of a ministerial reception. Elsewhere, the bombs took about 250 lives. Material damage was not great, but the raid gave a severe jolt to morale that was already sinking.

The French made what riposte they could. The Aéronavale, the French Navy's air arm, had acquired a large four-engined Farmann 223.4 originally built to carry mail to South America. Commandant Daillière of the Aéronavale converted the plane into a makeshift bomber and got permission to bomb the industrial suburbs of Berlin. He and his crew took off on June 8, and after following a roundabout course, they dropped their bombs on a city they identified as Berlin and returned to France. Curiously, the German records do not indicate an air attack on Berlin for that night.

The token raid on Berlin gave the French newspapers a chance to print an encouraging headline, but it was virtually the only good news available in that second week of June 1940. On June 10 there was fresh catastrophe: Italy declared war and launched an offensive of its own in the south. Italy's entry into the war was not unexpected. The Allies had hoped to keep it out by suggesting that its cities were vulnerable to air attack. What is more, they had plans to attack those cities, so when Italy entered the war, the RAF began to shift bombers to the south of France. A raid was ordered for the night of June 12 but someone in the French government began to have misgivings. Frantic telephone calls did not resolve the differences of view, with the result that the British bombers had orders to fly and the French authorities at Salon airfield had orders to keep them from flying. As the British prepared to take off, the French drove trucks onto the airfield to block them. There was a very tense confrontation, and the British finally canceled the mission. Such scenes were common enough in that tragic, chaotic episode historians have labeled the fall of France.

The resounding collapse of France placed its ally in extreme peril, and the pluck and determination with which the English government and people faced that peril have won universal admiration. The British Air Staff, with an obstinacy and a single-mindedness of purpose remarkable for those distracted times, clung to its belief in the strategic air offensive. RAF bombers never completely abandoned the night skies of Germany, and in that disastrous summer they even found their way to Italian cities. Although Bomber Command was mobilized at that time to aid in the defense of the British Isles—no easy task for a force schooled exclusively in the offensive—its leaders nonetheless pored over schemes to deprive Germany of its oil, to burn off its forests with incendiary pellets, to wreck viaducts near Münster and factories in Mannheim. In a word, the RAF was fertile in plans and projects for a strategic air offensive, but the prospects of executing them were extremely poor, at least for the imminent future.

Across the Channel the situation of the Luftwaffe was just the reverse: fresh from one triumph, it stood poised for the next campaign without any clear idea of how to use the impressive means at its disposal. The three Luftflotten that were ranged about England (Luftflotte V in Norway, Luftflotte II in the Low Countries and northeastern France, and Luftflotte III along the French coast of the Channel) consisted of just under a thousand twin-engined bombers, an air armada that could deliver over England in a single day five times the tonnage of bombs dropped on it during all of World War I. But nearly two months elapsed between the fall of France and "Eagle Day"—August 13—the date on which Goering formally opened the air offensive against Great Britain. The delay was due in part to difficulties in working out strategy for the offensive. A sure and steady hand had guided the German air force through the Battle of France, but once the panzers reached the Channel the assurance disappeared. Faced with an island fortress that spurned the Führer's "appeal to reason" on July 19, Germany's leaders were not sure quite how to grasp the nettle.

This is not to say that the Germans lost what has come to be called the Battle of Britain simply because they failed to adhere to a master plan while the British did. In the combat conditions prevailing over much of the British Isles, the advantage swung to the defensive for several reasons, chiefly technical ones. The radar warning system overcame the "lag time" in interception, enabling Fighter Command to organize prompt and effective resistance, while the Luftwaffe learned in the skies of England what the RAF had discovered a few months earlier in its raids across the North Sea: neither the bomber's speed nor its armament could ensure its survival in daytime encounters with an enemy fighter force. It was also the turn of the Luftwaffe to discover shortcomings in its matériel: the Stuka dive-bomber was very vulnerable to British fighter attacks, and so was the twin-engined Messerschmitt 110, cast in the role of "heavy" fighter to escort the German bombers. Many other considerations colored the outcome of the Battle of Britain, such as morale; there was even a meteorological factor, for bad weather helped to delay Eagle Day and gave the RAF a much needed respite in the second half of August.

All in all, it seems clear that Luftwaffe planners did not seriously occupy themselves with the question of an air offensive against Great Britain until quite late. The first extensive study was made by Gen. Hellmuth Felmy late in 1938, and it offered little hope that the British could be brought to their knees by air action alone. Felmy fixed the most attractive targets as airfields and aircraft factories, the Royal Navy's ships and installations, and merchant shipping and port facilities. There were further studies in 1939, including *Studie Blau*—a kind of inventory of British industry something like the "Bomber's Baedeker," which the British Air Staff used in selecting targets in Germany. *Studie Blau* was followed closely by the Geisler report, which grouped bombing objectives into broad categories and priorities. What emerged from these studies were several distinct and often competing air strategies. First of all, there was the intriguing possibility that the British Isles might be starved out, or "strangled," the term used by "Beppo" Schmid, Luftwaffe intelligence chief and warm supporter of the plan. The scheme was esentially a new application of the blockade principle of World War I, although in the present case bomber and submarine would cooperate to close down Britain's lifeline. Another strategy, which originated even before 1914, was to employ the Luftwaffe against the Royal Navy in the hope of canceling out Britain's naval superiority. (This idea was particularly attractive in the summer of 1940, when Hitler and his advisers were contemplating a cross-Channel invasion.) There were proposals to hamstring the British war economy by bombing key industries and transport targets, and finally there were the suggestions of those who believed in the efficacy of "morale" bombing, among them Hitler himself.

Most of these ideas appear in the stream of directives and instructions that Hitler and Goering issued to the Luftwaffe through the summer and fall of 1940, even after it became obvious that the first

From Bomber to Transport. Bombing planes such as this German R-plane were rapidly converted to commercial uses after the armistice of 1918. In the interwar period, disarmament negotiators feared that commercial aircraft might in turn be converted into bombers. *Courtesy the Library of Congress*

Billy Mitchell. General Mitchell's thorough knowledge of the technical aspects of aviation set him apart from many other theorists of air power. *Courtesy the Library of Congress*

The Soviet TB-3. In the 1930s the Soviet Union possessed the largest fleet of heavy bombers in Europe, with several hundred TB-3s like the one pictured here. Highly advanced when it was introduced into serial production in 1932, it was outmoded when the Soviet Union entered World War II. *Courtesy the U.S. Air Force*

A Case of Gigantism. The Boeing XB-15 shown here dwarfing an accompanying fighter was the largest airplane in the world when it was completed in 1937. Although an important step in large bomber development, the plane was slow and underpowered. *Courtesy the U.S. Air Force*

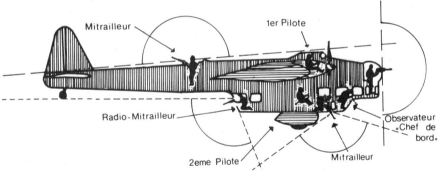

Mitrailleur — 1er Pilote

Radio-Mitrailleur

2eme Pilote

Mitrailleur

Observateur «Chef de bord»

The Amiot 143. This plane was the workhorse of French bombing squadrons on the eve of World War II. Although slow, it was heavily armed for its day, and as the diagram indicates, its guns were placed to cover every angle of attack. This design reflected the belief of Douhet and other theorists that the bomber's best defense was firepower. *Courtesy the Service Historique de l'Armée de l'Air*

The First B-17. It was completed in 1935 and known as Model 299. Not long after this photograph was taken, the plane was destroyed during flight trials. *Courtesy the U.S. Air Force*

The Five-Thousandth B-17. Visibly changed in nine years of evolution, this B-17G was completed in May 1944 and flew off to war bearing the name *Five Grand* and the signatures of several thousand workers at the Boeing plant in Seattle. *Courtesy the U.S. Air Force*

"The Flying Crusader." Two rows of tiny bombs painted along the nose on this B-24 Liberator of the U.S. Eighth Air Force indicate that it is the veteran of seventy-seven missions. *Courtesy the U.S. Air Force*

The AVRO Lancaster. This most successful of all British heavy bombers was an almost fortuitous creation, having been derived from the far less successful Manchester by lengthening the wings and mounting two more engines on them. *Courtesy the U.S. Air Force*

Opposite "The Best Heavy Bomber of WWII." So an East German historian describes the four-engined Soviet TB-7, although fewer than a hundred were built. The Western Allies got a close look at the plane in this photo when it brought Molotov to London in May 1942. *Courtesy the U.S. Air Force*

The Humble Drop-Tank Saved the Day. Auxiliary fuel tanks such as the ones being installed on this Mustang enabled Allied fighters to accompany bombers deep into Germany and reverse the tide of battle in 1944. *Courtesy the U.S. Air Force*

B-17 Waist Gunner. For high-altitude missions the gunner wore heated boots and gloves, an oxygen mask with goggles, earphones and microphone, and a flak "apron" armored with plates of manganese steel. *Courtesy the U.S. Air Force*

The Norden Bombsight. Not until 1945 did the U.S. government supply details of this device; then, press releases revealed it to be a $6,000 complex of mirrors, gyroscopes, and gears "about the size of a football." The unit shown here, attached to its automatic pilot on the lower left, is from the *Enola Gay*. *Courtesy the National Air and Space Museum, Smithsonian Institution*

Four-thousand-pound Bombs. These bombs, shown in a depot in England, dwarf both the American sergeant and his jeep. *Courtesy the U.S. Air Force*

Tallboy. Such was the name for this 12,000-pound blast bomb carried to Germany by such planes as the Lancaster seen in the background. *Courtesy the U.S. Air Force*

One Bomb in Five Did Not Explode. This bomb
was one of five that struck a machine-tool plant in
Cologne; well into the war most of the belligerents
were troubled by a similar proportion of duds.
Courtesy the National Archives

Life in the Underground. This was a familiar scene in London in 1940–41, although never more than a minority of Londoners sought refuge in mass shelters. *Courtesy the Library of Congress*

The *Enola Gay*. Perhaps the most famous bombing plane in history, the *Enola Gay* is now the property of the National Air and Space Museum. *Courtesy the U.S. Air Force*

Flakhelferin. In both Great Britain and Germany, thousands of women took an active part in the air defense systems. Here a young German woman mans a *Horchgeraet,* or "sound detector." *Courtesy the Library of Congress*

Life in the Ruins. This German has made a home for his family in the basement of a shattered building in Hamburg. *Courtesy the U.S. Air Force*

The V-Weapons Brought Random Violence. Here a V-1 "buzz bomb" has come down in a residential neighborhood of Bovington, England, in the summer of 1944. *Courtesy the U.S. Air Force*

The Final Ignominy. The shattered façade of the German Air Ministry building in 1945 is testimony to the Luftwaffe's ultimate failure to protect the air frontiers of the Reich. *Courtesy the U.S. Air Force*

Not Even the Führer Was Spared. Hitler's mountain retreat at Berchtesgaden was heavily damaged by air attacks. In this photo, a Twelfth Air Force Thunderbolt is flying over the ruins. *Courtesy the U.S. Air Force*

B-29s over Osaka. Many inhabitants of the city thought it would be spared .
was ablaze. *Courtesy the U.S. Air Force*

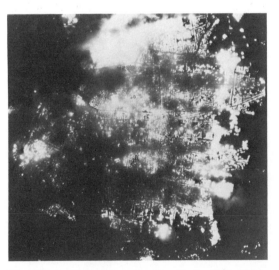

The Death of Toyama. On August 1, 1945, B-29s
attacked this city of 127,000 with 1,500 tons of
bombs, destroying 99.5 percent of its built-up area in
a single raid. *Courtesy the U.S. Air Force*

but on June 4, 1945, B-29s deluged it with bombs, and within minutes much of the city

The Marunouchi District of Tokyo, 1945. According to the U.S. Strategic Bombing Survey, safes such as this one were "probably the most common landmarks showing where combustible businesses had been located." *Courtesy the U.S. Air Force*

Frau Jaeger. A photograph taken before the
ruins of her home at Cordierstrasse 59,
Frankfurt. *Courtesy the Stadtarchiv, Frankfurt am Mein*

task—and the indispensable prerequisite for accomplishing the other tasks—was to beat down the British air defense system so that the German bombers could range freely. In the narrow sense, the Battle of Britain was a duel of sorts, a direct confrontation between two air forces. The Luftwaffe's chief goal was to shatter Fighter Command, to kill or exhaust its pilots, and to destroy its Spitfires and Hurricanes not only in the air but on the ground and even on the assembly lines. The British had to make this effort prohibitively expensive for the Germans, and ultimately this is what they succeeded in doing. A battle of this sort could be fought only in daylight hours; it filled the long summer days of August and September 1940 and culminated in the vast air battles on Sunday, September 15, which cost the Luftwaffe sixty aircraft and Fighter Command twenty-six. Thereafter, Goering was forced to take a long, sobering look at his bombing offensive; by the end of September it had cost the Germans over fifteen hundred aircraft and crews, with little evidence that Britain's air defenses had been seriously impaired. With September the great daylight raids came to an end. Henceforth, the German bombers would strike under cover of night.

The abandonment of massive daylight raids meant also the end of precision bombing and consequently of the attacks on smaller targets. Initially the Luftwaffe set great store by two systems of radio guidance (the *X-Geraet* and *Knickebein*) in which the bombing planes would fly "on the beam" straight over the objective, releasing their bombs at the right moment in accordance with a signal. Elite crews were trained in the technique to form Kampfgruppe 100, whose purpose was to mark the target for the main bombing force that followed. But the British got wind of the system early in the summer and managed to interfere with its operation—the beginning of a "high-frequency war" involving increasingly sophisticated "black boxes" and elaborate jamming techniques. The short-term result was to deprive the Luftwaffe of its first radio-guidance navigational aids. (An exception was on the night of November 14, 1940, when the British failed to jam the *X-Geraet* that led German bombers to Coventry, resulting in a devastating raid on the city's center.)

The switch to night bombing thus meant a change to broader definitions of objectives and to area bombing, but this change worked no great hardship, for it coincided roughly with a change of emphasis in the whole bombing offensive. Even before the outcome of the battle for air supremacy over England was clear, Germany's leadership was increasingly drawn to the idea of an attack on the cities, and on London particularly, in the hope that it could drive the British out of the war. Hitler especially seems to have regarded an all-out air assault on the British capital as a trump card to be held and then played at the most opportune moment. In his first war directive, dated August 31, 1939, he reserved for himself the decision to attack London, and it was the only Allied city singled out in that way. He no doubt had London in mind when he told his military leaders that he was meditating an air offensive "against the heart of the British will-to-resist." [6]

It was important to Hitler for the British people to know that their cities were in grave danger, and he missed no opportunity to tell them so in his speeches that summer. English translations of the texts were usually dropped over England in leaflet form. Even in his July 19 speech to the Reichstag, the Führer mixed menace into his appeal for peace. He accused Churchill of having begun an air war against harmless civilians in May and did not blush to cite the attack in Freiburg of May 10. So far, Germany had not replied in kind, but its patience was nearing an end. The Luftwaffe stood ready to bring "dreadful sorrow and misfortune" to the people of England. [7]

By August 1940 the German leadership had received intelligence reports—inaccurate ones, as it turned out—indicating a significant slump in morale, particularly in London. A directive prepared in the middle of the month on the projected invasion called for an air raid on the city to coincide with the landing. The bombing would make the population of London stampede out of the city, choking the roads and blocking the movement of British military units to the landing areas. By August 19, Goering had ordered preparation of a heavy night raid on Liverpool, set for August 28. On the night of August 24, the first German bombs fell on central London. The planes that dropped them did not intentionally attack the British capital; they were looking for Rochester and oil storage tanks along the Thames, but their navigation was faulty. Winston Churchill did not know this, and he ordered an immediate retaliatory raid on Berlin, which was executed the following night. Eighty-one Hampdens and Wellingtons started on the long trip, but no more than twenty of them found and bombed Berlin. British bombers struck three more times within the next week. None of the attacks were serious, but they probably caused Goering and his allies to hasten the preparation of their own attack on London. In the meantime, the Luftwaffe had begun night raids on Liverpool.

Preliminary orders for the first bombing assault on the British capital went out on August 31, and the attack itself took place on September 7. But before the bombers struck, Hitler made another speech. He began by denouncing the "night pirates" of the RAF, who came to bomb villages, farms, and residential areas: "Wherever they see a light they drop a bomb." Henceforth, they would be paid back, night for night, bomb for bomb. "And if the British air force drops two or three or four thousand kilograms of bombs, then we will drop in a single night 150,000, 180,000, 230,000, 300,000, 400,000, a million kilograms. If they announce that they will attack our cities on a large scale, then we shall wipe their cities out!"[8]

Shortly before five o'clock on the evening of September 7, the warning sirens sounded in London. A first wave of three hundred German bombers appeared over the city, opening an attack that would last for twelve hours. When the last raiders had gone, 306 Londoners were dead and some thirteen hundred were wounded. At least a thousand fires broke out within the city, and several of the larger ones were still burning the following day. The Luftwaffe came again that evening, killing an additional 412 Londoners; still another raid on the night of September 9–10 added 370 more fatalities. The "Blitz" had begun in earnest, and for the time being, London came in for the worst of it. Not until early November did the city spend a night free from raids and alarms.

Just what motives guided the German high command during the bombing offensive against Britain's cities is not altogether clear. The pattern of attacks in the last months of 1940 and the first half of 1941 has been described as "a confused arrangement looking much more like the aimless destructive outbursts of a child with conflicting impulses than the results of clear, decisive planning often regarded as the prerogative of totalitarian leadership."[9] An air assault on London was to coincide with the launching of Operation Sea Lion, the German cross-Channel invasion, and the British assumed from the raid of the seventh that the invasion was imminent (it was in fact still officially "on" until canceled by Hitler on September 17). But as hopes faded in Berlin that the Luftwaffe would gain the air superiority needed for the invasion attempt, the idea of attacking Britain's cities became more attractive, particularly since they could be struck at night. Certainly Hitler was still juggling with options at the beginning of September, but he made a significant observation on the tenth of that month. German naval authorities were anxious for the Luftwaffe to move on to bombing of the Channel ports, an operation crucial for the success of Sea Lion, but in conference with the Führer they did not press the point, because he told them the air assault on London might be critical. His pronouncement was recorded in the Kriegsmarine war diary for that day: "A systematic and long-drawn-out bombardment of London might produce an attitude in the enemy which will make Operation Sea Lion unnecessary."[10]

The Führer and his entourage were tantalized by the idea the British people might be close to the breaking point, as intelligence reports seemed to indicate. If the British were feeling the pressure, there was no better way to increase that pressure than to strike at the great metropolis which contained a fifth of the island's population. The belief that the British were at the end of their endurance was not confined to official circles in Germany, for the news was too good not to share it with the German public. Throughout the fall the German press returned to the theme. On October 13, Dr. Goebbels's newspaper *Das Reich* reported the repeated blows of the Luftwaffe had delivered so severe a shock to Londoners that Churchill's government had "grave anxieties" about their morale.

In truth the British war cabinet was not at all sure how the city's inhabitants would hold up, and it too watched carefully for the first signs of panic or despair. On September 11, Winston Churchill addressed his nation by radio, and he chose words not only to pay tribute to the embattled population of the capital, but also to stiffen its resolve: "All the world that is still free marvels at the composure and fortitude with which the citizens of London are facing and surmounting the great ordeal to which they are subjected, the end of which or the severity of which cannot yet be foreseen."[11] On September 23, King George VI went on the air to pay his tribute and to announce that he was creating the George Cross and the George Medal to honor those who distinguished themselves on the home front. This gesture was particularly well received, for a few days earlier a single German bomber had made a daylight attack on Buckingham Palace, thus uniting the monarch and his people in a common peril and generating an outpouring of affection for the royal family.

For the moment an indomitable spirit was London's chief weapon against the German bombers, along with civil-defense measures. A more active defense of the city against night attacks was very difficult to mount. When the first raids occurred London was defended by 92 heavy antiaircraft guns; the number soon doubled, and by May 1941 no fewer than 1,691 guns stood guard over the city. But no matter how numerous they were or how furiously they fired, they did not bring down many German bombers. At night their fire could be directed only by means of searchlights and sound-detection equipment, and neither of these devices worked very well at locating the high-flying and fast-moving bombers of the Luftwaffe. The only other technique was barrage fire, in which the batteries tried to put into the sky a curtain of projectiles into which, it was hoped, the enemy planes would fly. The solution to better accuracy lay in the use of radar to aim the guns, but promising as the idea was, it had not been realized in 1940.

The night fighter, the other potential weapon against the nocturnal bomber, was in a very early stage of development in 1940, for in this instance the British had lagged behind both the Germans and the French. The hastily constituted night-fighter units of 1940 rarely found their targets, and although there were certainly prospects of improvement with airborne radar, actual improvements did not come until later. The incessant pounding of the antiaircraft guns was comforting to Londoners, and both guns and night fighters added something to the stress that German aircrews had to face, thus perhaps contributing to accidents, which in this period seem to have accounted for more German bomber losses than any other cause. But this was little recompense for the vast defensive efforts both on the ground and in the air. Gen. Sir Frederick Pile, who helped organize the air defenses of the London area, confessed, "We seemed as far as ever from solving the great problem of the night bomber."[12]

Largely undeterred, then, Luftflotten II and III continued their campaign against the British capital. Through September and October the attacks went on, with a nightly average of 160 raiders. For the month of October the Luftwaffe released on the city 7,160 tons of high explosives and 4,735 canisters of incendiaries. In November came a shift of emphasis, with more attacks directed at other British cities. Coventry lost much of the city center and five hundred of its citizens in the devastating raid of November 14, and Plymouth and the Merseyside area came in for repeated attacks. In December, raids upon the capital were spasmodic, partly because of bad weather. But the raid of December 8–9 was particularly heavy, and both Westminster Abbey and the House of Commons were hit. Then, on the night of

December 29, much of London's center was damaged by spectacular fires. The raid that night was not a particularly heavy one, but several factors combined to make it devastating. It was a Sunday night, and many buildings were locked, with no firewatch posted. When the thousands of incendiaries were released, many fires burned for a time undetected, fanned in some cases by a stiff wind. Fire fighters were further hindered in their work by ruptured water mains and very low water in the Thames. Much of the square mile that constituted the City of London was burned out. Saint Paul's was saved by the closest margin, but eight other Wren churches were consumed on that night.

The pace of the German air offensive slackened for the first two months of 1941, once again because of bad weather and sodden airfields in France (hard-surface runways were still uncommon). In March the tempo picked up again, and from March to May the Luftflotten carried out some seventy major raids (those that killed fifty people or more). Of these, only eleven struck London; the rest were scattered among a score of cities, Plymouth, Hull, and Liverpool being the most frequently hit. The raids began to taper off, with a final heavy assault on London on May 10, 1941. The reason for the gradual slackening of the offensive lay in Hitler's decision to attack the Soviet Union. As early as April, 150 bombers were shifted to the Balkans, and in the next month Luftflotte II also departed. By the time Operation Barbarossa was unleashed on the Soviets on June 22, two-thirds of Germany's air strength was concentrated in the east.

For the British the Blitz was over, except for the harassing attacks and minor raids that Hitler ordered continued throughout the war. Three years later, the British would have to face a second ordeal with attacks on London and the southeast of England by the two V-weapons: the V-1 flying bomb, of which perhaps 5,000 reached England in the summer of 1944, and the much more sophisticated V-2 rocket, of which about a thousand were fired at the island between September 1944 and March 1945. Challenging as both of these weapons were, they did not rival the bombers of 1940–41 in destructiveness. Of the sixty thousand Britons who lost their lives to air attacks (half of them Londoners), about forty thousand were killed in the Blitz. Of the estimated 71,000 metric tons of explosives and incendiaries the island absorbed, 57,000 were dropped by December 1941.

What lessons could be drawn from this first extended bombing campaign of the war, which lasted some nine months? The campaign failed, of course, in its very first objective, which was to destroy the RAF. Here the analogy between sea and air warfare broke down, as some of the early theorists said it would. It proved far more difficult to drive the enemy fleets from the skies than to sweep them from the seas. Command of the air, as Douhet called it, proved a tenuous, elusive thing, not to be won against serious opposition in just a matter of weeks. And without air superiority there could be no Operation Sea Lion. The invasion was probably a last resource anyway, a chancy thing no one could approach without trepidation. Thus balked by an insular foe, the Germans turned to the bomber as the only weapon that could strike the enemy in its vitals. Hitler was certainly familiar with the idea of bringing an enemy to its knees by the destruction of key facilities; he boasted that with two hundred bombers capable of flying at 450 miles an hour, he could destroy all the power stations in a country and force it to capitulate within six months. But Germany had no such bombers in 1940, and those it did have were vulnerable if used in daylight raids on precision targets. The shift to nighttime operations was inevitably a shift to the larger target. While the specified objective might be a factory or an arsenal, and the German people were assured that the Luftwaffe went after "military targets only," most of the bombs would go into the surrounding urban complex. If enough bombs went into enough cities, the British would come to terms. At bottom, this strategy was nothing more than arm twisting; but it had worked before, and the Führer held to it through thick and thin.

The British learned a number of lessons during the Blitz, and many of those lessons would prove valid in other countries as well. The first and most heartening revelation was that under intense aerial bombardment the loss of life was far less widespread than anticipated, with perhaps five people killed for every ton of bombs dropped and three times that number injured. On the other hand, property damage was extensive and was much increased by fire losses. Rehousing proved a major problem. Some hazards had not been anticipated, such as getting about in the darkness of a blacked-out city or dealing with the large number of unexploded bombs; at one time London contained several thousand such bombs, including a monster one-ton projectile that sank into the earth beside Saint Paul's. But, all in all, the cities proved remarkably able to absorb punishment, and this was particularly true of London. The German medium bombers of 1940 could not deliver anywhere near the massive tonnages that would be used later in the war, and the very vastness of London—over seven hundred square miles—largely negated the limited effort the Luftwaffe mounted.

The great unknown factor at the beginning of the Blitz was the reaction of the population. In the first few days, there were some rumblings in London's East End, where the poorer districts near the London Docks suffered heavy damage, but they ended when the city came under more general attack and the fashionable West End began to receive its share of bombs. A Home Security report for September 25 could strike a reassuring note: "The German attack upon London has had no fundamental ill effect upon the capital or on the nation. Its first impact caused bewilderment and there was some ill-temper. . . . this loss of temper . . . has almost completely vanished and a general equanimity prevails."[13]

There was no real evidence of panic, no chaotic stampede from the city when the first bombs fell, and no appearance of the feared "deep-shelter mentality." In fact, a survey in November 1940 indicated that the great majority of Londoners did not seek out the subway tubes or the public shelters when the sirens sounded; six out of every ten continued to sleep in their homes. Much the same reassuring picture emerged in the provincial cities that came under attack, although there the authorities were somewhat concerned about the reappearance of "trekking," the phenomenon, noticed in the previous war in some Italian cities, of an exodus into the countryside each evening either for greater safety or simply for an undisturbed night's sleep.

So the Londoner and the Liverpudlian endured with "general equanimity" and went on with their lives as best they could. Their spirit would be fittingly praised in Churchillian prose. But the qualities they displayed were not exclusively British. In the following years, the bomber would bring the same threat to other cities and peoples, and they too would stand the test.

CHAPTER 8

THE BEGINNINGS OF THE ALLIED AIR OFFENSIVE

THE LUFTWAFFE ASSAULT ON GREAT BRITAIN was an operation that began with great fanfare and then gradually and almost imperceptibly declined into little more than harassment raids. The campaign that Bomber Command waged against Germany developed in just the opposite way. It began almost unnoticed on the night of May 15, 1940, when fewer than a hundred Hampden bombers crossed the Rhine; it was carried out by fits and starts and then rose to a terrifying climax in the last months of World War II.

Bomber Command emerged from the catastrophe of June 1940 with its share of losses. Scores of Fairey Battles had been lost, and the Blenheims of 2 Group, designated for use in conjunction with the army, had been badly mauled. But the workhorses of the bombing force of 1940—the seventeen squadrons of Hampdens, Wellingtons, and Whitleys—were largely intact. Among the chief casualties of those first months of war was the belief that a force of bombers could defend itself successfully against fighter attacks by means of close-formation flying and concentrated fire. And when that theory proved false, so did the concept of day bombardment. While brief penetrations into enemy airspace by daylight might still be possible with fighter escort, any deep, massive thrust could be carried out only under cover of darkness. This lesson had been learned at considerable cost, and Bomber Command took it to heart: in the last four months of 1940, its planes made twenty nighttime sorties for each one flown by day. And two years later, when the American Eighth Air Force was preparing to send its Fortresses and Liberators into the daytime skies of Germany, the pessimism in Bomber Command was ill concealed.

The conversion to night operations put severe limitations on bombing. While the fighters and flak batteries of the Luftwaffe were much less of a problem, nature posed some formidable obstacles. First of all, the raid could not stretch much past the hours of darkness, or else the bombers could be intercepted on the way to the target as well as returning from it. In practical terms, this meant that in summer, with its shorter nights, a bombing force could not fly to Berlin, Leipzig, or Stettin and back. These cities thus became "winter" targets, at least for the time being.

Darkness imposed still another restriction on bombing. During only a fourth of the nights each month would the moon be in correct phase—the "bomber's moon"—for sighting and identifying most objectives. (There were some exceptions, such as blast furnaces and targets that could be fixed by their relationship to bodies of water, these often being visible on darker nights.) Any cloudiness would complicate the bombardier's task even further. The towns in the Ruhr were notable for being partly shielded by the industrial haze that hung over the region. The search was on for better navigation aids and "blind bombing" devices, but for the time being, the success of a night bombing mission depended largely on the keenness of the human eye.

Assuming the British bombing force could reach and find its objectives, in 1940 it was severely limited in the amount of damage it could inflict. Just two years previously, Bomber Command had fixed on the type of aircraft it would need—one that could take a twelve-thousand-pound load of bombs to Berlin. The four-engined Lancasters, Halifaxes, and Stirlings, which could meet this requirement, would not begin to emerge from the production lines until 1941. In January 1942, Bomber Command had only 42 of these "heavies" available, and by the end of the year the figure stood at 261. Even these gains would not be painless. Crews had to be "converted" to the newer planes, a time-consuming process. The Lancaster proved to be by far the best of the new bombers. It alone could take aloft the twenty-two-thousand-pound "Grand Slam," the heaviest aerial bomb used in World War II. But the Lancaster had "teething" problems, which delayed its use. Not until early 1944 could Bomber Command boast a thousand planes, all of them "heavies" and more than half of them Lancasters.

The British bombing force of 1940 was thus a weapon to be reforged, and at the same time, political and military leaders were asking themselves how it might best be used. In the perilous summer of 1940, the bomber, like every other weapon at Winston Churchill's disposal, was used first and foremost to parry the invasion threat. Bomber Command sent its planes against enemy ports, shipping facilities, and barge concentrations, and several squadrons were put to "gardening," a code name for the sowing of coastal mines. But it was Churchill who ordered the first raid against Berlin on August 25, 1940, and who sanctioned further nocturnal raids into Germany. The RAF's night bombers could at least perform the eminently gratifying task of bringing the war home to the enemy, and some historians have concluded that the first two years of the British bombing offensive did more to bolster the morale of the British people than it did to harm their enemies.

Those who believed in the strategic air offensive expected it to produce more than satisfying headlines. Prewar planners had examined the potential target categories in the late thirties and had incorporated most of them into the various "Western air plans." Perhaps the most sophisticated approach called for an assault on a single branch of the German war economy, one that was both vulnerable and critical. The targets would be carefully selected and destroyed with deftness and precision. In the "Ruhr plan," the productivity of the entire complex could be brought to a standstill by smashing its power stations and its coking plants; in another variation the industrial complex would be "blockaded" by shattering rail and canal lines. Some saw the transportation network generally as the Achilles heel of Nazi Germany, although the oil plan still retained its partisans.

For approximately a year and a half, down to the end of 1941, the bulk of the air staff's directives called for the bombers to strike precise targets figuring in one of the plans. It was impossible to carry out all the plans simultaneously, of course. The bombers were still of limited range and bomb-carrying capacity, and it was rare that more than a hundred of them ventured into the night skies over Germany. The Ruhr plan was not implemented because targets such as power stations were particularly hard to locate and German air defenses were especially strong there. Sir Arthur Harris, named chief of Bomber Command early in 1942, recorded that his predecessors had "done nothing more than scratch at the Ruhr."[1] The oil plan enjoyed considerable vogue in the first months, although directives from the highest authorities—the cabinet and the chiefs of staff—often diverted the bombers to other objectives—for example, to submarine construction facilities in September 1940 and again in March 1941.

In the summer of 1941, the targets assigned to Bomber Command began to change. Attacks on oil facilities showed no signs of handicapping the German war effort or, indeed, of slowing it down in the least. The transportation system of the Reich became the preferred target, with rail centers the most frequently designated objectives. The switch in targets masked a subtle but significant change in the rationale of strategic bombing, for it brought to the surface the factor of morale. A specific campaign to break the enemy's will to resist did not figure among the sixteen Western air plans, but it was never completely absent from discussion of air strategy. Even before the war, the air staff speculated that simply dropping notices of impending attacks on Ruhr towns might "cause great panic and seriously disorganize the industrial life of the Ruhr."[2]

Those who advocated "psychological warfare" against Germany made the profound mistake of assuming that the state of mind of the German people at the outset of World War II was similar to what it had been in 1918, and their view seems to have been confirmed by grossly inaccurate reports they received on German morale. In July 1941 the air staff claimed to have "many signs" that morale had declined in towns attacked by its bombers, and the attacks ordered on the communications system were designed to contribute to that decline. Sir Arthur Harris recalled, "The targets chosen were in congested industrial areas and were carefully picked so that bombs which overshot or undershot the actual railway centers under attack should fall on these areas, thereby affecting morale. This programme amounted to a halfway stage between area and precision bombing."[3] At about the same time, bomber crews were instructed not to bring bombs back from Germany, even if they were unable to locate their objectives.

The RAF's night raids over Germany in June and July 1941 were distinctive in that planes equipped with cameras took extensive night photographs of the bombing runs in an attempt to find out just how accurate night bombing was. The technique had been tried briefly during the Battle of France the year before, when it had yielded fragmentary but disturbing evidence that British night bombers were very much off target. Even so, air-staff calculations continued to give aiming error in hundreds of yards; now the extensive photographic analysis of the summer of 1941 would supply a more reliable indication of bombing accuracy, and as it turned out, a thoroughly disheartening one. The Butt Report, which incorporated the findings, put the proportion of bombers that placed their payloads within five miles of the target as about one-fifth. In the Ruhr, with its special challenges to the night bomber, perhaps seven planes in a hundred released their bombs anywhere within the most general neighborhood of the objective.

The Butt Report made it quite clear that the RAF could no longer speak of night operations and precision bombing in the same breath. There was hope for improvement in bombing accuracy, for several new techniques were under study. (Two years later, Bomber Command would claim that three-fifths of its crews put their payloads within three miles of the aiming point.) But for the time being a very disheartened air staff had to concede that the strategic-bombing program it had prescribed was incapable of execution. In November came orders to reduce the intensity of the air offensive over the Reich.

In February 1942, Bomber Command embarked on a new offensive. The tempo of its attacks rose again, but now the air offensive had a new leader and a different thrust. A directive of February 11 set the new course: "It has been decided that the primary objective of your operations should now be focussed on the morale of the enemy civil population and in particular, of the industrial workers."[4] Accompanying the directive was a list of targets, and leading the list were Essen, Duisburg, Düsseldorf, and Cologne. The Ruhr, then, was to be the primary target, with the intention of making life difficult and work impossible for its industrial labor force. (In that connection Churchill would speak of "dehousing" the German worker.) The concept of precision bombing of key installations did not disappear completely, for Appendix B contained a list of power stations and synthetic oil and rubber plants. Bomber Command was to "consider the practicability" of attacking these if it could do so with sufficient accuracy. But the primary targets in the Ruhr were virtually the cities themselves, where the bombers were to strike at "transportation and general industries."

One can read into these phrases a significant shift in British air strategy. Britain's bombing force had not made a very effective rapier; now it would be used as a cudgel.

Nine days after Bomber Command got its new orders, it got a new leader who would oversee its operations to the end of the war, Air Marshal Sir Arthur Harris. The official history of the British strategic air offensive described his leadership as "vigorous," and there is no reason to quarrel with this description. A man of clear-cut notions tenaciously held, Harris knew where his bombers could do the most good—or, more properly, the most harm—and he persisted in directing them to those objectives despite the opposition of the Luftwaffe and sometimes despite the wishes of his superiors.

Harris did not believe that the enemy's morale should be his chief target. In his view, the leaflet campaigns of the first months of the war had done nothing to change the outlook of the German people; they had only supplied their needs in toilet paper for the rest of the war. Furthermore, bombs would not have the desired effect in a police state such as Hitler's; people might be demoralized, but they would be kept working all the same. Nor did the air marshal have any use for the precision bombing of key factories, which he called "panacea bombing." On paper the scheme was sound enough, but in the night skies of Germany it was unworkable. The power stations and synthetic-rubber plants could not be found; even it they were, they could not be hit.

As deputy chief of the air staff, Harris had been a witness to the Blitz. During the worst nights, he watched from the roof of the Air Ministry, and he vividly remembered Saint Paul's standing out in the middle of a sea of flames. The Blitz convinced Harris that "a bomber offensive of adequate weight and the right kind of bombs would, if continued for long enough, be something that no country in the world could endure."[5] Harris intended to attack Germany's industrial cities and the production units within them, weighing his success not in individual plants destroyed, but in acres of city devastated. The fundamental goal was physical destruction. If morale were shattered in the process, so much the better; but Harris preferred to consider it an imponderable. Thus, the cities themselves were the targets. They were to Germany what ganglia are to a living body. If enough of them were destroyed, the body would succumb.

Convinced that smashing the industrial cities of the Reich was the proper work of Bomber Command, Harris was loath to send his planes anywhere else. He was cool to the idea of attacking dams in the Ruhr

Valley, for he considered them panacea targets and believed—rightly, as it turned out—that their destruction would have little lasting effect. He was particularly unhappy at having to divert his attention to objectives of naval importance: "I was required to attack targets of immediate strategic importance—a euphemism for targets chosen by the Navy."[6] He regarded raids on the submarine pens at Saint-Nazaire and Lorient as a gross misuse of air power that devastated two French towns and had no effect on the submarine installations, sheathed as they were in thousands of cubic yards of reinforced concrete. (The submarine pens still stand to this day, the French having decided that it would not be worth the immense cost to undertake their demolition.)

Harris even insisted on choosing targets within Germany himself. Unhappy at the results of the raids against the Ruhr cities, he shifted his bombers elsewhere; the Battle of the Ruhr would not take place until the following year. In the autumn of 1942, Harris successfully resisted pressure to undertake a bombing campaign against Berlin, which Churchill thought might hearten the Russians. Harris had good reasons for declining. Throughout 1942 his force of heavy bombers remained very modest; at the time he was being urged to attack Berlin, he had fewer than a hundred Lancasters available. He also suffered something of a disappointment in the electronic navigation aid known as Gee, which was used for the first time operationally on the raid against Essen on the night of March 8, 1942. The Gee device carried by some of the bombers received radar impulses from England, enabling the navigator to "fix" the bomber's position, and some experts believed it would be sufficiently accurate to serve as a blind-bombing device—that is, one that could bring the bomber squarely over the target city and have it release its bombs at the right moment even though the bombardier could not actually see his objective. As it turned out, Gee could help the bombers find their way to the vicinity of Essen, but it could not position them over their target.

Nevertheless, the bombing campaign of 1942 was marked by considerable progress, first of all in testing the theory that the incendiary was the bomber's most effective weapon. The test was conducted on the city of Lübeck on the nights of March 25–29. Lübeck was at considerable range from England, far beyond the limits of Gee. But moonlit nights enabled the bomber crews to spot the city, thanks to its location on the Trave River. A total of 234 RAF bombers passed over in two waves, releasing some three hundred tons of bombs, nearly half of that weight in incendiaries. Lübeck was an old town with narrow streets and heavily timbered houses, so the flames destroyed much of it before they could be brought under control. The loss of life was far from negligible; for the first time, a German town had casualties in four figures. The earlier bombing attacks had been pinpricks, but this one stung. And hardly had the impact of the Lübeck attack sunk in than the RAF paid visits to the nearby Baltic port of Rostock on four successive nights. It too proved highly flammable. Harris estimated that in the two Baltic cities he had destroyed over seven hundred acres.

The Nazi leaders seem to have been particularly incensed that the RAF should have attacked Lübeck, a city they regarded as a cultural landmark. Goebbels was confident that the population could absorb its losses, for he judged the North Germans to be particularly tough. But he noted in his diary, "Stupendous works of art have fallen victim to the British craze for destruction."[7] Hitler too dwelt at length on the cultural loss; he had ambitious plans for rebuilding the city and told his dinner guests that he would send artists to Ypres so that they could copy the marvelous hues on the roof tiles there.

But retribution was foremost in the Führer's mind. In his speech to the Reichstag on April 26, he warned the British that reprisal was on its way. Since Churchill had begun the bombing war in May 1940, "this man should not wail or whine if I now feel myself obliged to make a response which will bring grief to his people. Henceforth I will repay blow for blow."[8] Hitler and Goebbels discussed possible targets and agreed that it was a waste of time to send the Luftwaffe against munitions factories. The targets must be centers of culture, like Lübeck, so that the British would understand the message clearly, for according to Hitler, they belonged to "a class of human beings with whom you can talk only after you have knocked out their teeth."[9] A spokesman for the Propaganda Ministry promised that the Luftwaffe would attack every English town that had three stars in Baedeker.

Luftflotte III was charged with carrying out the Baedeker raids, as they came to be called, and they were well under way before Hitler made his Reichstag speech. German bombers attacked Canterbury on the night of March 31, and during April they struck at Exeter, Bath, York, and other historic towns. Hitler boasted to Goebbels that the destruction in Bath was more extensive than that suffered by Rostock. He planned to keep the campaign up until the British were "sick and tired of terror attacks."[10] The Baedeker raids did not have this effect, but they did lead several members of Parliament to ask whether it might not be possible to negotiate a gentleman's agreement to spare cultural and historical centers. At the same time, Goebbels tried to bring pressure to bear on the British public. He prepared leaflets that showed scenes of destruction in Lübeck and Rostock; these were accompanied by the text of Hitler's promise of reprisal. The Luftwaffe was to drop the leaflets over English towns, and Goebbels confided in his diary that he expected them to have considerable psychological impact.

Winston Churchill's government rejected any idea of moderating the air offensive, and in May 1942, Bomber Command took another step in intensifying its effort. On May 30 it mounted its first "thousand" raid, against Cologne, and the following month it staged thousand-plane raids on Essen and Bremen. Bomber Command did not have anywhere near a thousand bombers operational in its squadrons; four hundred would have been more accurate. But by mobilizing aircraft and crews from the "rear," chiefly from training units, Harris was able to put into the air the magic number of a thousand bombers. Harris considered the attack on Cologne to be particularly successful. The city received fourteen hundred tons of bombs, about two-thirds of the tonnage being incendiaries. Air-reconnaissance photographs indicated six hundred acres razed. On the other hand, the June 1 raid on Essen was a severe disappointment. The night was cloudy and the Ruhr cities were shrouded by a ground haze. The bombers so scattered their loads that the German high command did not even recognize Essen as the objective; it simply reported widespread bombing in western Germany. Weather also interfered with the attack on Bremen on the night of June 25–26.

The "thousand" raids received great publicity, although it was of course not widely known that they were a makeshift effort which the RAF could not sustain. (Not until 1944 would Bomber Command again put a thousand planes over a single target.) For Air Marshal Harris they were extremely useful, since they enabled him to experiment with his ideas on massive and concentrated bombardment, a technique as yet unused in night operations. At the beginning of the war, both the Luftwaffe and the RAF used the night-bombardment techniques dating from 1918. The bombers were dispatched at intervals and arrived over the target either singly or in small detachments, so that a sizable raid could last many hours. This procedure of stringing out attacks had a dual advantage: it prolonged the period of danger for the enemy population in the target area, robbing people of sleep and wearing them down emotionally, and at the same time, committing the bombing planes in "penny packets" reduced the risks of midair collisions, thought to be serious for concentrated masses of aircraft flying at night.

Harris thought the weaknesses of the system outweighed these advantages. First of all, the enemy's air defense system was presented with a succession of targets, rather like the ducks that pass by in a shooting gallery. The antiaircraft fire could be concentrated on each in turn. But if the bombers came over in great masses, the plethora of targets might overwhelm the defenses, and in any event the danger to each bomber would be reduced. Even more important to Harris's way of thinking was the prospect of overwhelming the civil-defense and fire-fighting teams in the target area. The air marshal felt that the Germans might have accomplished this in London, with catastrophic results for the British capital; instead, the showers of incendiaries spaced throughout the night had started a succession of fires that the efficient London fire brigades extinguished one after the other. But if much of a city could be blanketed with incendiaries so that many fires sprang up at once and if, at the same time, a deadly rain of high explosives kept the fire fighters from their task, then the fires might soon escape all control. With this deadly recipe the RAF could gut the cities of the Reich one by one.

But as a first step, Bomber Command had to demonstrate that it could achieve what Harris called "the principle of concentration in time and place," that it could form and take over the target masses of aircraft in close succession (what came to be called a "stream" of bombers). The "thousand" raids were the successful culmination of experiments the RAF had been carrying on for months, utilizing moonlit nights to concentrate its bomber formations. Over Cologne, Harris achieved the concentration he had been seeking; the raid, which would normally have lasted seven hours, was cut to two and a half. Despite the concentration, there had been no disastrous collisions, especially in the hectic period over the target. What is more, there was every indication that the attack had overwhelmed the enemy's air defenses not only over the city itself but also on the western frontier of the Reich, with its belt of defenses known as the Kammhuber Line. Harris was ready to accept the loss of a hundred planes on the Cologne raid, but only thirty-nine failed to return. If there was any cause for disappointment over the raid, it was in its lack of destructive punch. The average bombload was under a ton and a half, chiefly because most of the aircraft used were still twin-engine types with modest capacity.

By the summer of 1942, then, Air Marshal Harris had the recipe for his bombing offensive. What he still lacked was the means to carry it out. He would need more "heavies," and they were coming off the production lines. He also needed a means to guide them to their targets in any kind of weather, since a few weeks after the "thousand" raids the Germans began jamming Gee transmissions. In August 1942 an elite unit called the Pathfinder Force came into existence, with the task of finding and marking the target for the main force of bombers, which followed it. To aid in this work, British scientists soon had ready two new electronic aids. Oboe was a device that enabled a plane to fly along a radio beam until it reached a predetermined point, and while the principle was similar to that of Gee, Oboe was more accurate—so accurate, in fact, that it could be used for blind bombing. The second aid was H2S, an airborne radar set that could be used to scan the earth below. Since different types of ground gave back different radio echoes, features such as rivers, coastlines, and built-up areas of cities made "prints" on the cathode tube, enabling the operator to locate the position of his bomber and sometimes that of the target. Oboe became operational in December 1942, and H2S, one month later. By early 1943, Air Marshal Harris had a daily average of five hundred bombers available, the majority of them four-engined craft. "At long last," he wrote in his memoirs, "we were ready and equipped."[11]

In this new phase of the air offensive against Germany, Bomber Command would not be alone, for on January 27, 1943, B-17 and B-24 bombers of the American Eighth Air Force penetrated Germany for the first time. It was little more than a token raid—ninety-one bombers were dispatched—but it was remarkable in two respects. The Americans struck in broad daylight, and they came without fighter escort, for their objective, the port city of Wilhelmshaven, was well beyond the operating range of any Allied fighter of the time. And, properly speaking, the Americans had not come to destroy the city itself but a number of precise targets in, and around, it, the foremost being the Marinewerft submarine construction yards.

An American contribution to the bombing offensive against Germany had figured in prewar thinking and was incorporated with the Rainbow 5 plan, drawn up shortly before Pearl Harbor. Even so, Gen. Hap Arnold, who headed the U.S. Army Air Forces, found it a painfully slow process to create a strategic bombing force in Europe. Unlike the RAF, the service he headed had very clear obligations to assist in the struggle both on land and at sea. Furthermore, the demands of the Pacific theater were intense in the first months of the war. The first contingent of B-17s were poised to cross the Atlantic early in June when an urgent directive sent them off to the West Coast. The Battle of Midway was shaping up and the bombers might be needed. As a result, when Maj. Gen. Carl Spaatz opened headquarters of the Eighth Air Force on June 18, 1942, he did not have a single bomber in the British Isles. The first B-17 flew in on July 1, but the buildup of Brig. Gen. Ira Eaker's VIII Bomber Command was agonizingly slow, with many planes and crews siphoned off for Operation Torch (the landings in North Africa), planned for November. By the end of the year, the Eighth Air Force had only a hundred heavy bombers operational on its fields in Huntingdonshire and East Anglia.

The American bombers carried out their first mission on August 17, when a dozen Flying Fortresses struck the Rouen-Sotteville marshaling yards. Bombing accuracy was encouraging, and all the bombers returned without mishap (or nearly so, for two crewmen in one of the B-17s were slightly injured when a pigeon crashed into the nose of their plane). Other missions followed, all of them confined to precision targets in German-occupied France, Belgium, and the Netherlands: railways, factories, and submarine pens. Although it was true that the bombers employed fighter escort on most of their missions, they did on occasion have sharp clashes with German fighters. The American bombers came off rather well in such encounters; the Flying Fortress, particularly, seemed likely to live up to its name. The more optimistic at Eighth Air Force headquarters felt that once they were available in sufficient numbers, Fortresses and Liberators would be able to venture deep into Germany unescorted and return with losses of under 5 percent. General Eaker was confident that his planes could put 40 percent of their bombs within five hundred yards of the aiming point. His colleagues in the RAF were polite but dubious. British bombers still made occasional daytime forays into Germany and invariably showed that the game was not worth the candle. (A daylight raid on a diesel engine factory at Augsburg on April 17, 1942 cost Bomber Command seven of the twelve attacking Lancasters.) The leaders of the RAF were not impressed with the argument that what the American bombers sacrificed in bomb-carrying capacity, they gained in ability to defend themselves; the British had given the early models of the Fortress and the Liberator limited trials and were not greatly impressed by either aircraft. The year 1943 would see the Americans' concept of strategic bombing put to the test and some of the misgivings of their British allies confirmed.

The coming battles would work a significant change on the Luftwaffe. Whereas previously the Luftwaffe had been a weapon forged for offensive use, now it had to be set to the task of defending the Reich. Curiously, the initiative often came from below, for the highest leadership in Nazi Germany was slow to admit that defensive measures were needed or even that the Reich was vulnerable to air assaults. Once the air offensive began in earnest, Germany's leaders, especially Hitler, could think of no way to combat it save massive reprisal. In reality, the solution was a straightforward one: the Luftwaffe had to make the enterprise so costly that the Allies would abandon it; in the case of the British, German air defense systems had only to destroy seven of every one hundred bombers on each raid, for this was a rate of loss that Bomber Command knew it could not sustain.

Reichsmarschall Hermann Goering had taken control of every aspect of Germany's air defense, and there seems little doubt that it was he who bore chief reponsibility for its ultimate failure. Although the night fighter was to prove the most deadly enemy of the RAF bomber, the Reichsmarschall had proclaimed at the beginning of the war, "Night fighting will never happen."[12] The Luftwaffe's prewar experiments with night interceptions had been dropped, but after the war broke out, pilots in several units continued the effort on their own initiative, and in April 1940 a Messerschmitt 110 operating from a field in Denmark made a nighttime interception of a British bomber. Other pilots reported successful contacts, and in July a pilot of Jagdgeschwader II succeeded in bringing down an RAF Whitley. By then the Luftwaffe leadership had become interested again, for in June 1940 it created the first night-fighter unit, Nachtjagdgeschwader I. Gen. Josef Kammhuber took command of night-fighter activities and embarked on a number of tests of both *dunkel Jagd,* literally "hunting in the dark," and *helle Jagd,* in which the night fighter found its target with the aid of a searchlight. These experiments led to a defensive belt, the Kammhuber Line.

Initially Kammhuber had most success with a *helle Jagd* system that employed radar, fighters, and searchlights working together, with a "team" of these covering a *Raum,* or "box" twenty-seven miles wide and twenty-one deep. Essentially the technique was as follows: a Freya early warning radar set would locate an incoming enemy bomber and "pass" it to a Würzburg set, which had less range but greater accuracy in fixing location; the Würzburg would guide the searchlight to the enemy aircraft, and then the light would reveal it to the patrolling fighter. By early 1941 there were eighteen of these boxes stretching from Hamburg to Liège, and subsequently, the line was extended by the addition of more boxes.

Kammhuber added other improvements, including *dunkel Jagd* zones on either side of the *helle Jagd* belt. He experimented with *kombinierte Nachtjagd,* using searchlights, night fighters, and antiaircraft guns all at once. This technique was tried over several German cities but was ultimately abandoned because the operators of the searchlights and cannon had difficulty distinguishing enemy craft from their own and sometimes shot down the latter. Another procedure, far more promising, retained the box principle but omitted the lights. The Freya radar still detected the oncoming bomber and passed it to a Würzburg operator; but now a second Würzburg followed the waiting interceptor, and with both aircraft represented on a plotting board, a ground controller could guide the fighter to its prey, or very near it. A final link in this radar interception system appeared early in 1942, when German night fighters began to carry telltale "antlers," the projecting antennae of onboard radar sets. With the Lichtenstein set, it was possible for the radar operator in the night fighter to "see" his quarry on the cathode tube.

Luckily, this new *dunkel Jagd* system had proved itself by the spring of 1942, for in May, Hitler ordered the Kammhuber Line stripped of its searchlights; they were moved to German cities, about which the Führer was increasingly concerned. In the aftermath of the Lübeck raid, he was chiefly anxious about historic towns such as Weimar and Nuremberg. "Factories can be rebuilt," he told his entourage, "but works of art are irreplaceable."[13] He spoke of giving every German village its own battery and searchlight detachment; blinded by a continuous sea of lights, the British pilots would not be able to see anything. Besides being ambitious in the extreme, Hitler's inclination to defend everything would thwart the development of Kammhuber's plans. The cities of the Reich were not to be denied; Berlin saw its complement of antiaircraft batteries doubled after the

RAF raids in the late summer and fall of 1940; by early 1941 it had its own line of boxes defending its western approaches. The gauleiters clamored for more protection for other towns, often with success.

Hitler also intervened to put an end to a promising development in night-fighter tactics pioneered by the pilots of Nachtjagdgeschwader II. The aircraft used for night interceptor work were two-engined craft such as the Messerschmitt 110 and the Junkers 88, chosen initially because their greater endurance allowed more time to stalk an enemy than would be the case with the single-engined Messerschmitt 109. The considerable range of the Junkers 88 and the Dornier 17, which was also used for night operations, led some pilots to undertake what was called *Fernnachtjagd*—attacking the enemy bombers where they were most vulnerable, over England. It was an easy matter to locate the enemy bombers by their radio traffic as they formed for the outbound flight or to follow them back and attack as they glided toward the haven of their home bases. In October 1941, Hitler ordered an end to *Fernnachtjagd* sorties. The kills made over England could not be verified; the planes that defended the Reich should do so in their own airspace, where their efforts could be seen and appreciated. Despite the Führer's order some night fighting of this sort continued, but it soon became the specialty of RAF Mosquitoes, whose "intruder" operations made them a menace around German air bases.

The second major element in the German air-defense system was the Flakartillerie, with its batteries of guns and searchlights. In 1935 this service left the control of the German Army and became a part of the Luftwaffe, and it is quite probable that the transfer ultimately robbed the service of much of its potential. In order to head off a movement by the army to supply its own antiaircraft defenses in the field, Goering motorized a part of the Flakartillerie and sent it off to accompany the army of the blitzkrieg campaigns of 1939–41. These units, quickly grouped into two Flak Corps, won a good deal of praise for their participation in the land battles as well as for their success against enemy aircraft. But the elements that remained at home for air defense of the Reich had little chance to distinguish themselves in those first years of the war, when the RAF's attacks were no more than pinpricks. According to their historian, these units suffered from an "inferiority complex."[14] Their morale was not improved by the scoldings they received from Goering when British bombers began to roam the night skies of Germany almost at will. The Reichsmarschall found the same shortcomings in his flak forces that he would later find in his fighter units: the failures were in the men, rather than in the matériel.

At the start of war Germany possessed an antiaircraft artillery that compared favorably with that of any other belligerent. In the summer of 1939, the Flakartillerie numbered slightly over 100,000 officers and men, an important percentage of the 373,000 total in all branches of the Luftwaffe. The service possessed about 650 heavy flak batteries, the kind chiefly used in the air defense of the Reich. The cannon in use was the efficient 88mm, a 1918 design improved in 1936 and 1937. Its chief limitation was its range, the fire being effective to a height of about twenty thousand feet. This was considered quite adequate in 1939, for the early generation of British Wellingtons, Whitleys, and Hampdens bombed from altitudes that kept them well within range. But as the war progressed, bombing altitudes tended to increase; the B-17, for example, was designed for operations at 25,000 feet and could be taken to nearly 40,000. The Flakartillerie found an answer in the 88mm model 1941 cannon, a weapon of phenomenal ballistic qualities. Unfortunately, the new cannon required about a thousand more pounds of steel than the older model, and for reasons of economy its production was blocked until the spring of 1944.

The Flakartillerie's matériel needs never seem to have enjoyed high priority. Often equipment destined for it was siphoned off by the army and navy, which resolved to build their own flak defenses. At the end of 1941, the Flakartillerie decided on a heavier, 128mm gun, hoping to base it on a gun of that bore used by the German Navy; but the navy would give no help, so the Luftwaffe had to do its own research and development. As a result, by May 1944 there were only twenty-four of the 128mm units in operation. An even heavier gun, of 150mm bore, was under development by Krupp in 1939. The work was suspended on orders from above; the Flakartillerie did not get permission to pursue the project again until 1944, too late for the gun to see service.

The most critical problem German ground defenses faced in the first years of the war was achieving accurate fire at night. The *Kommandogerät,* or "predictor," used by the heavy batteries relied chiefly on visual contact with the target, therefore on the ability of the search-lights to find and hold an enemy aircraft at night—not always an easy task. The ideal solution was to link the fire-control system to a radar set, a scheme the Telefunken Company was working on in 1939. But the first available radar sets, the Würzburgs, were routed to other uses, on the grounds that they were not sufficiently accurate for gun-laying. Yet, when improved radar more suitable to this purpose appeared, it too was allocated to competing services. Ultimately, the heavy flak batteries got updated Würzburg radar equipment, but even this was slow in coming. By the end of 1941, a great many heavy-flak batteries lacked any kind of electronic fire-control system for night work.

By the beginning of 1943, German flak units were in a considerably better state, and so for that matter was the whole air-defense system, all of which was under the command of a Luftwaffe general carrying the title Luftwaffebefehlshaber Mitte. The flak units would help defend the cities both day and night. The Kammhuber Line offered a formidable obstacle to the night intrusions of the RAF. Finally, there was the threat of heavy daylight raids from the Americans, although at the end of 1942, this danger was no more than a cloud on the horizon. Most of the Luftwaffe's day-fighter units were on the fighting fronts; as late as 1941 there were only two hundred day fighters covering the Reich frontier from Denmark to eastern France.

These improvements in Germany's air defenses had not gone undetected by Allied intelligence, but in London the view prevailed that the tide had begun to swing in favor of Allied forces, bringing an all-out bombing offensive close to reality. The British chiefs of staff said as much in a report dated the very last day of 1942: "We have gained a lead in quality over the German defenses, and we do not believe that they will be able to develop countermeasures sufficient to offset our advantage."[15] The chiefs of staff went on to prescribe day and night attacks on Germany, which would have as their goal "the progressive destruction and dislocation of the enemy's war industrial and economic system, and the undermining of his morale to a point where his capacity for armed resistance is fatally weakened."[16] This phrase reappeared virtually without alteration in the Casablanca Directive, approved by Churchill, Roosevelt, and their respective chiefs of staff early in 1943. The RAF and the U.S. Army Air Forces had their orders for a strategic-bombing offensive of unparalleled scope and intensity.

CHAPTER 9

THE BATTLE
OF GERMANY

ON THE EVENING OF MARCH 5, 1943, thirty aircraft from Bomber Command's Pathfinder Force took off for Germany, followed by a main force of 442 bombers. Their destination was Essen and its vast Krupp works, the most important manufacturing complex in the Ruhr. A full year had elapsed since Air Marshal Harris ordered his first, disappointing strike at Essen; now he expected far better results. For one thing, he had available an average striking force of between seven and eight hundred bombers; and to guide them he had a new electronic device known as Oboe. This navigation and blind-bombing method relied on impulses sent by radar-equipped transmitters in an aircraft and at two ground locations in England; the radar sets permitted extremely accurate measurements of the aircraft's position and bomb-release point, limited only by the fact that the impulses did not follow the earth's curvature and so could be used only to a range of about 250 miles for bombers flying at twenty-eight thousand feet. Most of the Ruhr fell within easy reach, although targets like Berlin were far out of Oboe's range.

The raid on Essen on the night of March 5–6, 1943, met Harris's highest expectations. The Oboe-guided Mosquitoes placed their red marker bombs precisely, providing an aiming point in the center of Essen for the craft that followed. Photographs taken during and after the raid showed heavy damage to the center of the city and to the

Krupp works in central Essen. What is more, losses were very light on the raid, with only fourteen bombers failing to return. The mission against Essen was part of a bombing effort that continued until July 1943 and is frequently referred to as the Battle of the Ruhr. In those five months Bomber Command staged forty-three major raids, and while the Ruhr cities were frequent targets, the night bombers also struck Berlin, Munich, and Nuremberg. All of the raids were not as well executed as the first attack on Essen, nor did the bomber force always escape so lightly. Still, the offensive seemed to be producing impressive results.

No one knew this so well as Adolf Hitler. After the first Essen raid, he had an angry scene with Goering; the Reichsmarschall was not at hand when Hitler learned of the Nuremberg raid a few nights later, so the Führer had the Luftwaffe's Gen. Karl Bodenschatz pulled from his bed and gave the hapless general an early morning lecture on air power. That same March, Hitler confided to Goebbels that it was the air war that was keeping him up at night. Goebbels was able to see for himself the impact of the new bombing offensive when he visited Essen shortly after the third big raid, which occurred on April 3. He was appalled at the extent of the destruction. He noted in his diary, "Now at last I have a real picture of what English air warfare means."[1]

Hitler and Goebbels agreed that the only proper response was a savage reprisal on the cities of Britain, particularly on the "pluto-cratic" quarters of London. Unfortunately, the Luftwaffe was not then capable of delivering the retribution the Führer wanted, and for that he held Goering chiefly responsible. But Hitler also railed against Marshal Hugo Sperrle, who, he claimed, had grown sybaritic in the easy life in occupied France, while the pilots of his Luftflotte III had forgotten the way to London.[2]

Although the Führer breathed fire and vengeance and would talk only of *Vergeltungswaffen,* or "reprisal weapons," the renewed bombing offensive obliged Germany's leaders to look to their air defenses and to take further civil-defense measures. General Kammhuber tried to adjust his defensive line to the concentrated bomber streams now coming over the Reich and experimented with a system in which a single controller on the ground could direct several intercepting night fighters. In the summer of 1943, a Luftwaffe pilot named Hajo Hermann developed a new night-fighting technique known as the *wilde*

Sau, or "wild boar" method. This involved the use of high-flying single-engined fighters whose pilots would try to spot enemy bombers silhouetted against the glow of searchlights or fires burning in the target area. That same summer the Luftwaffe high command ordered the withdrawal of fighter units from the various fronts and occupied countries—two Jagdgeschwader from the eastern front, one from France, and parts of several Geschwader from Italy. The units were rapidly integrated into the air defense system.

Flak units also multiplied in 1943 and now used radar both for gunlaying and for directing searchlights. There were not enough heavy flak guns for the units now being created, so they used captured weapons, including sizable numbers of Russian and Czech models. Beginning in 1943, the flak units began to draw on the Reich Labor Service for personnel; over a hundred thousand women worked in the antiaircraft batteries, where they were joined by Hitler Youth, Croatian and Italian laborers, and Russian prisoners of war. Goering joked that his flak units were like the League of Nations, while Goebbels worried about "miscegenation" in the batteries.

The German civil-defense system had already been shaken out of its complacency in 1942, following the raids on Lübeck, Rostock, and Cologne. (The German press gave considerable coverage to the raid as *Terrorangriffe,* or "terror attacks," but carefully avoided indicating the loss of life or the extent of the destruction.) The distinct danger that fire seemed to present was now recognized, and there was a shake-up in the Amtsgruppe Feuerwehr, the office in the German Air Ministry concerned with fire fighting. Hans Rumpf took the post of Generalinspekteur des Feuerlöschwesens and began the task of strengthening and unifying the fire-fighting forces in the towns and cities of Germany. The year 1943 saw substantial progress in the construction of air-raid shelters, an activity that had lagged in a number of cities. The new cycle of raids was an obvious incentive, but if the inhabitants of Germany's cities needed any further reminder, it was supplied in the leaflets that Air Marshal Harris was having dropped. After the RAF visited Frankfurt one night in 1943, the city's inhabitants found the streets littered with a message from the head of Bomber Command: "Adolf Hitler has led you into this hurricane. What you experienced this past night was like the first raindrops which announce a coming storm. For the moment they are light, but they will beat down upon you ever more heavily and more destructively until you can no longer resist the hurricane's force. Take heed!"[3]

In another of his leaflet messages, Harris told the German people that shortly the bombing offensive would be intensified by the arrival of the Americans. He described for them the vast Ford works at Willow Run, where every two hours the workers completed a new bomber that could deliver four tons of explosives to any city in Germany. "Soon," he promised, "we will be coming every day and every night, through rain or storm or snow—we and the Americans."[4]

This particular threat was some time in materializing, for the buildup of the American bombing force proceeded with painful slowness during the spring of 1943. Much was still being diverted to the North African theater of operations, and even when bombers began to arrive in sizable numbers, the ground crews that were to maintain them were held up by a shortage of ocean transport. The Americans still subscribed to the belief that their Fortresses and Liberators could battle their way to targets inside Germany and then home again in broad daylight without fighter escort—but only if they flew in sufficiently large formations. They needed a base force of about seven hundred bombers and a raiding force of three hundred in order to give their theory a fair chance. Until they had sufficient planes and crews, they could only conduct probing experimental attacks, "nibbling the edges" of the Reich. Several of these experimental raids in the spring of 1943 seemed to confirm the view that small forces of American bombers were vulnerable to German fighters. An attack on Hamm in March led to the loss of four of the fourteen Fortresses that participated; a bombing mission against the Focke-Wulf factory in Bremen by 115 American bombers cost the attackers 1 plane in 10.

The Combined Bomber Offensive, prescribed at Casablanca, did not officially get under way until mid-1943, with the issuance of the "Pointblank" directive of June 10, which was to guide the operations of the two bombing fleets. Since the American offensive was based on the precision-bombing principle, the directive listed in order of priority specific target groups, beginning with aircraft production facilities, then the ball-bearing industry, then petroleum installations, and so forth. These were of course many of the same panacea targets that the RAF had considered three years previously. Not surprisingly, the RAF's commitment to the Pointblank program was only limited. While the U.S. Army Air Forces would go after specific industrial objectives by day, Bomber Command would attack the cities "associated" with those objectives by night; but the British were to hit the Pointblank target categories only "as far as practicable." In fact, Air

Marshal Harris retained a rather free hand over his operations. The associated cities were in most cases targeted for destruction anyway, and both air forces were in agreement that the German fighter was their most dangerous enemy and deserved high priority. So, through a concurrence of interests rather than a closely integrated campaign, the Combined Bombing Offensive began in mid-1943.

The most spectacular raids of that summer were without question those directed at the city of Hamburg; the attacks were known collectively as the Battle of Hamburg. Air Marshal Harris had targeted the city as early as May, when he estimated it would take 10,000 tons of bombs to destroy it (and that was the word he used). He planned to deliver this tonnage in several successive raids, and to improve the chances for success, he timed the raid to coincide with the first use of "Window," strips of paper ten and a half inches long, coated with aluminum. Discharged into the air in large quantities, these strips would effectively cloud or jam the Würzburg radar that the Germans were using both for gunlaying and for directing their night fighters. (The British had held back the use of this particular jamming technique for fear the Germans would use it in turn and wreck their own radar detection system; only in July 1943 did the government agree to its use.)

Bomber Command's first raid took place on the night of July 24–25; the bombing force was composed of 791 planes, all but 73 of them four-engined bombers. The Pathfinders put down their markers not far from the aiming point, the center of the city. The main force sowed a path of destruction across the northwest section of Hamburg. The raid was heavy but hardly crushing, akin to the strikes already made against the Ruhr cities. Some of the fires had not been extinguished two days later, and perhaps fifteen hundred inhabitants lost their lives. Among the casualties was the house in which Johannes Brahms composed his "Lullaby" and the municipal zoo. (The bombing liberated a number of monkeys, which took to the city's trees.) As the British anticipated, the German air-defense system had been hopelessly confused by the use of Window. Few night fighters appeared and ground fire was very inaccurate; searchlights probed the skies in vain. Only twelve British bombers failed to return.

On the twenty-fifth and again on the twenty-sixth, American B-17s made daytime appearances. Their participation in the Battle of Hamburg was modest and so were their accomplishments. Only 252 American bombers attacked the city. They were after precision targets: a submarine yard and an aircraft engine factory. Both objectives were either obscure or completely hidden by smoke, part of it generated for that purpose by the Germans, but much of it coming from fires ignited by the British raid. The Americans bombed as best they could and scored some hits, but the tonnage dropped was small and the damage soon made good. (The American bombardments accounted for only about 1 percent of the casualties Hamburg suffered during the battle.) The Anglo-American cooperation over Hamburg would be much touted in the Allied press, but for the U.S. Army Air Forces, it was a far from satisfying experience.

On the night of July 27–28 the RAF struck Hamburg again in what was to be one of the most memorable actions of the war. This time the bomber stream contained 787 bombers with an increased weight of incendiaries, some twelve hundred tons of them. They were preceded by Pathfinders that put down clear, well-grouped marker bombs, but about two miles east of their aiming point, the city center. The main force bombed on the markers with unusual concentration, with the result that veritable showers of four-pound incendiaries clattered down on the eastern section of Hamburg, most of it heavily built-up residential areas with buildings five or six stories in height. The weather was warm and the humidity low; many of the city's fire fighters were still at the other end of the city fighting blazes ignited in the raid of three days earlier.

Even the crews of the departing British bombers could see that this raid was different; the vastness of the fire below was unprecedented, the brillance it reflected into the sky awesome. One airman recalled that the illuminated clouds looked like cotton dipped in blood. Within half an hour of the first bombing wave, a fire storm appeared, growing in intensity for perhaps two hours and subsiding only at six or seven in the morning. The blaze may have begun in a lumberyard, but soon the surrounding area began to burn fiercely, with temperatures soaring to 800 degrees Centigrade and powerful currents of air developing as the fire "drew" like a giant chimney. People in shelters could hear the roar of the wind over the crash of exploding bombs; those caught in the streets were hurled to the ground and sometimes sucked into the conflagration. The winds carried sparks and burning debris, drawing all of the fires into one vast inferno.

The Hamburg chief of police estimated the burned-out area of the city at thirteen square miles. Loss of life within the area of the fire storm was extremely heavy. The next morning rescuers found charred bodies on the streets, shrunken in size by the intense heat. In some underground shelters the dead appeared to be asleep; death had come to them stealthily in the form of carbon monoxide and other gases. In one basement in which scores had taken refuge nothing remained but a layer of gray ash. Initial estimates put the dead at 100,000, but they have been revised downward, so that a recent work lists 42,600 bodies found and another 2,000 who simply vanished.

The authorities arranged the hasty evacuation of the city's population on the assumption that the British bombers would return. They came again on the night of July 29–30, 777 strong. They had no difficulty finding their target, for Hamburg was a glow on the horizon as they approached, and they could see that many fires were still burning. This time the eastern end of the city was struck again, with the bombing pattern overlapping somewhat the area of the fire storm. There was no second conflagration, and casualties were low among that portion of the civilian population that had refused to leave the city. A fourth raid on the night of August 2–3 was largely ineffectual. Mercifully for Hamburg, storms and strong winds blew the bombers about and scattered their bombs.

News of the fate of Hamburg spread gradually through Germany. Refugees from the stricken city scattered to other localities, taking with them stories of Hamburg's martyrdom. Inevitably the tragedy compelled city authorities elsewhere to reexamine the situation of their own populations. In Berlin the authorities drew up plans for the evacuation of a portion of the inhabitants, beginning with the schoolchildren. The destruction of Hamburg also made a strong impression among Hitler's entourage. Goering was stunned, and no doubt saw in the catastrophe the omen of a further decline in his personal fortunes. Hitler was apparently less affected, partly because he was simultaneously struck by a blow from an entirely different quarter. On July 25, a few hours after the first attack on Hamburg, Benito Mussolini fell dramatically from power and became a prisoner of the new government of Pietro Badoglio. When Hitler greeted Badoglio's emissary on July 30 he told him straightaway of the recent bombings of Hamburg and the Ruhr and then added characteristically, "The day will come, maybe three hundred years from now, when we will be able to avenge ourselves."[5]

Italy offered an interesting interlude in the bombing war during that summer of 1943. The political crisis there threatened to expose the whole southern flank of Hitler's Europe, and the Allies, of course, did what they could to bring about Italy's defection from the Axis. Winston Churchill had believed from the outset that Fascist Italy was the weak link in the Axis, and in the perilous summer of 1940 he had sent RAF bombers to harass Italian cities. In the fall of 1942, the British bombers hit Turin and Milan several times. The Alps proved to be the chief obstacle the raiders encountered, for Italian air defenses were far weaker than those in Germany. Mussolini had asked Hitler for flak guns as soon as Italy entered the war, and although some help was forthcoming, in 1942, the Duce could do little more than call the British "brutes, barbarians."[6] Churchill was as much encouraged by the raids as the Duce was discomfited. In December 1942 he decided that "the heat should be turned on Italy,"[7] and instructions to that effect went to Bomber Command. The cities of the industrial north were clearly the most promising targets; hence, in February 1943 the RAF struck Turin, Milan, and the Italian naval base at La Spezia. As the authors of the official *Strategic Air Offensive* acknowledge, "the Italian diversion did not amount to much."[8] Air Marshal Harris was husbanding his forces for the coming Battle of the Ruhr; unenthusiastic about any operations that kept his bombers from their proper work in Germany, Harris made only a minimal commitment: four separate attacks in 1942, with 336 sorties in all.

Within a few months, the buildup of Allied air power in the Mediterranean presented a new opportunity to "turn on the heat." Part of the buildup was the creation of the Northwest African Strategic Air Force (NASAF). NASAF bombers performed a notable feat in reducing Pantelleria, a 47-square-mile island that stood between the Allies in Tunisia and their next major target, Sicily. From May 14 to June 10, Allied bombers pounded Pantelleria with 6,200 tons of bombs, with such effect that the island's garrison surrendered before the invasion forces could get ashore. As early as April, American bombers had begun to hit targets on the Italian mainland, chiefly air bases in the southern half of the peninsula. Rome was within reach and an increasingly inviting target. The British were much in favor of bombing it, and the Americans less so, perhaps because Franklin Delano Roosevelt had sizable Catholic and Italian constituencies, while Winston Churchill had neither. In any event, the official historians of the Army Air Forces make it obvious that bombing Rome was an action fraught with political risks, including the possibility of unfavorable reaction from the Roman Catholic Church, as well as from many artists, architects, historians, and others throughout the world. Yet on the edge of the Eternal City were legitimate military targets, two of which were very tempting: the Littorio and San Lorenzo marshaling yards, which handled almost all of Italy's north–south railway traffic. Moreover there was the possibility of a great dividend in demoralization of the enemy; the Allies hoped an attack "might even drive a strong wedge between Mussolini and the bulk of the Italian people."[9]

If the attack were to be carried out, the Americans could cut the risks with a precision daylight raid that would restrict the damage to legitimate targets and at the same time emphatically demonstrate Allied air might to all of Rome. By the second half of July, the American bombing forces were no longer needed for the conquest of Sicily, which was proceeding apace. Consequently, on July 19 a force of more than five hundred planes attacked objectives on the outskirts of Rome, chiefly rail yards and airfields. The attack had been meticulously planned and executed, and when the Allied command issued its version of the attack, it could claim that damage to nonmilitary targets was minimal. (Some seven hundred Italians were killed in the raid, and another fifteen hundred were wounded; the Church of San Lorenzo, which was in the middle of the target area, was heavily damaged.)

The attack probably did deliver a shock to the inhabitants of Italy's capital. Most of them believed with the king of Italy that "the Pope is our best antiaircraft battery"[10] and that the city's religious and cultural role would ensure its being spared from air attacks, as in the previous war. Pope Pius XII protested and sought to get Rome declared an open, demilitarized city, but the only other strong objections to reach Washington came from Spanish bishops. Six days after the bombing of Rome, Mussolini fell from power. The Allies began long and tedious negotiations with the new Italian regime, which, finding itself between the hammer and the anvil, was at the same time trying to propitiate Hitler. The Allies were torn between giving the new government a breathing space and trying to push it into an armistice by bombing its cities. A second raid on Rome was planned for August 4, but it was canceled on orders from Gen. George Marshall. President Roosevelt was still troubled over bombing the city and inclined to accept the papal idea of declaring the city "open." Churchill was opposed, and it was no doubt on his urging that the American bombers returned to Rome on August 13, hitting rail targets and airfields, demolishing one church, and badly damaging another. Pope Pius went immediately to comfort the latest victims and returned to the Vatican with his cassock stained with their blood. The following day the Italian government proclaimed Rome an open and undefended city, whereupon a British spokesman announced the declaration was not binding on the Allies. But when the American planes flew over Rome again on August 20, they dropped only leaflets.

Since the Badoglio government seemed to be dragging its feet in armistice negotiations, the British war cabinet was inclined to increase the pressure, or to use the expression of Harold Macmillan, "turn on the rough stuff."[11] This could be done by Bomber Command, fresh from its triumph over Hamburg. On August 8, 13, 15, and 16, RAF bombers carried out night attacks on Milan, and on August 8, 13, and 15 they struck Turin. Milan was particularly hard hit, receiving 2,600 tons of bombs, including 380,000 incendiaries. There was no fire storm as at Hamburg, but damage was extensive. After the August raids, 60 percent of the buildings in Milan had to be repaired or totally rebuilt. The loss of life was heavy, with a thousand people killed in the heavy attack of August 13.

The inhabitants of Italy's northern industrial cities could not understand why they were being attacked: "Mussolini is no longer here, we've torn up our party cards, we're throwing away our badges, so why are we being bombed?"[12] Many of them had celebrated the Duce's fall, and mass demonstrations made it obvious that they wanted an end to the military partnership with Germany. The Badoglio government, finding it difficult to keep control of the distracted country, proclaimed martial law on July 26; this action had led to clashes between troops and workers in the north, and the RAF's missions were basically designed to increase the government's difficulties in the region. They seem to have been successful, for on August 19 a general strike broke out in Turin and similar movements developed elsewhere in the north.

In the meantime, the Italian government was moving closer to an armistice, which was secretly arranged in the city of Syracuse at the beginning of September. When the Italian negotiator, General Giuseppe Castellano, had last-minute reservations, the British army's Gen. Harold Alexander told him that the Allies had already assembled on the airfields of Tunisia the most powerful air armada ever seen: "If the armistice isn't signed within twenty-four hours we will be obliged to raze Rome to the ground."[13] Even after the armistice was signed, the Allies continued to attack Italian cities until the agreement became public; thus, Naples was the victim of a very punishing attack on September 6, two days before the armistice was officially announced.

In Italy the Allies clearly used bombing as a form of coercion, and Sir Arthur Harris held that the strikes on Italian cities did more than anything else to bring about the fall of Fascism. In truth, they probably did no more than exacerbate preexisting problems, so that in the political and diplomatic climate of 1943 they were more catalyst than cause. At the time, however, this was not clear, and it was easy to see in the bomber a very useful instrument for "turning on the heat." This was probably a consideration when the Combined Chiefs of Staff sent Allied bombers to attack Sofia in November 1943, but the Bulgarians did not sign an armistice until eleven months later.

It was just as well that the Allied strategic-bombing forces claimed a share of the credit in Italy, for in the second half of 1943 their offensive against Germany reached something of a impasse. First of all they were making no apparent headway in the primary goal of the Pointblank directive, which was to reduce the strength of the German air force. Bomber Command was devoting only part of its energies to this effort. (Neither the spectacular raids against Hamburg nor the Battle of Berlin later in the year contributed very much to weakening the Luftwaffe.) The American air force, which adhered to the directive much more rigorously, was not having an easy time of it. Precision raids on aircraft factories were limited by periods of bad weather and by the fact that many of the more important installations were deep inside Germany. To help the Eighth Air Force in this work on distant targets, the American high command mobilized its air resources in the Mediterranean; but the Fifteenth Air Force, based in Italy, did not come into existence until November 1943; before then, U.S. bombers from the Mediterranean had made only a few tentative strikes at aircraft plants in southeastern Germany and Austria.

It was not simply that the targets were a long way off; the skies in which the Fortresses and Liberators had to fly were becoming increasingly dangerous. The German day-fighter forces were growing in numbers and perfecting their tactics. The deeper the penetration the American bombers carried out, the more they exposed themselves to danger.

Even before midsummer there were some doubts in the American camp that heavy bombers could successfully defend themselves and battle their way to a distant target without prohibitive losses, and events in July and August showed that these fears were only too well grounded. On July 28, thirty-nine B-17s attacked an aircraft factory at Oschersleben, ninety miles south of Berlin; fifteen of them did not come back. Four days later, a force of 147 Liberators flew from North African bases to the Rumanian oil refinery at Ploesti, where they made a low-line attack into heavy antiaircraft fire; 54 Liberators failed to return. Then, on August 17, 376 B-17s left England to hit two separate targets, both of them deep inside the Reich: the ball-bearing facilities at Schweinfurt and the Messerschmitt factory at Regensburg. The air battles over Germany were particularly severe that day. Some sixty Fortresses went down, a loss of 16 percent of the attacking force.

For the next five weeks the American bombers struck targets nearer at hand; then, in the week from October 9 to October 14—"Black Week," as it came to be known—the Eighth Air Force made four deep penetrations of German airspace. The last mission of the four, that against Schweinfurt, was something of a milestone. A total of 291 B-17s headed for Schweinfurt in two groups, the Allied fighter escort turned back over Aachen, and from that point on, the bombers were continuously assailed by waves of German fighters, as aggressive as they were numerous. They made attacks with rockets and explosive cannon shells and attempted to bomb the Fortresses. The American bombers made it doggedly to their target and placed their bombs accurately—but they paid a staggering cost. Sixty Fortresses, or one bomber in five, fell to German fighters and flak. The toll for the four missions of Black Week was more staggering still: 148 Fortresses lost. For the rest of the year, the Eighth Air Force made no more such raids into the Reich. The official historians of the U.S. Army Air Forces acknowledged that after the Schweinfurt raid "the Eighth Air Force had for the time being lost air superiority over Germany."[14]

In a word, Pointblank's objective was not achieved. German air defenses seemed if anything stronger at the beginning of 1944 than they had been twelve months before: some sixteen hundred fighters of all types guarded Germany and the western front, five hundred more than were available in early 1943. This was partly because the German fighters in the air were able to protect those still on the assembly lines, and whatever damage was done to the German aircraft industry was soon set aright. Under the skilled direction of Albert Speer, German fighter production continued to increase well into 1944.

The failure to destroy the German fighter force caused considerable concern to the Allied planners, who were now preparing Operation Overlord, the cross-Channel invasion of France. It was also disturbing to the leaders of the RAF, whose night-bombing missions into Germany were turning up evidence of a renaissance in the German night-fighter force. The Luftwaffe's air-defense system recovered rapidly from the confusion created by Window, and the rigid Kammhuber Line gave way increasingly to a new method in which ground controllers directed swarms of night fighters to the bomber stream; at the same time, improved airborne radar gave the fighter a better chance of finding its quarry. As the German night fighters improved, Bomber Command's losses began to rise. For the last quarter of 1943 they crept over the 5 percent mark; in three raids on Berlin in late August and early September the rate rose to 7 percent.

The attacks on the German capital were in fact the opening rounds of the Battle of Berlin, for Air Marshal Harris had chosen the city for his next major effort. The battle got under way in earnest in November, and by the end of the year, the city had received 14,000 tons of bombs. The campaign against Berlin continued until March 1944, with sixteen major assaults over a four-month period. At the outset, Harris was very optimistic. "We can wreck Berlin from end to end," he told Churchill, "if the U.S.A.A.F. will come in to it. It will cost us 400–500 aircraft. It will cost Germany the war."[15] The damage done to Berlin was certainly great. Goebbels, who saw it at firsthand, was much worried. "Issue no denials of the English claim to have killed a million in Berlin," he instructed officials in the Propaganda Ministry. "The sooner the English believe there's no life in Berlin, the better for us."[16]

Yet the attacks on Berlin produced none of the spectacular results seen in Hamburg. The city was more modern and more open in its construction. Although the raid of November 22–23 produced serious conflagrations, there was no fire storm. Moreover, the British bombardiers found it hard to place their bombloads where they wanted them. Berlin was far beyond Oboe range and often so obscured by clouds that H2S radar had to be used; unfortunately for the British, the various features of the city did not show up well on the radar tube. Moreover, the air defenses of Berlin were particularly well developed.

Goebbels had overall charge of the system and sufficient authority to commandeer what he needed for the city's defense, including mobile flak units, the fire brigades of other cities, and night-fighter forces from as far away as France and Denmark. Furthermore, Berlin was at the other end of the Reich; in reaching it, British bombers ran a long and deadly gauntlet that contributed much to their general loss rate of 5 percent. The final attack of the campaign, which took place on the night of March 23–24, 1944, cost over 9 percent. Air Marshal Harris acknowledged that when compared to the Hamburg raids, the Battle of Berlin "did not appear to be an overwhelming success."[17] Other writers do not hesitate to call the bombing effort of late 1943 and early 1944 against Berlin and other cities a clear defeat.

With the coming of 1944, the Allied strategic air forces began a new bombing program in preparation for the Normandy invasion; the demands of Overlord began to supersede those of Pointblank, and in April the strategic-bombing forces passed under the control of Gen. Dwight Eisenhower. Many of the targets were in German-occupied western Europe, particularly in France; attacking them inevitably carried the risk of injury or death to populations the Allies were pledged to liberate, and when the bombing intensified in the late spring of 1944, it produced something of a crisis in the Allied camp.

The British had faced the issue early in 1942, deciding that area attacks would not be used in France except on the French Atlantic ports, where German battleships and submarine pens were priority targets. Bomber Command wrecked both Lorient and Saint-Nazaire so thoroughly that Admiral Karl Doenitz reported, "No dog or cat is left in these towns. Nothing but the submarine shelters remain."[18] The Royal Navy wanted Air Marshal Harris to order attacks on the ports of Brest and Bordeaux as well, but he refused.

For other targets in occupied France, the British and American bombing forces tried to adhere to guidelines drawn up by the British Air Ministry in October 1942: the raids were to be directed only at legitimate military objectives; the bombardiers had to identify those objectives and then take reasonable care in the attacks to avoid loss of life among the civilian population. Even before these guidelines were promulgated the Eighth Air Force had a bad bombing experience at Lille on October 9, 1942. It was the first major sortie of the Eighth Bomber Command's Fortresses and Liberators; over a hundred of them sought as their objective the Lille-Fives rail complex with its yards and workshops. As a precautionary measure Allied radio broadcasts had already warned in a general way of the danger of living near such targets, but they could not, of course, pinpoint Lille as the coming objective. The area around the rail complex was still thickly populated, and a number of bombs went into residential quarters, producing over a hundred casualties and the first ripples of protest.

During 1943 the problem came up again, with the Americans most often the subjects of complaints and protests from both the French resistance and the French government in exile. The problem may have come in part from Allied propaganda, which pictured American bombing accuracy as far greater than it really was. Sometimes the Americans were just unlucky. In a raid on a ball-bearing works in Annecy in November, planes from the Fifteenth Air Force in Italy overshot the target, and their bombs fell into the town, where, the resistance reported, they did terrible damage. The French were not the only victims. An American raid on Antwerp in April produced sizable civilian casualties and a protest from the Belgian ambassador in Washington. The Germans saw immediately the propaganda value of the incident. They accorded a public funeral to the victims, and Goebbels hoped the Allies would bomb other cities, thus giving him more grist for his propaganda mill.

This was inevitably what happened in April, May, and June of 1944 as British and American bombers struck at rail and industrial targets in France. In April alone, they killed 250 people at Juvisy, 200 at Toulon, 500 at Lille, 850 at Rouen, and 650 at Paris. Marshal Henri Philippe Pétain visited the capital at the end of the month to commiserate with its inhabitants, the trip being facilitated by the German authorities. The British war cabinet monitored the situation carefully. Churchill wrote Roosevelt early in May that the cabinet was "very much concerned." Earlier studies had shown that the bombing operations might result in eighty thousand casualties to French civilians, including twenty thousand dead. Now Air Marshal Sir Arthur Tedder was saying that "about 10,000 killed, apart from wounded, will probably do the job."[19]

The protests continued to mount, chiefly on the grounds that the attacks were haphazard and that those who ordered them and carried them out were indifferent to the fate of the population. A telegram from a French official one day after D Day summed up the feeling: "The population understands the necessity of bombing military and industrial objectives and accepts the risks, but it is showing serious discontent over attacks which seem unjustified and carried out almost by chance."[20] Within France, resistance leaders were saying that they could destroy the objectives with far less risk and that the Allies should entrust such missions to them. There was even some feeling that the resistance should stop furnishing information on prospective targets. Beyond that, Churchill feared the bombing might alienate the French people and have serious political consequences after the war. But the bombing continued, for "the logic of military necessity in a total war proved unanswerable."[21] Once the actual liberation of France began, the level of protests seems to have declined; in any event, by September the Allied strategic-bombing forces were once again training their sights on Germany.

A return to full-scale air assaults on the Reich meant renewed reckoning with the day- and night-fighter forces of the Luftwaffe, which seemed to grow in strength despite all Allied efforts to reduce them. Even after "Big Week," an intensive bombing effort in February 1944 that put ten thousand tons of bombs into German aircraft production facilities, the Messerschmitts and Focke-Wulfs seemed more numerous and more aggressive than ever. In April, Air Marshal Harris framed a request for night fighters to help protect his squadrons over Germany.

Yet the scales in the air war over the Reich were about to tilt in favor of the Allies, and this time they would hold the advantage to the end of the war. For one thing, the problem of protecting daylight bombers was solved by the long-range fighter escort. The U.S. Army Air Forces had been working steadily on the escort fighter since late in 1942; it took nearly two years to find the ideal craft—the P-51B Mustang equipped with auxiliary gas tanks. As Anthony Verrier has written, "the humble drop-tank saved the day."[22] In March 1944 the first Mustangs appeared over Berlin, showing that they could provide a greater measure of security for Allied bombing missions into the farthest corners of Germany. But there were other developments, among them the growing disproportion of forces as the Allies, and especially the Americans, drew upon seemingly endless resources. By June 1944, Bomber Command had a thousand "heavies" in its squadrons. The Eighth Air Force had two thousand and two crews for each bomber. The U.S. Fifteenth Air Force, which became operational late in 1943 at Foggia, Italy, had twelve hundred heavy bombers, and by the end of 1944, it too had the luxury of two crews for each plane.

With a total force of over four thousand heavy bombers, it was possible to mount raids in endless varieties and combinations, to pummel Germany in several places at once.

Then there were other forces whose incursions into Germany further taxed its air-defense system. There was the RAF's Light Night Striking Force, which was equipped with elusive Mosquitoes and specialized in harassing and diversionary raids; and there was the U.S. Ninth Air Force, which shifted its base of operations to the Continent in the late summer of 1944. The Ninth was essentially a tactical force, but the advances of the Allied armies brought western Germany within easy reach of its medium bombers and even its fighters, whose forays into Germany complemented the destruction being carried out by the strategic air forces.

The forward movement of the Allied armies paid another indirect dividend in the air war, for the Allies were soon able to destroy the Luftwaffe's early-warning radar system. First, the installations along the French coast were lost, then those in Belgium and the Netherlands. And as the German network shrank, that of the Allies expanded. New Oboe installations on the Continent extended the range of this accurate blind-bombing device. But the Germans were losing the high-frequency war in other respects, because Allied technology pulled ahead with ever more sophisticated spoofing and jamming techniques. The RAF's 100 Group, activated in December 1943, flew planes crammed with electronic equipment designed to interfere with German radar and radio. This it did with increasing effectiveness, blinding and baffling the German night fighters. On the night of February 13, 1945, when the RAF staged its terrible night raid on Dresden, only twenty-seven German night fighters rose to meet the attackers; all the others were kept on the ground, their communications blotted out in a blizzard of man-made static.

The day fighters of the Luftwaffe probably suffered irremediable losses in the air battles of 1944. While the machines could be replaced, seasoned pilots could not, and this loss of personnel may have been the critical factor in the Luftwaffe's decline. That the loss was accelerating seems clear: from June 1941 to June 1944, the German air force lost thirty-one thousand flying personnel; in the five-month period from June to October 1944, the loss stood at thirteen thousand. Replacements were hastily and imperfectly trained and rushed into operational squadrons, where their inexperience was sometimes obvious even to the enemy.

From the spring of 1944 on, the Luftwaffe no longer mounted the maximum effort to block each and every Allied raid; it chose its opportunities like a combatant husbanding his strength; but when the German fighters did come up to meet the intruders, they fought with courage and determination. Sometimes they fought with makeshift and expedient; they occasionally rammed Allied bombers, and from 1943 on, Allied flyers reported seeing during day battles German aircraft with the telltale black paint and radar antlers of the night fighters. Sometimes the Luftwaffe even sprang ahead in technology; the Messerschmitt 262 jet fighter might well have tilted the balance once again, had it been committed sooner and in larger numbers to the air battles over the Reich. German flak also remained dangerous to the end, switching gradually to larger guns with greater ranges. In the last year of the war, American bombers considered flak a more troublesome enemy than the fighter. German science never matched the American proximity fuse, which greatly improved the efficiency of antiaircraft guns by ensuring that the shell would explode as it passed close to an aircraft; but at the end of the war, the Germans were far along in the development of the "Schmetterling" rocket, a thousand-pound missile capable of homing in on an enemy bomber. Other surprises were in preparation when the war ended, so the Allies were wise to regard the air superiority that they finally acquired as a fragile asset to be assiduously guarded.

The summer of 1944 did not see any sudden or dramatic shift in the operations of the Allied strategic air forces. Until September they remained under Eisenhower's control, and they were sometimes called in support of the land battles long after that date. To their lingering obligation to Overlord could be added their Crossbow missions—those flown against V-1 and V-2 missile installations. Into August, Bomber Command made more raids on France and Belgium than on Germany, although in that month Harris got authorization for twelve area attacks on German cities. General Eisenhower and his deputy, Air Marshal Arthur Tedder, favored a campaign against German transportation facilities. General Spaatz, now head of the U.S. Strategic Air Forces, wanted to unleash the Eighth and Fifteenth Air Forces against oil targets and sought the aid of Bomber Command. The head of that force, having successfully met challenges to his leadership within the RAF, wanted to get on with his own version of the air war. These various views produced a compromise of sorts that gave first priority to oil targets and second place to transportation objectives, leaving considerable latitude to each of the Allied air forces.

Although the strategic air offensive in the last year of the war was not a carefully coordinated effort, it nonetheless stands apart from all the bombing campaigns that preceded it. First of all, in its scope and intensity it dwarfed anything seen before. In the last ten months of the war—from July 1, 1944 to May 8, 1945—the Allies hit Germany with almost three times the tonnage of bombs they had dropped in all their preceding campaigns against it. In 1943 most "major" raids still involved less than a thousand tons of bombs; in 1944 and 1945, from 1,000 to 4,000 tons were common for such an operation. It was in this latter period that fifty of Germany's great cities were reduced to rubble and ashes. By the spring of 1945, both Allied air forces were having a difficult time finding targets worthy of their destructive power. In March they put another 4,700 tons of bombs into Essen, where they did little more than turn over the rubble. In April they lavished 1,100 tons on Hitler's mountain retreat at Berchtesgaden.

Other differences separate the last phase of the bombing war from the earlier campaigns. The American strategic-bombing force moved gradually away from its doctrine of precision bombing and came to adopt a policy not very dissimilar to that of Bomber Command. In part, the change was required by the U.S. Army Air Forces' obligation to assist in the land struggle. As Allied armies began to penetrate into Germany, American bombers pounded the towns and cities that lay in their path, trying to destroy centers of resistance and speed the Allied advance. But beyond this, the Americans had to adjust their policy to European weather conditions, which often shrouded the target from view. Blind bombing was the only solution if the U.S. Army Air Forces was to keep up its tempo of operations; for this purpose the Americans adopted H2X, a version of the British radar device. The first experimental missions took place at the end of 1943, but by the last quarter of 1944, about 80 percent of Eighth Air Force missions involved blind bombing with radar aids. At the beginning of 1945, the circular error with this method was about two miles; the official history of the U.S. Army Air Forces is frank to acknowledge that such attacks "depended for effectiveness upon drenching an area with bombs."[23]

The shift in American bombing techniques may well be linked to another phenomenon in the latter stage of the war—an increased interest in attacks directed specifically at the German people. Both Allies advanced schemes and projects for such attacks with the avowed intention of "breaking" German morale and hastening the end of the war. The British favored razing a "sample" area in a way that would send a shock through Germany: "Operation Thunderclap" would obliterate Berlin, while "Hurricane I" would sow destruction through the entire Ruhr. The Americans proposed unleashing on Germany "war-weary" B-17 bombers packed with twenty thousand pounds of explosives and controlled by radio; General Arnold thought this might have significant psychological effect. Another American scheme was the "Jeb Stuart" plan; later elaborated as "Operation Clarion," it called for fighter and bomber raids throughout Germany, seeking out transportation targets in the smaller German towns and villages where the populations had so far been spared. It was expected to produce "a stupefying effect on morale."[24]

How can we account for the vogue of these schemes toward the end of the war? They probably represent a casting about for options in that frustrating period of the conflict when the ultimate victory was assured but the road to that victory was long and any shortcut tempting—all the more tempting since the enemy no longer had the possibility of replying in kind. It is significant that the British opposed the American scheme for B-17 "flying bombs" on the grounds that the Germans could use similar weapons against the British Isles. There are a number of indications that whatever inspired this policy trend, the Allies were moving toward an air war clearly waged against the enemy population. Within the U.S. Army Air Forces, resistance to area bombing declined, and in February 1945, both air forces carried out Clarion (although with indifferent results). On February 3 the Eighth Air Force carried out a devastating raid on Berlin that may have taken as many as twenty-five thousand lives. Ten nights later, the RAF put the torch to Dresden, an old and vulnerable city jammed with refugees. The inferno that resulted was as terrible as the Hamburg fire storm. The total number of dead will never be known; estimates have ranged between twenty-five thousand and a half million.

The German government was also party to the increasing ruthlessness of the struggle in the air. It made its own contribution to terroristic and indiscriminate warfare with the V-1 and V-2 weapons: aimed at a target the size of London, they might come down anywhere in southeastern England. What is more, Hitler and his entourage considered measures against captured Allied armies that would have had profound repercussions had they continued. Starting with the raid on Lübeck, the German press had called the Allied bombing attacks *Terrorangriffe* with such regularity that the term passed into general usage. If the Allied airmen bombed to instill terror in the population, they were criminals and should be treated as such. This was the argument put forward by Goebbels. When he learned in the spring of 1943 that the Japanese government was placing on trial American airmen who had bombed Tokyo the year before, Goebbels urged Hitler to do the same. The Führer refused, not because it was against his principles but because "he fears the English may have too many possibilities for reprisals."[25]

In 1944 there were several occasions on which Allied airmen who had bailed out over Germany were manhandled and even beaten to death by irate crowds of German civilians. Here was another propaganda opportunity for the Germans to exploit. On May 29, 1944, Goebbels wrote in the *Völkische Beobachter,* "It seems to us hardly possible and tolerable to use German police and soldiers against the German people when it treats murderers of children as they deserve." Both Heinrich Himmler and Martin Bormann let it be known that the police were not obliged to protect captured airmen from the popular wrath. These invitations to the German people to lynch downed flyers became more explicit in 1945, and in the final days of the Third Reich, there was even talk of renouncing the Geneva convention and meting out summary justice in the prisoner of war camps.

Fortunately, the fighting ended in Europe before these threats could be carried out or the air war further envenomed. But in the Far East the struggle went on: three weeks after the destruction of Dresden, American bombers dealt Tokyo and its people a staggering blow, opening a bombing campaign of unparalleled violence and destructiveness.

CHAPTER 10

JAPAN: ORDEAL BY FIRE

SHORTLY AFTER DAWN ON APRIL 18, 1942, a Japanese patrol vessel encountered an American task force eight hundred miles or so east of Japan. The chance encounter triggered one of the more memorable operations of World War II, one that proved to be the opening round of the strategic-bombing war in the Pacific. The American force intended to move to within five hundred miles of the Japanese home islands and then launch against them the sixteen B-25 bombers crowded on the deck of the carrier *Hornet.* Now that their approach had been detected, Col. James Doolittle decided to take his bombers on their way immediately. Three hours later, just after midday, Doolittle attacked Tokyo, while other planes in the force struck at Kobe, Yokohama, and Nagoya; then the bombers flew on toward a haven in China, having struck several factories and military installations but also, unfortunately, a hospital and six schools. (Of the eight participants in the Doolittle raid who fell into Japanese hands, three were executed and the rest condemned to life imprisonment.)

The Doolittle raid was more symbolic than anything else, like so many of the operations that opened the bombing war in Europe. It would give the Japanese pause, but more than anything else, it would provide welcome relief from the grim headlines that American newspapers were carrying in those first disastrous months of the war in the

Pacific. This may have been what initially attracted President Roosevelt to the scheme and to others like it as early as January 1942.

The idea of a bombing war against Japan antedated Pearl Harbor by many years. A number of American officers, among them Billy Mitchell, had come to believe that an armed confrontation with the Japanese was inevitable. In 1924, Mitchell penned a report based on his visit to Japan in which he called attention to the vulnerability of its congested and flammable cities. The terrible proof of that vulnerability had been the earthquake and fire of 1923, which took an estimated hundred thousand lives. This consideration was also in the minds of the Committee of Operations Analysts, a panel created in December 1942 to study possible targets for strategic-bombing offensives against Germany and Japan. In its report to General Arnold eleven months later, the committee listed as the most rewarding targets merchant shipping, aircraft plants, steel production, the ball-bearing and electronics industries, and "urban industrial areas," which they judged particularly susceptible to incendiary attacks.[1] Six cities were prime candidates: Tokyo, Yokohama, Kawasaki, Nagoya, Kobe, and Osaka.

By the time the various target systems had been studied and categorized, American military planners had found a way to bring those targets within range of the U.S. Army Air Forces' bombers. The plan carried the code name "Operation Matterhorn" and had as its goal the "early sustained bombing of Japan"; in conception, it was a refinement of schemes proposed early in 1942 calling for a bomber force operating from India and "staging" through bases in China. In the spring of 1944, the vehicle for this operation came into existence as the Twentieth Air Force, specializing in long-range strategic bombing and designed to operate under the direct orders of the Joint Chiefs of Staff in Washington, through General Arnold as their agent. And finally, for this new venture there would be a new bomber—the Boeing B-29 Superfortress.

Since the B-29 was used exclusively in the Pacific theater, it is easy to assume that it was designed for the peculiar needs of that area, but this was not the case. Initially, it had been slated for use in the European theater of operations, with units earmarked for such places as England and Egypt. The decision to commit the B-29 in the Pacific was motivated first of all by the fact that it became available in appreciable numbers after the second half of 1944. (By then the strategic-bombing offensive against Germany had hit its stride with the bomber types already available.) Second, strategic air operations in the Pacific required a bomber of exceptional range and the B-29 fulfilled this requirement.

The B-29 took shape on the drawing board in·1940 and first flew in September 1942; it was conceived in the heyday of the American theory of daylight precision bombardment. It was exceptional in any number of ways, the first of which was its size. From wingtip to wingtip, it measured just over 141 feet, or half the length of a football field. Its basic weight was 74,500 pounds (roughly twice that of the B-17), but fully armed it could weigh 135,000 pounds, or 67.5 tons. Its four 2,200-horsepower engines drove propellers 16.5 feet in diameter. The plane was enormous, but it was no monster. Aerodynamically, it was an extraordinarily clean aircraft. Its skin was flush riveted and had no camouflage paint to cover its brilliant silver finish. In addition the plane was a stable platform for the Norden bombsight. It could also deliver—in theory, at least—a 10-ton payload at a distance of 1,500 miles. It could cruise in excess of 300 mph and at 30,000 feet and above. If its speed and ceiling could not ensure its safety, its twelve .50-caliber machine guns and one 20mm cannon would.

While this formidable weapon was being readied, the Japanese government was doing relatively little to strengthen its air defenses. In November 1941, Premier Hideki Tojo reviewed the air defenses and found them satisfactory. Three hundred planes were available for defense of the home islands, along with seven hundred antiaircraft guns. The aircraft were of the obsolescent Type 97 fighter variety and would be flown by personnel drawn mostly from flight schools on the islands. The antiaircraft guns were 75mm cannon, capable of reaching no higher than twenty-five thousand feet. Yet, modest as these weapons were, they were sufficient. The primary defense Japan could rely on was its great distance from its enemies. Since it had limited resources and could not be strong everywhere, it felt that priority should go to the fighting fronts.

Tojo conceded that the Allies might from time to time succeed in breaching the outer defensive perimeter and send bombers over the home islands—the Doolittle raid was not unexpected. But Japanese aircraft could generally keep enemy carriers at a distance and could be counted on to neutralize any air bases the enemy might try to establish in China or possibly in the Soviet Union. Thus, only tip-and-run raids seemed likely, and they would be few and of minor concern. For much of the Pacific war, this was true; the Doolittle raid had no sequel for two years. Nevertheless, the Imperial Japanese Army, which had chief responsibility for air defense, pushed for improvement in two directions in the aftermath of the Doolittle raid. The first was the quest to produce better antiaircraft guns, notably the 120mm with its greater range; the second was perfection of the radar system, in which Japan was woefully behind. For the first two years of the war, fighter defense remained a makeshift, with outmoded aircraft and pilots "borrowed" from training establishments. But by the spring of 1943, Japanese intelligence had some knowledge of the new American bomber, which it expected to begin operations that fall. The high service ceiling seemed its most dangerous characteristic. Japanese authorities thus pushed the production of the 120mm gun and began searching for new types of fighters that could take greater firepower into the higher altitudes. But they had not completed their search when the first B-29s flew over Japan in June 1944.

The debut of the Superfortresses was a surprisingly modest one. This was partly because there was only a small number of B-29s available that summer and partly because they were operating under an incredibly complex logistical arrangement. The planes had as their home base a series of airfields around Kharagpur, India, not far from Calcutta, but to strike at targets in Japan or Japanese-held Manchuria, they had first to fly "over the Hump" to advance, or "staging," airfields around Chengtu, China—a distance of some twelve hundred miles. At Chengtu they refueled and flew on to their objectives, perhaps another twelve hundred miles. They had to stage at Chengtu on their return, so that each mission involved nearly five thousand miles and more than twenty hours of flying time. This was a demanding schedule even in the best of circumstances.

Perhaps only the Americans would have made such a lavish commitment of resources in order to operate a sophisticated weapon in adverse conditions. The B-29 needed runways of extraordinary length—1.5 miles—and these were built. Its four engines consumed enormous quantities of aviation gasoline—six thousand gallons for a twelve-hundred-mile flight. The fuel with which the bombers filled their tanks at Chengtu had to be brought over the Hump by air, and the transports sometimes consumed twelve gallons to deliver one gallon. Chengtu offered nothing but the barest necessities to crews staging there. The historian of XX Bomber Command complained that "full colonels walked two miles to their airplanes."[2]

By the end of May a full complement of 112 B-29s had reached Twentieth Bomber Command's Fifty-Eighth Wing and were poised for action on its bases around Kharagpur. On June 5, ninety-eight of them took off for a "practice" raid on Bangkok. Then, on the night of June 15–16 they carried out their first attack on Japan. The target chosen was the Imperial Iron and Steel Works at Yawata, which produced a quarter of Japan's steel; the B-29s came away virtually unscathed, but reconnaissance photos revealed that the Imperial Iron and Steel Works had also escaped undamaged.

Steel plants, and particularly coking ovens, were at the top of the target list, so in July the B-29s also went after the Showa Steel Works in Manchuria; they struck it a second time, as they did the steel plant at Yawata. They flew both by day and by night, and at various altitudes; they bombed visually when the weather permitted and with radar when it did not. They struck at an aircraft plant at Okayama by day and then tried a night incendiary raid on Nagasaki (with negligible results). In all, the Twentieth Bomber Command flew forty-nine missions up to March 31, 1945, when it was deactivated. It dropped about 11,000 tons of bombs, but only 800 tons fell on the Japanese home islands. Considering the effort expended to bring Japan within bombing range, the record was modest indeed. Twentieth Bomber Command never activated more than one wing of B-29s, the Fifty-Eighth, and even the operations of that limited force were severely hobbled by logistical problems.

As early as March 1944, it was clear to the American Joint Chiefs of Staff that the big bombers would need a less precarious base; to that end, they ordered the taking of the Marianas, only twelve hundred miles from Tokyo. On June 15, the same day the B-29s invaded Japanese airspace, U.S. Marines stormed ashore at Saipan. Even before the island was secure, Seabees had begun work on the enormous runways. (Guam and Tinian would have airfields as well.) On October 12 the first B-29 touched down on Saipan's Isley Field. Six weeks later a force of 110 Superfortresses lifted off that same field bound for Tokyo.

The pilots who flew the first B-29s from Saipan took with them a valuable fund of knowledge about what their bombers could do and could not do in the skies of Japan, and that knowledge had been amassed—sometimes very painfully—by the men who had flown the big bombers out of Chengtu and Kharagpur. First of all, the bombers could be operated both by day and by night without serious loss; rarely did the loss rate exceed 5 percent, and for all B-29 operations during the war, was under 2 percent. At thirty thousand feet the Superfortress had little to fear from flak. Enemy fighters could operate at that altitude but could rarely manage more than a single pass through a formation, because of the big bomber's speed. Sometimes, when the weather conditions were right, the B-29 could place its bombs with remarkable accuracy. But the weather proved to be the great limiting factor in the precision bombing for which the plane had been built, since, as in the case of the European theater, targets were all too often obscured by cloud cover. And whereas in Europe it was fairly easy to determine from England what the weather would be like over Mannheim, since the weather generally moved from west to east, this same phenomenon made it extremely difficult to know what kind of weather might move from Siberia or central Asia over the Japanese home islands.

The problem of Japanese weather tended to grow even worse in the fall and winter, as the men of Brig. Gen. Haywood S. Hansell, Jr.'s Twenty-first Bomber Command soon discovered. Hansell believed strongly in the precision-bombing doctrine, which he had helped formulate, so he set his men and planes to work on the Japanese aero-engine industry, most plants of which were well known. The very first raid from Saipan was directed at the Musashi engine works in northwest Tokyo, which produced 27 percent of all Japanese aircraft engines. The Musashi plant, "target no. 357," was destined to become famous, or infamous, to the men who flew B-29s. During the raid of November 24, there were strong winds at thirty thousand feet, and the target below was almost completely obscured. Three days later, the Superfortresses returned to Tokyo to find the Musashi works completely blanketed by cloud. On December 3 the plant was visible, but bombing was scattered because of high winds.

In all, there were eleven major raids on the Musashi works between November 1944 and May 1945; they cost the attackers fifty-nine Superfortresses. Air crews drilled relentlessly to hit the works. (Some still in the United States made practice bombing runs on the Continental Can Company's plant in Houston, which was about the same size.) Only the last two raids were effective; all the others were balked by adverse weather. At thirty thousand feet, wind was often more of a problem than cloud, for it could reach in excess of 150 knots. On

one downwind bombing run, a B-29 went rocketing over the M
plant at a ground speed of more than five hundred mph. The sto
not much more encouraging at the other eight high-priority t
In three months of effort, not a single one had been destroyeu. ɴo
more than 10 percent of the bombs dropped seemed to be landing anywhere near the objective. Even the Japanese noticed the erratic pattern of the bombing. So many bombs exploded in Tokyo Bay that a
joke started to make the rounds of the Japanese capital: The Americans were going to starve the Japanese into submission by killing all
the fish.

In the meantime, an alternative approach to strategic bombing was
emerging in Washington. General Arnold's Committee of Operations
Analysts had pursued its investigations into incendiary raids to the
point of building models of Japanese structures and testing their
flammability. The committee proposed several Japanese cities for
incendiary attacks, and General Arnold sent out instructions in
November to conduct a test raid. General Hansell's heart was not in
this sort of bombing. He made a small and inconsequential fire raid
on Tokyo on the night of November 29–30, but when he received word
to mount a full-scale incendiary effort on Nagoya, using a hundred B-
29s, he protested. Nevertheless, Hansell was a good soldier, so he sent
his bombers to Nagoya on the night of January 3–4. The damage
caused was slight; bad weather kept reconnaissance planes from getting the photographic evidence for some twenty-seven days. By that
time, General Hansell was no longer leading Twenty-first Bomber
Command; on January 20 his command had passed to Maj. Gen. Cur-
tis E. LeMay.

The official history of the Army Air Forces indicates strongly that
Hansell's preference for precision bombing cost him his job, and this
may indeed be the case. The man who succeeded him did not have the
same commitment to doctrine. He had the reputation of a "driving
operator" who had already taken over Twentieth Bomber Command
and breathed energy into its operations. But, for a month and a half,
LeMay made no radical departures in operations from the Marianas.
At first, he rode two horses at once: he continued the high-altitude
daylight precision raids against the aircraft plants that were now
becoming so familiar to his crews; at the same time, he pushed experimentation with incendiary attacks, with which he already had some
experience—his XX Bomber Command had succeeded in burning

much of Hankow in December 1944. On February 3 he sent the B-29s to Kobe, where they dropped 159 tons of incendiaries and burned out a thousand buildings, a fairly encouraging result. On February 25 a maximum-effort fire raid on Tokyo produced an impressive level of destruction: a square mile of the city was burned out and over twenty-seven thousand buildings were destroyed.

It was early in March that LeMay made the basic changes in B-29 operations, and on those changes he no doubt staked his career. The fact was that up to that point his bombing force had not "delivered the goods"; that is to say, it had not justified its existence by striking telling blows at the enemy. After three months of operations, the big bombers had delivered about 7,000 tons of bombs, a very modest figure; half of the sorties had ended with the bomber unable to attack the primary target. The clear solution was to drop more bombs and drop them where they would count.

LeMay felt that massive incendiary raids carried out by night against the cities of Japan offered several advantages. First of all, very often the precision targets were located within an urban matrix, so that if the city were burned, the factory or arsenal would go up in flames as well. That the cities were particularly vulnerable to fire was already well established; in many of them 95 percent of the structures were flammable. The attack on a city was an area attack, so it could be conducted in adverse weather and, if necessary, by radar. An attack of this sort had several advantages if delivered by night. It would help neutralize Japanese defenses, which at night were nowhere near as formidable as those LeMay had known in Germany, for the Japanese night fighter was still in its infancy and lacked airborne radar. Japanese flak was sometimes intense but not a grave danger at night. The night attack paid another dividend in that it could be executed at fairly low altitude, as low as five thousand feet. At this height there was less strain on the engines than at thirty thousand feet, and fuel consumption was appreciably lower, so that the bombload could be increased accordingly. And LeMay took a further gamble by ordering his bombers to fly stripped of guns and ammunition; normally the B-29 carried 1.5 tons of armament. This weight too would now be carried in bombs.

The key to the successful raid was saturation and just the right concentration, as Air Marshal Harris had proved over Hamburg, so when LeMay sent his bombers against Tokyo on the night of March

9–10 he sent an extremely large force—a total of 334 bombers rying 2,000 tons of bombs, the vast majority of them incendiaries first pathfinder planes passed over the city shortly after midnig mark the target area: a rectangle about three miles by four, containing a hundred thousand inhabitants per square mile, or roughly 1.25 million people. There was no tightly organized bomber stream that night, and the last bombers did not pass over Tokyo until about three hours after the attack had begun. By then, Tokyo was a sea of flames. Tail gunners in the returning B-29s could see the glow of the city 150 miles away; it was a man-made dawn on the horizon, and the first of many that would light the skies over Japan.

The raid on Tokyo on the night of March 9–10, 1945, was the most destructive air raid ever carried out, not excluding the nuclear attacks on Hiroshima and Nagasaki. The loss of life that night has officially been fixed at 83,793, but other estimates have placed it at over 100,000. The vast fires burned out some sixteen square miles of the immense city and destroyed a quarter of a million structures. Several factors contributed to making the attack particularly destructive. Both the air defense and the Tokyo fire brigades were caught off guard by the new tactics, over a hundred firemen lost their lives in the conflagration, and nearly that number of fire trucks were consumed by the flames. Worst of all, that night the *Akakaze,* or "Red Wind," was blowing across Tokyo, and it took the flames with it. There was no true fire storm over Tokyo that night. Martin Caidin has written, "Because of the wind, the potential fire storm was transformed into an even deadlier force—the sweep conflagration."[3] A tidal wave of fire moved across the city, the flames preceded by superheated vapors that felled anyone who breathed them.

Forty-eight hours after their attack on Tokyo, the B-29s struck Nagoya and then moved on to Osaka and Kobe. Within a ten-day period beginning March 9 the bombers dropped 9,373 tons of bombs and burned out 31 square miles of city. LeMay pushed the firebombing with such energy that by the end of March his depots began to run low on incendiary bombs, and the shortage was not overcome until June. City burning was becoming something of a science, as LeMay's men tried various weapons and techniques. The M50 thermite incendiary used in Europe had "excessive" penetration. It would often pass entirely through a Japanese structure and ignite in the earth beneath it, occasionally perforating water mains. The best weapon was the

M69, a small incendiary bomb, many of which were dropped in a single casing: "Each of these clusters, arranged to explode at 2500 feet altitude, was constructed to release thirty-eight incendiary bombs, made to fall in a random pattern, this arrangement furnishing the basis for the big bombing success to come. The orderly design or distribution from one bomber with an intervalometer setting, or spaced fall, of one bomb every fifty feet, could burn about sixteen acres, as each Superfort had a full bomb load of 16,000 pounds." The basic procedure, concludes this passage, "was like throwing many matches on a floor covered with sawdust."[4]

As these descriptions indicate, the destruction was most effective if carried out systematically. With "impressionistic" bombing—that is, with each bombardier trying to place his bombs where they would extend the damage—the ultimate yield was less than if there was a general pattern. In some cases radar bombing was more effective than visual aiming. Two hundred and fifty tons of bombs per square mile, adequately distributed, virtually guaranteed total destruction of the area. Everything combustible would be consumed, and the fierce temperatures generated would ensure that by radiant heat alone the conflagration would cross streets and canals. In some cases the heat would soften the asphalt in the streets, so that fire equipment mired down and was lost to the flames. Water sprayed on the fire would simply vaporize; glass panes would soften and drip from metal window frames. Here and there, incredibly, concrete melted. No living thing could survive in such an atmosphere.

Every major city in Japan was slated for this sort of destruction save one; the historic town of Kyoto. Each target city was divided up into zones, or "urban areas," and these bore the designations UA/1, UA/2, and so on. As the B-29s destroyed each of these, they would be checked off. When enough of them had been razed, the city was removed from the target list. By the end of May, Tokyo had lost 56 square miles to the flames and was no longer considered a priority target. For a time, Yokohama seemed to be spared; rumor had it in Japan that the Americans were saving it because they planned to land there. In fact, Yokohama UA/1 had a B rating on the target list, relegating it to the "second phase." But Yokohama's turn came on May 29, when 454 Superfortresses came over in a high-altitude daylight raid and rained down twenty-five hundred tons of incendiaries. Yokohama UA/1 went up in flames, as did much of the rest of the city—nearly seven square miles. The inhabitants of Osaka clung to the belief that the rest of their badly damaged city would be spared. There were, it was said, "connections" between the Americans and important commercial families of Osaka, "the Manchester of the Orient." But the B-29s came on June 1 and finished the city off.

There was very little that the Japanese government could do, short of capitulation, to prevent the incineration of its great cities one after another. The menace from the Marianas was growing every day. By June, General LeMay was mounting raids with five hundred Superfortresses, and by September he would have a thousand at his disposal. In March, American P-51 fighters began to move to bases on Iwo Jima, and by April they were appearing over Japan. From February on, the attacks from LeMay's B-29s were supplemented by those from carrier-based planes, which periodically appeared to harass the home islands.

Japan's early-warning network had begun to disintegrate, like that of Germany. The increasingly mighty American navy had destroyed Japanese picket ships or driven them toward the shelter of the home islands. The type-B radar, with its range limited to 150 miles or so, was an inadequate substitute. The Japanese fighter force probably made its heaviest impact on the raids in January 1945, when B-29 losses rose to 5.7 percent; thereafter, the Japanese fighters had less success, although the pilots were plucky and aggressive to the end. The Tenth Air Division held the Kanto Sector, covering the highest-priority targets, Tokyo and Yokohama. On the night of the great March raid in Tokyo, they put eight fighters in the air; there were at that time only three hundred fighters for the defense of all Japan plus two hundred machines available in the training schools. Some pilots tried to make up the deficiencies by extraordinary measures, such as ramming the B-29s. This tactic was first used against the B-29 in August 1944 and from time to time afterward; late in 1944 the Japanese high command ordered the formation of "special duty" units whose pilots were to ram the American bombers. In statistical terms, the policy seemed justified. The Japanese pilot took with him eleven American crewmen and a bomber twelve times the size of his fighter plane. But many Japanese commanders violently opposed the policy of ramming. Japan was already running short of experienced pilots, and this practice would take the lives of those who were left.

Some Japanese fighter pilots pinned their hopes on the Shusui jet-powered fighter, which could climb to thirty thousand feet in a scant four minutes, but the fabled weapon came too late. In July, air force authorities were working on a daring plan called the *Ken* operation. Transport planes would fly special demolition teams to the Marianas, where they would storm the airfields and destroy the Superfortresses on the ground. The scheme collapsed when the transport planes were destroyed in an air raid. For lack of radical solutions, the air defense authorities continued with traditional methods. They decided not to challenge every air attack, but to husband their strength for the big bomber incursions. Japanese intelligence tried to "read" American radio traffic and predict when and where attacks might take place. The flak forces, woefully insufficient, were moved about according to the readings; at one point, nearly a third of Japan's flak units were being shifted about between potential targets.

The Japanese authorities did what they could in the way of passive defense. Beginning in June 1944, they began evacuating young children from urban areas and ultimately other groups as well. Although Japan was losing much of its industrial capacity with the burning of its cities, the authorities did not order dispersal and relocation of critical industries until the spring of 1945. They probably delayed because they knew that war production, already slumping in late 1944, would dip further as the firms shifted their operations to new localities. Within each Japanese city, the local authorities tried to prepare for fire attacks, filling water reservoirs and cutting firebreaks, often by demolishing whole blocks; municipal authorities made agreements to lend fire-fighting apparatus back and forth between threatened cities.

These measures were completely justified in light of the way the American bombing offensive was growing in intensity. In March, LeMay's bombers had released 13,000 tons of bombs on Japan; in July the figure was 42,000, and by the end of the summer it was expected to exceed 100,000 tons per month. By the middle of June, the Superfortresses had burned out all the largest cities in Japan, so they began on the lesser cities in a campaign that lasted two months. Now the raids were "multiple-target" missions, in which four wings of B-29s took off, each wing hitting a different city. Yet LeMay never completely abandoned the strategic-bombing concept. Whenever the weather was favorable, the bombers took high explosives to precise targets; when it was not, they hauled incendiaries to another city. The B-29s also found time to sow some twelve thousand naval mines and to scatter 4.5 million leaflets.

There was never any doubt that the towns and cities of Japan were the prime target. Of the 135,000 tons of bombs the B-29s dropped in the last months of the war, 104,000 went to urban areas. By July the bombers were attacking cities with populations of 100,000–200,000; the last cities attacked in August had fewer than 50,000 inhabitants. Toyama, with a population of 127,000, was deluged with 1,500 tons of bombs, which destroyed 99.5 percent of its built-up area. In the final weeks of the war against Japan, the bombers seemed to be having the same difficulty they had experienced over Germany: they were running out of targets worthy of their powers of destructiveness.

There was another parallel with the final phase of the air war in Europe, and an ominous one: the fire attacks on the cities of Japan were part of a general intensification and escalation of the conflict. On the Japanese side, there was no hope for new weapons of enhanced destructiveness, but shortcomings here could be offset by a higher level of human commitment. The Japanese high command ordered an extravagant yet calculated expenditure of lives. Kamikaze aircraft attacks began in the fall of 1944; by the following April, they had become such a serious menace that LeMay's B-29s turned from their customary targets and tried to neutralize the Kyushu airfields from which the suicide planes set out. April was also the month in which the Americans landed on Okinawa, and the mighty Japanese battleship *Yamato* steamed toward that strategic island on a kamikaze mission of its own, only to be sunk by American planes long before it reached its destination. On Okinawa, as on Iwo Jima two months before, the invaders encountered garrisons that fought with utmost determination. The Americans paid a heavy price for both islands, but they could expect the toll to be higher still on the beaches of Honshu and Kyushu: the Japanese government began the formation of the Peoples Volunteer Corps, a sort of *levée en masse* that would commit the bulk of Japan's adult population—men and women—to the defense of the homeland.

While those in power in Tokyo were making plans to offer up the Japanese people wholesale to stave off defeat, political and military planners in Washington were looking for ways to consummate the victory they saw ahead with a minimum investment of American lives. Not surprisingly, they mobilized technology in order to spare men. At the tactical level, napalm made its debut in the fall of 1944; delivered by air, it proved an efficient way to "burn out" pockets of resistance. Confronted with sobering losses at Okinawa and Iwo Jima, the American Joint Chiefs of Staff discussed going a step further and using poison gas, but in the end they decided against it. Meanwhile, the air offensive against the home islands swelled in intensity, preparing the way for the invasion that most American leaders believed would be necessary. The attacks had the dual function of reducing the enemy's ability to resist both materially and psychologically. The fire raids were presumably doing both, but after May they were supplemented by air attacks from Okinawa. While the B-29s brought destruction to the inhabitants of Japan's cities, Okinawa-based fighters and medium bombers brought it to hamlet and countryside. They ranged over Japan as they had ranged over the expiring Reich, attacking trains, bridges, and whatever targets of opportunity presented themselves—missions described at the time as "general hell-raising." Their operations blurred further the distinction between military and civilian objectives. At least twice, returning fighter pilots reported they had strafed groups of civilians in the fields and along the roads. A spokesman for the Fifth Air Force offered a rationale for such attacks: since the Japanese government was mobilizing the people generally to resist the invasion, it followed that "the entire population of Japan is a proper military target."[5]

It was in such a climate that the ultimate air weapon of the war made its debut. When the first atomic bomb was being readied, a group of scientists involved in its development proposed that it first be used in a harmless demonstration that would be given the widest publicity. But the panel of civilians who advised President Truman on atomic affairs recommended that the bomb be used on a Japanese target and without any prior warning about its nature. So it was that Col. Paul Tibbets took the *Enola Gay* and its bomb over Hiroshima on the morning of August 6, 1945. A second nuclear bomb struck Nagasaki three days later, as the inner council of the Japanese government was considering Allied peace proposals—which it accepted on August 14. Both Hiroshima and Nagasaki were dual targets, containing installations of military value and sizable civilian populations; as such, they were no different from other cities that B-29s had deluged with incendiaries. And in their immediately perceptible results, the nuclear attacks resembled the conventional fire raids—so much so that some survivors felt they had experienced just such a raid. The Hiroshima and Nagasaki bombs were only the second and third nuclear devices exploded, and by modern standards they were puny indeed. Bombing experts estimated shortly after the war that they could have produced the same level of death and destruction with

2,100 tons of conventional bombs, about half of them incendiaries. This tonnage was well within the capacity of the B-29 fleet.

So while the bomb itself was new and extraordinary, no new or extraordinary use was made of it. Nuclear fission replaced incendiaries and high explosives in an ongoing, escalating air offensive. To many partisans of strategic bombing, the mushroom cloud was like the fire storm, a milestone in the realization of a doctrine a half-century old. And to those partisans, the surrender of Japan while its shores were still inviolate brought triumphant affirmation of the doctrine and the dream. The air weapon had become the supreme weapon—or so it seemed.

CHAPTER 11

THE BOMBING WAR IN RETROSPECT

"ITS MYSTERY IS HALF ITS POWER."[1] J. M. Spaight once described the bomber this way, and perhaps no other phrase captures quite so well the peculiar ambiance in which this weapon was conceived and developed. The aura of mystery and power surrounded aerial bombing when it was still only an idea; by the 1930s the strategic air weapon had become an awesome, overshadowing presence that preoccupied men quite as much as nuclear arsenals do today. While the bomber worked on the imagination of the Sunday-supplement writer and the public who read his exposés, at the same time it affected the men who flew it and knew its powers at firsthand. The history of aviation in general is the story of machines and of men, but also of a kind of interaction between the two. To men like Mitchell and Douhet, the power of the air weapon came with the force of revelation. They believed and then they became evangelists.

The bomber was an idea long before it was a reality, and this discrepancy, if one may call it that, has remained a feature of its history. The realization would always lag behind the conception; performance never quite caught up with expectations. "The potential of the strategic air offensive was greater than its achievement"[2]—this was the judgment that Bomber Command's official historians rendered on its operations against Germany, but the same words might serve as epitaph for almost any strategic-bombing campaign in either world war. Perhaps it was not until the *Enola Gay* appeared over Hiroshima that strategic bombing met and exceeded the expectations of those who placed their faith in it.

From the very beginning, the partisans of air power expected too much of the bomber. They were dazzled by the offensive possibilities it offered. Its "penetrativeness," as Spaight called it, brought the enemy's factories, arsenals, and towns within sight for the first time; and what the bomber could see, it could of course destroy. "From above one can see well and from above one can strike easily,"[3] Douhet, writing in 1910, put it simply. The early theorists also accorded to aerial bombardment a special efficacy. Somehow, by a process they never quite explained, fifty pounds of explosives coming to earth in the form of an aerial bomb would wreak more havoc than a similar weight of explosives delivered by more conventional means. And the damage was not merely physical; it was psychological as well. A rain of bombs was less bearable to human beings than a salvo of artillery. These notions were virtually articles of faith by 1914, and they would linger to color the thought of later generations of strategists.

The unique potential for destruction that made the bomber a promising weapon also made it a dangerous one. Any number or people saw the danger before 1914: aerial bombing could extend death and destruction far beyond the customary parameters of warfare, erasing the distinction between combatant and civilian, between war zone and hinterland. At the Hague conference of 1907 the nations involved chose to permit aerial bombing of military objectives. In doing so, they virtually assured that the practice would spread and intensify, for the threshold to "illegal" bombing was not clearly marked. The air weapon might conceivably have been banned altogether while still in embryo; what helped save it was the argument that actually it represented "progress" in warfare, a means to bring speed and precision to military operations and thus make wars less bloody. This notion too would linger. In the 1920s, Mitchell and Douhet argued that a war decided in the air would be a merciful substitute for the hell of the trenches. And arguments about the economy and the humanity of the air war continued to be heard into World War II. Initially, much of the talk was about the fabled knockout blow, which would stun a belligerent in the first hours of conflict, delivering him up to the will of the attacker with a saving of lives and property all around; later, when the war was well under way, advocates of the strategic-bombing offensive put forth a more modest claim: it would save lives on "our" side.

The Great War scarcely gave the strategic bomber a chance to do more than try its wings; at the close of the conflict, it was a weapon imperfectly tested, but with a potential all the more inviting now that traditional methods of warfare had come into discredit. If there was a single episode in the war that served to demonstrate that potential it was the German air offensive against England, culminating in the cycle of raids on London in the summer and fall of 1917. No one grasped the lesson quite so well as those on the receiving end of the offensive; it was at the height of the attacks that the British cabinet took the key decisions that committed the country to a strategic air force of its own. And the episode made a strong impression on foreign observers, perhaps because Britain's cities had so long been inviolable. Long after the war, air power advocates invoked as their final argument the peril and the panic London had known.

But after the war the pendulum swung again. What had been a weapon for victory in 1918 became a menace to European civilization and the object of countless disarmament efforts. For the bomber to survive in the 1930s, it had to lend itself to new uses and appear to serve other causes—and sometimes it even had to change its name. Although it was a supremely offensive weapon, its proponents claimed that it would serve the cause of defense, that it no longer threatened attack, but only promised retaliation. With an unrivaled ability to erase distance, it served to promote a kind of isolationism, insulating the belligerent nation from too close contact with the horrors of war. Bomber Command offered the British a means to fight the enemy at arm's length, striking it from the security of their island. The American Flying Fortress would meet and turn back hostile forces that were still hundreds of miles offshore; and there were any number of armchair strategists in America who spoke of a "superbomber" that could strike across the Atlantic.

Of all the belligerents of World War II only Great Britain and the United States had made a strong commitment to the strategic air offensive before the conflict started, and only they were able to mount and sustain such offensives once the war began. In the end, this seems to have been more than anything else a result of priorities and resources. A strategic-bombing fleet of any size was a rich nation's weapon, and that nation had to be rich not only in money but in men and technology as well. It is doubtful that Japan could have found the wherewithal to construct such a fleet, and it is questionable whether Germany could have found the fuel to keep such a fleet in the air. Air Marshal Harris dreamed of a force of four thousand heavy bombers, but British industry could not give them to him if it was to continue meeting the needs of the land and sea services. As it was, the bomber offensive may at times have absorbed a third of the British war effort. Britain could not find the aircrews that Bomber Command required without drawing heavily on the Commonwealth. Only the Americans could afford to offer themselves a bomber like the B-29, which cost over $800,000—a staggering sum for the era—and gulped six thousand gallons of aviation gasoline on a single mission. And only the Americans could build them by the thousands and maintain them in style. In the summer of 1944, XX Bomber Command had fifty B-29s operational—and twenty thousand men working to keep them that way.

In 1939, as in 1914, the bombing war developed slowly; for the first few months, the Germans and the Allies scrupulously respected each other's cities and populations. Even after these restrictions disappeared, the impact of bombing was far less than expected. The strategic offensives of 1940–41, both German and British, revealed the bomber to be vulnerable and its destructive capacities disappointing. The British and the Americans persisted with this form of the air war; they had made a heavy commitment, so their bombing fleets were under clear imperative to produce results. Bomber Command had to reequip with better aircraft; since it could not strike precision targets by day, it had to attack larger ones by night. If the Americans could not see Stuttgart through their Norden bombsights, they would have to locate it with radar and bomb it through clouds. These things the two Allies did, and monthly tonnages rose accordingly.

Yet the story of the Allied bombing offensive is hardly one of smooth acceleration. In the skies over Germany, the advantage shifted several times between offensive and defensive forces; not until the last months of the conflict could the Allies enjoy anything approaching the fabled "command of the air." For most of the war, each mission was like a roll of the dice, its outcome dependent upon weather, enemy dispositions, sheer chance, and a host of other factors that could not be controlled. So it must have seemed to those who flew in the big bombers. They knew only that if they played the game long enough they were certain to lose. Martin Middlebrook has calculated that in 1943 only about a third of Bomber Command's crews made it through a first tour of thirty missions; one crew in six survived a second tour of twenty missions. Whenever the bombers had a particularly bad run of luck, as did the British in the Ruhr and the Americans over Schweinfurt, morale would drop perceptibly. It was a measure of the men that the bombers continued to fly.

Statistically, the most striking feature of the strategic air offensives against both Germany and Japan was their incremental nature. The great weight of bombs to descend on Germany came in the last year of war; in the case of Japan, 90 percent of the bombs were dropped in the final five months. The figures on physical destruction are eloquent: 7.5 million Germans and over 8 million Japanese homeless at the end of the war. This was "dehousing" on a grand scale indeed. Fire proved to be the greatest agent of destruction, with the incendiary bomb about five times more effective than high explosives. But aerial bombing was not an efficient way to take human life. It took three tons of bombs to kill a German, a ton and a half to kill a Japanese, with differences in building construction and population density accounting for the variation.

These figures and many others were meticulously compiled by research teams after the war and incorporated into the British and American strategic-bombing surveys. Much of the data collected there served later to buttress the arguments presented in the massive official histories: the four-volume *Strategic Air Offensive Against Germany,* which chronicles the efforts of Bomber Command, and the seven-volume *Army Air Forces in World War II.* The claims made for strategic bombing are, on the whole, not extravagant. Bomber Command "made a contribution to victory which was decisive."[4] The Americans also employed the word *decisive,* and they too perceived the bomber as just part of a larger effort. But in the postmortem of the Pacific campaign, they put forward an interesting argument: Even if there had been no atomic bomb and no Soviet declaration of war against the Japanese, "air supremacy over Japan could have exerted sufficient pressure to bring about unconditional surrender and obviate the need for invasion."[5] Unfortunately, historical questions and hypotheses that begin with *if* cannot be resolved.

But in the way the campaigns actually worked out, the supreme hope placed in the strategic air offensive by some of its partisans in the 1930s, and indeed in the early years of World War II, was not realized: the strategic bomber did not win the war by itself. It was used along with a variety of other weapons and its role has been called variously "decisive," "important" or "relatively modest" by different historians sifting through the same evidence. But to determine how really worthwhile strategic bombing was to the Allied war effort, one would need to know if the vast resources committed to that effort would have counted for more if invested in tactical aviation, armored divisions, or—as one historian has suggested—landing craft. This is another *if* question.

There is nevertheless a good deal to be learned from the Allied air offensives, for they put to the ultimate test strategic recipes that were refined and debated for decades—and a number of those recipes failed. One that did not was the American doctrine of precision bombing directed at the *points sensibles*. Complex industrial societies *can* be hamstrung by a judicious pattern of destruction. The assaults that the Eighth and Fifteenth Air Forces mounted on Germany's transportation and fuel installations in the last year of the war proved to be stunning successes; this was confirmed by Albert Speer, who was in an excellent position to judge. But the postwar surveys showed that this type of warfare might have been far more productive than it was: the Americans should have concentrated on these targets sooner, should have struck German power stations (in retrospect, an even more rewarding target) and should have given more attention to the Japanese railway system.

The British got somewhat lower marks from Speer. Although the damage they did was more widespread, it was less critical. The cities that they made their objectives proved surprisingly able to absorb punishment; with half the streetcars out of commission and the homeless crowding in with friends or relatives, life went on, and so did work. As the city was tenacious of life, so was the production center. Often the building was destroyed, but the tools and machinery saved, so that production lines soon opened again in makeshift quarters and sometimes simply in the open air. Both air forces discovered they had "underbombed." Targets thought to have been obliterated would have to be hit again and again or somehow they would come back to life; the German synthetic-fuel works at Leuna were a notorious case in point. And sometimes what had seemed to be an ideal target system proved not to be. The costly raids on the ball-bearing works at Schweinfurt did not slow down the German war machine. The British went to considerable effort to burn out Düsseldorf because it contained the headquarters of many German industries located elsewhere. But once rid of their head offices, those industries seem to have operated at an even higher pitch. All of this was learned later, of course.

During the war, the Allies were fundamentally handicapped by not knowing what effect their raids were having. Photographic intelligence could not tell them all they needed to know, and stories coming from enemy countries had to be heavily discounted. In this sense, both Allies were bombing blind. There was an even more fundamental shortcoming in intelligence: failure to perceive the excess capacity, the unused resources, and the "fat" that characterized the German economy well into the war. When Allied bombers began serious efforts to apply the brakes to German production in 1943, Albert Speer was just moving it into high gear. Well into 1944, his efforts effectively counteracted theirs.

All of the bombing offensives of the war, including that which the Luftwaffe waged against England in 1940–41, seem to have been launched with the expectations of quick and tangible results; when those results did not come, the bombers were directed against another target system and then another. But probably no target proved so frustrating, so elusive as morale. At some point, the offensive came to include this target, and at times, the chief objective of the raid was to demoralize the enemy civilian, to panic him, or, if necessary, to kill him. The punishment administered could be extremely severe: as a result of American bombing on dual targets, Japan suffered more casualties among its civilian population than among its armed forces on the fighting front. From Goering's Operation Seaside at the beginning of the war to Clarion and Thunderclap toward its end, there were innumerable schemes to produce a massive and debilitating shock to the enemy's population. The bombing of Rome was carried out largely for its shock value, as was the nuclear attack on Hiroshima. In these cases a shock certainly was produced, but it added to pressures already building on the Italian and Japanese governments, so its exact role is impossible to determine. On the other hand, the Blitz was a total failure psychologically, as was the Battle of Berlin in the winter of 1943–44.

Here and there, the air war against the cities triggered panics and stampedes, but these were exceptional. In March 1943, 197 Londoners were killed when a crowd rushing to shelter in a subway found its progress blocked. Seven months later, a similar crush in Milan cost the lives of 354 people; but this sort of tragedy can be produced anywhere excited crowds encounter unexpected obstacles—at soccer games and at rock concerts, for example. Perhaps the nearest thing to massive and spontaneous flight came in the immediate aftermath of the two nuclear attacks, both of which came virtually without warning. But within hours many of the inhabitants of Hiroshima and Nagasaki returned and rescue efforts were being organized.

Almost universally, morale bombing was a disappointment; the evidence that the bombing surveys offered to the contrary is not convincing. Some students of human behavior have argued that the bombing of the cities would have had a far greater psychological yield if it had been an all-out effort from the start, rather than one that built slowly in intensity, allowing urban populations to adjust to it. Be that as it may, when a city came under repeated attack and the air-raid siren became a familiar sound, the civilian at home proved as adaptable and as capable of living with danger as the soldier at the front. Indeed, embattled city dwellers often thought of themselves as combatants in the struggle against the bomber, even though their weapons were nothing more than sand buckets and blackout curtains. To be sure, in London, Essen, and Turin, the bombs exacted a price beyond the deaths and injuries they provoked. Bed-wetting increased among children, women had greater menstrual difficulties, and coronary occlusions among men were a common occurrence in the air-raid shelters. The human body coped with stress in its own way, and so did the human will.

Those who lived through the air raids did so largely by keeping their tempers, obeying the law, and holding to the bonds of family, friendship, and fellowship in common peril. They did not sustain themselves with dreams of vengeance or clamor for subjecting the enemy's cities to the same ordeal; polls and surveys were quite clear on this point. Sometimes they survived by calling on unsuspected capacities within themselves, like the old woman entombed alive in the wreckage of her London home who left an indelible impression on rescue workers: "She was buried for hours, and we could hear her swearing away down there. Can't think where she learned the words, a nice old lady like that."[6] Sometimes they could demonstrate an amazing coolness, like the Italian who dragged an unexploded bomb from his house and placed it at the curbside for the bomb-disposal squad. There were flashes of humor, even in time of greatest despair. A Berliner was heard to remark at the end of the war, "If anybody is still alive here it's his own fault; there were bombs enough for everybody."[7] If there was a lesson to be read in the ruins of Berlin, Coventry, and Hiroshima it was the terrible fragility of all man's works and treasures—and the tenacity and endurance of man himself.

A woman who survived the inferno in Hamburg recently said to an interviewer, "It was hell on earth. It was obvious that Hitler had to be destroyed, but did it have to be done this way?"[8] The question is a fair one. The strategic-bombing offensive has been criticized for its fundamental inefficiency, but it has been more roundly condemned for its no less fundamental savagery. The plain fact is that most people have had difficulty in accepting the argument that since the entire nation now makes war, any part of that nation may justifiably be attacked. Despite the bitterness of the conflict they fought, the generation of 1939–45 generally observed the distinction between soldier and civilian. Few Americans or Britons of that era would agree that a toddler of three or a widow on pension was a proper target for military operations, yet the Anglo-American air offensive destroyed thousands of such targets.

Since the hallmark of strategic air forces is their close control by the supreme military and political leadership, that is where some historians have sought the explanation for this discrepancy—and the culprits. Some would lay the blame at the door of the military—Britain's "bomber barons," for example, who got their way by a variety of questionable means, including deception. An American historian has recently argued that the leaders of the U.S. Army Air Forces carried the war to German civilians through similar means: "Official policy against indiscriminate bombing was so badly interpreted and so frequently breached as to become almost meaningless. . . . In the end, both the policy and the apparent ethical support for it among AAF leaders turn out to be myths; while they contain elements of truth, they are substantially false or misleading."[9] Others point the finger at the political leadership; the author of a recent book on the British bomber offensive maintains that "from beginning to end of the war, ministers prevaricated—indeed, lied flatly again and again—about the nature of the bomber offensive."[10] Another has painted a cover-up of sorts involving cabinet ministers, the air staff, and the media: "In some ways, area bombing was a three-year period of deceit practiced on the British public."[11]

None of the belligerents began the war with plans for an air assault against civilian populations—and this includes Nazi Germany. They were in fact all anxious to avoid such an air war, often because they were unsure how their own populations would stand up. And for the first few months of the conflict, they were able to limit the air war to clearly defined and isolated military targets, such as ships at sea. But this was insufficient employment for the bombing fleets, so they went after "legitimate" targets on land as well. Once this step was taken, escalation of the air war was inevitable, if for no other reason than the bomber's inaccuracy. An error or accident bred a reprisal, which in turn became a provocation. And when a nation's cities came under attack and its leaders proved unable to prevent those attacks, the leaders offered their beleaguered populations the next best thing—the spectacle of the enemy's cities even more savagely punished. But beyond this, there was always the possiblity that morale bombing might work, a possibility all the more alluring because the other bombing programs were not giving results.

Thus drawn or driven by a variety of pressures, those who controlled the bombers gradually unleashed them on the enemy populations. Many leaders did so unwillingly or with misgivings; the resistance in the U. S. Army Air Forces was notably strong. The escalation of the air war was made easier by the fact that those who directed the bombing offensives and those who carried them out remained curiously insulated and detached from the consequences of their work. Photographs taken at thirty thousand feet gave no clue to the human effects of a raid, nor did other sources. In this vacuum, imagination and extrapolation could picture the population of an enemy town deprived of its homes but not of life and limb or public transport reduced by 50 percent and belief in victory by the same amount. Anodyne, antiseptic phrases such as "dual target" and "area attack" further served to mask the fact that human lives were being destroyed.

If there was deception, there was also self-deception; and if there was a conspiracy to deceive, then the public, or at least the thinking portion of it, was party to that deception. In both Britain and America a few voices of protest could be heard. In March 1944, twenty-eight American clergymen drew up a letter of protest that was cited in the front pages of the *New York Times*. In the House of Lords, George Bell, Bishop of Chichester, spoke up, while a Labour member of Parliament named Richard Stokes asked endless and disconcerting questions about area bombing. But they found no echo. Most people simply wanted to get on with the war, to win it, and, at the same time, to keep intact the belief that a noble cause was not being prosecuted by barbarous or immoral means. In the final year of the war, the sheer intensity of the bombing resulted in attacks so great in their destructiveness that they aroused concern within minds and consciences in the Allied camps. The burning of Dresden certainly had this effect. Churchill, who had no small part in bringing the attack about, decided it was time to review "the question of bombing of German cities simply for the sake of increasing terror, though under other pretexts."[12] An Associated Press report on Allied terror bombing created a sensation a few days after the attacks on Dresden and gave General Arnold's chief of information grave cause for concern: "This is certain to have a nationwide serious effect on the Air Force as we have steadfastly preached the gospel of precision bombing against military and industrial targets."[13] In England, Bomber Command soon became the object of vague disapprobation. Air Marshal Harris's men were denied their campaign medal, and Harris himself was left out of the shower of titles and distinctions that followed victory. Utterly unrepentant, Harris wrote a ringing defense of his work from first to last. The crisis of conscience over Dresden, he felt, could best be explained by a psychologist: "It is connected with German bands and Dresden shepherdesses."[14]

There was no such dramatic turn of events in the United States, but after Germany and Japan were occupied and the enormity of the destruction became apparent, it produced a certain uneasiness. That uneasiness has lingered; it can be stirred in many Americans whenever Hiroshima is mentioned. The National Air and Space Museum receives a steady trickle of letters protesting the presence in its collections of the *Enola Gay,* and each year the flow increases around August 6. But there is another flow of inquiries asking why the most famous bomber in history is not put on public display. In the meantime, the *Enola Gay* remains in storage outside Washington and there it is likely to stay. Asked if the plane would ever be exhibited, a curator replied diplomatically, "It's too big for the museum."

NOTES

CHAPTER 1
A WEAPON IS BORN

1. Letter to Dr. Brockleby, October 6, 1784, quoted in John C. Cooper, *The Right to Fly* (New York: Henry Holt, 1947), p. 10.

2. J. C. G. Hayne, *Versuch ueber die neuerfundene Luftmaschine des Herrn Montgolfier, besonders in wie fern solche der Kriegskunst eine Aenderung machen und einem Staate nuezlich und nachteilig seyn koenne* (Berlin and Stettin: Nicolai, 1784), p. 36.

3. V. A. Popov, *Istoria vozdukhoplavania i aviatsii v SSSR: Period do 1914g.* (Moscow: Izdatel'stvo oboronnoi promyshlennosti, 1944), p. 32.

4. *Erinnerungen eines österreichischen Veteranen aus dem italienischen Kriege 1848/49* (Stuttgart and Tübingen: J. G. Cotta, 1852), p. 306.

5. C. F. S. Snowden Gamble, *The Air Weapon: Being Some Account of the Growth of British Military Aeronautics from the Beginnings in the Year 1783 until the End of the Year 1929.* Vol. I: November 1783–August 1914 (London: Oxford University Press, 1931), p. 67.

6. H. W. L. Moedebeck, *Handbuch der Luftschiffahrt mit besonderer Berücksichtigung Ihrer militairischen Verwendung* (Leipzig: E. Schloemp, 1886), p. 91.

7. Letter of September 14, 1893, reproduced in the work of the Kriegswissenschaftliche Abteilung der Luftwaffe, *Die Militärluftfahrt bis zum Beginn des Weltkrieges 1914,* 3 vols. (Berlin: E. S. Mittler, 1941), II, 13.

8. Jean de Bloch [Ivan S. Bliokh], *La Guerre,* 6 vols. (Paris: Guillaumin, 1898–1900), I, 203.

9. James Brown Scott, ed., *The Hague Conventions of 1899 and 1907* (London: Oxford University Press, 1915), p. xviii.

10. *Ibid.,* p. 117.

11. See Sir Hiram Maxim's Introduction to R. P. Hearne, *Airships in Peace and War* (London: John Lane, 1910), p. xxx.

12. Quoted in Angelo Lodi, *Storia delle origini dell'aeronautica militare 1884–1915: Aerostieri, dirigibilisti, aviatori dell'esercito e della marina in Italia nel periodico pionieristico,* 2 vols. (Rome: Bizzari, 1976), II, 39.

13. Henri Mirande and Louis Olivier, *Sur la bataille: Journal d'un aviateur français à l'Armée bulgare, au siège d'Adrianople* (Paris: Ambert, 1913), p. 136.

14. Pol Timonier, *Comment nous torpillerons Berlin avec notre escadrille d'aéroplanes des l'ouverture des hostilités* (Paris: Editions pratiques et documentaires, 1913), passim.

CHAPTER 2
THE GREAT WAR

1. *New York Times,* October 19, 1914.

2. General der Kavallerie Ernst von Hoeppner, *Deutschlands Krieg in der Luft. Ein Rückblick auf die Entwicklung und die Leistungen unserer Heeres-Luftstreitkräfte im Weltkrieg* (Leipzig: K. F. Koehler, 1921), p. 21.

3. Quoted in Jules Poirier, *Les bombardements de Paris (1914–1918): Avions-Gothas-Zeppelins-Berthas* (Paris: Payot, 1930), p. 65.

4. Von Hoeppner, p. 21.

5. Letter of October 24, 1912, reproduced in the work of the Kriegsmilitärische Abteilung der Luftwaffe, *Die Militärluftfahrt bis zum Beginn des Weltkrieges 1914,* 3 vols. (Berlin: E. S. Mittler, 1941), II, 89.

6. *Ibid.*

7. Quoted in Douglas H. Robinson, "The Zeppelin Bomber: High Policy Guided by Wishful Thinking," *Air Power Historian,* VIII (July 1961), 146.

8. R. P. Hearne, *Zeppelins and Super-Zeppelins* (London: John Lane, 1916), p. 2.

9. *Ibid.,* p. 6.

10. Raymond H. Fredette, *The Sky on Fire: The First Battle of Britain 1917–1918 and the Birth of the Royal Air Force* (New York: Holt, Rinehart and Winston, 1966), pp. 261, 264.

11. *New York Times,* October 14, 1917.

12. Quoted in Anthony Rhodes, *The Poet as Superman: A Life of Gabriele D'Annunzio* (London: Weidenfeld and Nicolson, 1959), p. 158.

13. Von Hoeppner, p. 57.

14. Andrew Boyle, *Trenchard: Man of Vision* (London: William Collins, 1962), p. 312.

15. Antonio Monti, ed., *Giulio Douhet: Scritti inediti* (Florence: Scuola di Guerra Aerea, 1951), p. 149.

16. *New York Times,* June 1, 1918.

17. *Ibid,* June 5, 1918.

CHAPTER 3
THE PROPHETS

1. J. M. Spaight, *Air Power and War Rights* (London: Longmans, Green, 1924), p. 6.

2. Quoted by P. R. C. Groves, *Behind the Smoke Screen* (London: Faber and Faber, 1934), p. 187.

3. Ferdinand Ferber, *L'Aviation: Ses débuts. Son développement. De crête à crête. De ville à ville. De continent à continent* (Paris and Nancy: Berger-Levrault, 1908), p. 159.

4. Clément Ader, *L'Aviation militaire* (Paris and Nancy: Berger-Levrault, 1909), p. 29.

5. Riley E. Scott, "Can the Panama Canal Be Destroyed from the Air?" *Sunset,* April 1914, p. 784.

6. Ader, p. 135.

7. Hans Ritter, *Der Luftkrieg* (Berlin: K. F. Koehler, 1926), p. 64.

8. Bernard Serrigny, *Réflexions sur l'art de la guerre* (Paris: Charles-Lavauzelle, 1921), p. 108.

9. William C. Sherman, *Air Warfare* (New York: The Ronald Press, 1926), p. 30.

10. *Ibid.*

11. Oliver Stewart, *The Strategy and Tactics of Air Fighting* (London: Longmans, Green, 1925), p. 190.

12. Colonel de Vaulgrémont, quoted in M. W. Royse, *Aerial Bombardment and the International Regulation of Warfare* (New York: Henry Vinal, 1928), p. 232.

13. Sir Walter Raleigh and H. A. Jones, *The War in the Air: Being the Story of the Part Played in the Great War by the Royal Air Force,* 6 vols. (Oxford: Clarendon Press, 1922–37), III, 247.

14. Raymond H. Fredette, *The Sky on Fire: The First Battle of Britain 1917–1918 and the Birth of the Royal Air Force* (New York: Holt, Rinehart, and Winston, 1966), p. 129.

15. Antonio Monti, ed., *Giulio Douhet: Scritti inediti* (Florence: Scuola di Guerra Aerea, 1951), p. 111.

16. Groves, p. 187.

17. Raleigh and Jones, V, 156–157.

18. Alfred F. Hurley, *Billy Mitchell: Crusader for Air Power* (New York: Franklin Watts, 1964), p. 44.

19. J. C. Slessor, *Air Power and Armies* (London: Oxford University Press, 1936), p. 65.

20. J. M. Spaight, *Air Power and the Cities* (London: Longmans, Green, 1930), p. 230.

21. Spaight, *Air Power and War Rights,* p. 13.

22. Spaight, *Air Power and the Cities,* p. 230.

23. Spaight, *Air Power and War Rights,* p. 4.

24. Spaight, *Air Power and the Cities,* p. 234.

25. Monti, *Douhet,* p. 126.

26. *Ibid,* p. 166.

27. *Ibid,* p. 265.

CHAPTER 4
BANNING THE BOMBER

1. Bertha von Suttner, *Memoirs of Bertha von Suttner: The Records of an Eventful Life,* 2 vols. (Boston: Ginn, 1910) I, 287.

2. Bertha von Suttner, *Die Barbarisierung der Luft* (Berlin: Verlag der "Friedens-warte," 1912), p. 7.

3. Viktor Silberer, *Die Wahrheit über den Stand der Luftschiffahrt* (Vienna: Verlag der "Allgemeinensport-Zeitung," 1913), p. 46.

4. *New York Times,* February 23, 1916.

5. Quoted in Alfred F. Hurley, *Billy Mitchell: Crusader for Air Power* (New York: Franklin Watts, 1964), p. 37.

6. John C. Cooper, *The Right to Fly* (New York: Henry Holt, 1947), pp. 306–307.

7. "General Report of the Commission of Jurists at the Hague," *American Journal of International Law,* XVII (October 1923), Supplement, 249.

8. "The Hague Rules of 1923," *Ibid.,* pp. 250–251.

9. J. M. Spaight, *Air Power and War Rights* (London: Longmans, Green, 1924), pp. 18–19.

10. *Ibid.,* p. 222.

11. *Ibid.*

12. William C. Sherman, *Air Warfare* (New York: the Ronald Press, 1926), p. 214.

13. L. E. O. Charlton, *Charlton* (London: Faber and Faber, 1931), p. 271.

14. E. J. Kingston-McCloughry, *Winged Warfare: Air Problems of Peace and War* (London: Jonathan Cape, 1937), p. 202.

15. Quoted in Uri Bialer, "Some Aspects of the Fear of Bombardment from the Air and the Making of British Defence and Foreign Policy, 1932–1939," Ph.D. thesis, University of London, 1974, p. 43, note.

CHAPTER 5
THE RISE OF
THE AIR FLEETS

1. Bernard Brodie, *Strategy for the Missile Age* (Princeton, N.J.: Princeton University Press, 1959), p. 75.

2. *Ibid.*

3. Olaf Groehler, *Geschichte des Luftkrieges 1910–1970* (Berlin: Militärverlag der Deutschen Demokratischen Republik, 1975), pp. 112, 124.

4. Reproduced in Sir Charles Webster and Noble Frankland, *The Strategic Air Offensive Against Germany, 1939–1945,* 4 vols. (London: H. M. Stationery Office, 1961), IV, 71–76.

5. Alexander Yakovlev, *Notes of an Aircraft Designer* (New York: Arno Press, 1972), p. 126.

6. D. C. Watt, *Too Serious a Business: European Armed Forces and the Approach to the Second War* (Berkeley and Los Angeles: University of California Press, 1975), p. 72.

7. Sir Walter Raleigh and H. A. Jones, *The War in the Air: Being the Story of the Part Played in the Great War by the Royal Air Force,* 6 vols. (Oxford: Clarendon Press, 1922–37), I, 488.

8. Reproduced in Karl-Heinz Völker, ed., *Dokumente und Dokumentarfotos zur Geschichte der deutschen Luftwaffe* (Stuttgart: Deutsche Verlags-Anstalt, 1968), p. 470.

9. Giuseppe Santoro, *L'Aeronautica italiana nella Seconda Guerra mondiale,* 2 vols. (Rome: Edizioni Esse, 1957), I, 17.

10. *Ibid.,* I, 35.

11. A. D. Tsykin, *Ot 'Ili Muromtsa' do raketonostsa: Kratkii ocherk istorii dal'nei aviatsii* (Moscow: Voennizdat, 1975), p. 16.

12. A. N. Lapchinskii, *Bombardirovochnaia aviatsia* (Moscow: Gosudarstvennoe Voennoe Izdatel'stvo, 1937), p. 43.

13. Alexander Boyd, *The Soviet Air Force Since 1918* (New York: Stein and Day, 1977), p. 70.

14. H. H. Arnold, *Global Mission* (New York: Harper, 1949), p. 52.

15. Wesley Frank Craven and James Lea Cate, eds., *The Army Air Forces in World War II,* 7 vols. (Chicago: University of Chicago Press, 1948–58), I, 68.

16. *Ibid.,* I, 52.

CHAPTER 6
ON THE EVE

1. J. P. Dunbabin, "British Rearmament in the Thirties: A Chronology and a Review," *Historical Journal,* XVIII (1975), 607.

2. Quoted in P. R. C. Groves, *Behind the Smoke Screen* (London: Faber and Faber, 1934), p. 156.

3. Hans Baasch, *Die Entwicklung der Luftverteidigung mit terrestrischen Mitteln* (Zurich: Kommissionsverlag Beer, 1960), p. 12.

4. Karl-Heinz Völker, *Die deutsche Luftwaffe 1933–1939: Aufbau, Führung und Rüstung der Luftwaffe, sowie die Entwicklung der deutschen Luftkriegstheorie* (Stuttgart: Deutsche Verlags-Anstalt, 1967), p. 213.

5. Lucien Rebatet, *Mémoires d'un fasciste*, 2 vols. (Paris: Pauvert, 1976), I, 198.

6. Quoted in Hilton P. Goss, *Civilian Morale Under Aerial Bombardment, 1914–1939* (Maxwell AFB: Air University, 1952), p. 58.

7. John Langdon-Davies, *Air Raid: The Technique of the Silent Approach, High Explosive, Panic* (London: George Routledge, 1938), p. 47.

8. N. de P. MacRoberts, *A.R.P. Lessons from Barcelona: Some Hints for Local Authorities and for the Private Citizen* (London: Eyre and Spottiswoode, 1938), p. 5.

9. Major Helders [Robert Knauss], *The War in the Air, 1936* (London: John Hamilton, 1932), p. 81.

10. Committee of the Cambridge Scientists' Anti-War Group, *Air Raid Protection: The Facts* (London, 1938), p. 57.

11. J. L. Nayler, "Additional Fire Risks from Air Raids," *Fire Protection and Air Raids Precaution Review,* I (May 1938), 22.

12. Lieutenant Colonel Clerc, *Causeries sur la D.A.T. à l'usage des militaires français libérales* (Paris: Charles-Lavauzelle, 1936), p. 9.

13. *Manual of Tactics, Air Raid Warden Service* (New York Police Department, 1942), p. 15.

14. Curt Wachtel, *Air Raid Defense (Civilian)* (Brooklyn, N.Y.: Chemical Publishing, 1941), p. 42.

CHAPTER 7

TOWARD TOTAL WAR

1. *Trial of the Major War Criminals Before the International Military Tribunal,* 42 vols. (Nuremberg, 1947–49), IX, 175.

2. Hans Krannenhals, "Massenhysterie beim Ausbruch des deutschen-polnischen Krieges," *Deutsche Studien,* VIII (1970), 131.

3. Speech of September 9, 1939, quoted in Max Domarus, *Hitler: Reden und Proklamationen, 1932–1945,* 2 vols. (Munich: Süddeutscher Verlag 1965), II, 1350.

4. William A. Swint, "The German Air Attack on Rotterdam," *Aerospace Historian,* XXI, no. 1 (March 1974), p. 16.

5. Walther Hubatsch, *Hitlers Weisungen für die Kriegführung 1939–1945* (Frankfurt: Bernard and Graefe, 1962), p. 53.

6. Quoted in Sir Charles Webster and Noble Frankland, *The Strategic Air Offensive Against Germany, 1939–1945,* 4 vols. (London: H. M. Stationery Office, 1961), I, 136, n. 2.

7. Domarus, II, 1558.

8. Speech of September 4, 1940, *ibid.,* II, 1579–1580.

9. Richard M. Titmuss, *Problems of Social Policy* (London: H. M. Stationery Office, 1950), pp. 304–305.

10. Quoted in Constantine Fitzgibbon, *The Winter of the Bombs: The Story of the Blitz of London* (New York: W. W. Norton, 1958), p. 93.

11. Charles Eade, ed., *The War Speeches of the Rt Hon Winston S. Churchill,* new ed., 3 vols. (London: Cassell, 1963), I, 256.

12. Sir Frederick Pile, *Ack-Ack: Britain's Defence Against Air Attack During the Second World War* (London: George G. Harrap, 1949), p. 144.

13. Quoted in Derek Wood, with Derek Dempster, *The Narrow Margin: The Battle of Britain and the Rise of Air Power, 1930–1940,* new ed. (London: Arrow Books, 1969), p. 239.

CHAPTER 8
THE BEGINNINGS OF THE ALLIED AIR OFFENSIVE

1. Sir Arthur Harris, *Bomber Offensive* (New York: Macmillan, 1947), p. 76.

2. Sir Charles Webster and Noble Frankland, *The Strategic Air Offensive Against Germany, 1939–1945,* 4 vols. (London: H. M. Stationery Office, 1961), I, 100, n. 1.

3. Harris, pp. 77–78.

4. Reproduced in Webster and Frankland, IV, 144.

5. Harris, p. 53.

6. *Ibid.,* p. 90.

7. Louis P. Lochner, ed., *The Goebbels Diaries, 1942–1943* (New York: Doubleday, 1948), p. 154.

8. Max Domarus, *Hitler: Reden und Proklamationen, 1932–1945,* 2 vols. (Munich: Süddeutscher Verlag, 1965), II, 1875.

9. Lochner, p. 190.

10. *Ibid.*

11. Harris, p. 144.

12. Quoted in Asher Lee, *Goering: Air Leader* (London: Duckworth, 1972), p. 142.

13. *Hitler's Table Talk, 1941–1944,* with an introductory essay by H. R. Trevor-Roper (London: Weidenfeld and Nicolson, 1953), p. 668.

14. Horst-Adalbert Koch, *Flak: Die Geschichte der deutschen Flakartillerie, 1935–1945* (Bad Nauheim: H. H. Podzun, 1954), p. 36.

15. Webster and Frankland, IV, 265.

16. *Ibid.*

CHAPTER 9
THE BATTLE OF GERMANY

1. Louis P. Lochner, ed., *The Goebbels Diaries, 1942–1943* (New York: Doubleday, 1948), p. 324.

2. *Ibid.*, p. 313.

3. Reproduced in Armin Schmid, *Frankfurt im Feuersturm: Die Geschichte der Stadt im zweiten Weltkrieg* (Frankfurt: Verlag Frankfurter Bücher, 1965), p. 46.

4. *Ibid.*, p. 45.

5. Quoted in Melton S. Davis, *Who Defends Rome? The Forty-Five Days, July 25–September 8, 1943* (New York: Dial Press, 1972), p. 214.

6. Giorgio Bonacina, *Obiettivo Italia: I Bombardamenti aerei delle città italiane dal 1940 al 1945,* 2nd ed. (Milan: Mursia, 1970), p. 159.

7. Quoted in Sir Charles Webster and Noble Frankland, *The Strategic Air Offensive Against Germany, 1939–1945,* 4 vols. (London: H. M. Stationery Office, 1961), II, 97.

8. *Ibid.*, II, 8.

9. Wesley Frank Craven and James Lea Cate, eds., *The Army Air Forces in World War II,* 7 vols. (Chicago: University of Chicago Press, 1948–58), II, 463.

10. Davis, p. 239.

11. Harold Macmillan, *The Blast of War, 1939–1945* (London: Macmillan, 1967), p. 309.

12. Davis, p. 239.

13. *Ibid.*, p. 319.

14. Craven and Cate, II, 705.

15. Quoted in Webster and Frankland, II, 190.

16. Lochner, p. 536.

17. Sir Arthur Harris, *Bomber Offensive,* (New York: Macmillan, 1947), p. 187.

18. Quoted in Craven and Cate, II, 317.

19. Francis L. Lowenheim, Harold D. Langley, and Manfred Jones, eds., *Roosevelt and Churchill: Their Secret Wartime Correspondence* (New York: Saturday Review Press, 1975), p. 493.

20. Quoted in Emmanuel d'Astier de la Vigerie, *Les dieux et les hommes* (Paris: Juilliard, 1952), p. 140.

21. Craven and Cate, II, 321.

22. Anthony Verrier, *The Bomber Offensive,* rev. ed. (London: Pan Books, 1974), p. 326.

23. Craven and Cate, III, 723.

24. *Ibid.,* p. 732.

25. Lochner, p. 367.

CHAPTER 10
JAPAN: ORDEAL BY FIRE

1. Wesley Frank Craven and James Lea Cate, eds., *The Army Air Forces in World War II,* 7 vols, (Chicago: University of Chicago Press, 1948–58), V, 27.

2. *Ibid.,* p. 88.

3. Martin Caidin, *A Torch to the Enemy: The Fire Raid on Tokyo* (New York: Ballantine Books, 1960), p. 117.

4. William Boyd Sinclair, *The Big Brothers: The Story of the B-29s* (San Antonio: Naylor, n.d.), pp. 87–89.

5. Quoted in Craven and Cate, V, 696, note.

CHAPTER 11
THE BOMBING WAR
IN RETROSPECT

1. J. M. Spaight, *Air Power and the Cities* (London: Longmans, Green, 1930), p. 227.

2. Sir Charles Webster and Noble Frankland, *The Strategic Air Offensive Against Germany, 1939–1945,* 4 vols. (London: H. M. Stationery Office, 1961), III, 310.

3. Antonio Monti, ed., *Giulio Douhet: Scritti inediti* (Florence: Scuola di Guerra Aerea, 1951), p. 111.

4. Webster and Frankland, III, 310.

5. Wesley Frank Craven and James Lea Cate, eds., *The Army Air Forces in World War II,* 7 vols. (Chicago: University of Chicago Press, 1948–58), V, 756.

6. Quoted in Constantine Fitzgibbon, *The Winter of the Bombs: The Story of the Blitz of London* (New York: Norton, 1958), p. 93.

7. Werner Girbig, ... *Im Anflug auf die Reichshauptstadt* (Stuttgart: Motorbuch-Verlag, 1970), p. 141.

8. Quoted in Martin Middlebrook, *The Battle of Hamburg: Allied Bomber Forces Against a German City in 1943* (New York: Scribners, 1980), p. 338.

9. Ronald Schaffer, "American Military Ethics in World War II: The Bombing of German Civilians," *Journal of American History,* LXVII, no. 2 (September 1980), 319.

10. Max Hastings, *Bomber Command* (New York: Dial Press, 1979), p. 170.

11. Middlebrook, p. 343.

12. Quoted in Hastings, p. 343.

13. Quoted in Schaffer, p. 331.

14. Quoted in Hastings, p. 344.

BIBLIO-
GRAPHICAL
NOTE

Just as a single book of modest length can only sketch the history of strategic bombing in the broadest strokes, so this essay on sources can only indicate the works that proved most useful in its preparation and that can take the reader further into various aspects of a vast and complex subject. The literature is vast and varied, but unfortunately it is not cataloged in a single, comprehensive bibliography. Still, there is an excellent point of departure for all researches into aerial warfare generally in Karl Köhler, *Bibliographie zur Luftkriegsgeschichte* (Frankfurt: Bernard and Graefe, 1966). For the period of World War I, there is a handy volume by Myron J. Smith, *World War I in the Air: A Bibliography and Chronology* (Metuchen, N.J.: Scarecrow Press, 1977).

Air power has been succinctly treated by Basil Collier in *A History of Air Power* (London: Weidenfeld and Nicolson, 1974) and by Robin Higham in his *Air Power: A Concise History* (New York: St. Martin's Press, 1972). The East German historian Olaf Groehler has written an ambitious history of aerial warfare: *Geschichte des Luftkriegs 1910 bis 1970* (Berlin: Militärverlag der Deutschen Demokratischen Republik, 1975). More recently still, R. J. Overy has produced a masterful treatise, *The Air War, 1939–1945* (New York: Stein and Day, 1981), which is full of sound judgments and useful insights into strategic bombing and carries a very rich bibliography. A number of authors have produced general works on bombing: Air Marshal Sir Robert Saundby, *Air Bombardment: The Story of Its Development* (New York: Harper and Row, 1961) draws heavily on the British experience, as does Alfred Price in *The Bomber in World War II* (London: Macdonald and Jane's, 1979). Policy implications of strategic bombing have found their historian in George H. Quester; his *Deterrence before Hiroshima: The Air Power Background to Modern Strategy* (New York: John Wiley, 1966) is widely cited.

There is a dearth of modern works on the general development of military aeronautics before 1914, but the void can be filled with studies for each of the major powers. For Great Britain, there is Charles F. Snowden Gamble, *The Air Weapon: British Military Aeronautics, 1783–1929* (London: Oxford University Press, 1931), and for Italy, the recent and beautifully illustrated work of Angelo Lodi, *Storia delle origini dell' aeronautica militare 1884–1915: Aerostieri dirigibilisti aviatori dell' esercito e della marina in Italia nel periodo pionieristico,* 2 vols. (Rome: Bizzari, 1976). Early developments in Germany are covered by a publication of the Kriegswissenschaftliche Abteilung of the Luftwaffe: *Die Militärluftfahrt bis zum Beginn des Weltkrieges 1914,* 2nd ed., 3 vols. (Frankfurt: E. S. Mittler, 1965–66), 66), and by John Morrow, *Building German Air Power, 1909–1914* (Knoxville: University of Tennessee Press, 1976). For Russia, there is V. A. Popov, *Istoria vozdukhoplavania i aviatsii v SSSR: Period do 1914g.* (Moscow: Izdatel'stvo oboronnoi promyshlennosti, 1944). There is no recent monograph on French military aviation before 1914, but the period is well covered in the recent general history by Gen. Charles Christienne, Gen. Pierre Lissarrague, and others, *Histoire de l'aviation militaire française* (Paris and Limoges: Charles-Lavauzelle, 1980).

During World War I, the Germans made the most extensive use of long-range bombing, and the literature on their efforts is correspondingly rich. The nearest thing to an official account is Gen. Ernst von Hoeppner, *Deutschlands Krieg in der Luft: Ein Rückblick auf die Entwicklung und die Leistungen unserer Heeres-Luftstreitkräfte im Weltkrieg* (Leipzig: K. F. Koehler, 1921). The bombing campaign against the British Isles is described by Raymond H. Fredette in *The Sky on Fire: The First Battle of Britain, 1917–1918 and the Birth of the Royal Air Force* (New York: Holt, Rinehart and Winston, 1966). The role of the zeppelin is covered by Douglas H. Robinson, *The Zep-*

pelin in Combat: A History of the German Naval Airship, 1912–1919 (London: G. T. Foulis, 1962), and by Ernest Dudley, *Monsters of the Purple Twilight: The True Story of the Life and Death of the Zeppelins* (London: George G. Harrap, 1960). G. W. Haddow and Peter M. Grosz treat the later raids in *The German Giants: The Story of the R Planes, 1914–1919* (London: Putnam, 1962).

The British strategic-bombing effort in the Great War is dealt with by Sir Walter Raleigh and H. A. Jones in *The War in the Air: Being the Story of the Part Played in the Great War by the Royal Air Force,* 6 vols. (Oxford: Clarendon Press, 1922–37), but should be supplemented by Neville Jones, *The Origins of Strategic Bombing: A Study of the Development of British Air Strategic Thought and Practice up to 1918* (London: William Kimber, 1973), and Barry D. Powers, *Strategy Without Slide Rule: British Air Strategy, 1914–1939* (London: Croom Helm, 1976). By far the best book on French bombing in the period is René Martel, *L'Aviation française de bombardement (des origines au 11 novembre 1918)* (Paris: Hartmann, 1939); while developments in Russia are recounted in A. D. Tsykin, *Ot 'Ili Muromtsa' do raketonostsa: Kratkii ocherk istorii dal'nei aviatsii* (Moscow: Voennizdat, 1975). Although there is no good monograph on Italian bombing in the Great War, these operations are treated in Felice Porro, *La guerra nell'aria,* 5th ed. (Milan: Corbaccio, 1940) and in Luigi Contini, *L'Aviazione italiana in guerra* (Milan: O. Marangoni, 1934). The modest achievements of the American bombing squadrons are well covered in James J. Hudson, *Hostile Skies: The Combat History of the Army Air Service in World War I* (Syracuse, N.Y.: Syracuse University Press, 1968).

The First World War also saw the emergence of air defenses, and their early development is treated in two general works: Ian V. Hogg, *Anti-Aircraft: A History of Air Defence* (London: Macdonald and Jane's, 1978); and Hans Baasch, *Die Entwicklung der Luftverteidigung mit terrestrischen Mittlen* (Zurich: Kommissionsverlag Beer, 1960). More detailed studies were made by the Luftwaffe's Kriegswissenschaftliche Abteilung, *Entwicklung und Einsatz der deutschen Flakwaffe und des Luftschutzes im Weltkriege* (Berlin: E. S. Mittler, 1938), and by Jean Lucas, *La D.C.A. de ses origines au 11 novembre 1918* (Paris: Baudinière, 1934).

A considerable number of books have appeared recently on air developments between the wars, although there are few syntheses treating all the great powers. H. Montgomery Hyde has dedicated six hundred pages to *British Air Policy Between the Wars, 1918–1939* (London: Heinemann, 1976), while Brian Bond has fitted air power into a broader context in *British Military Policy between the Two World Wars* (New York: Oxford University Press, 1980). Robin Higham has done much the same thing in his *Military Intellectuals in Britain, 1918–1939* (New Brunswick, N.J.: Rutgers University Press, 1966). Works on the Luftwaffe are legion, but perhaps the most useful for the interwar period are two volumes by Karl-Heinz Völker: *Die Entwicklung der militärische Luftfahrt in Deutschland, 1920–1933* (Stuttgart: Deutsche Verlags-Anstalt, 1964), and *Die deutsche Luftwaffe, 1933–1939* (Stuttgart: Deutsche Verlags-Anstalt, 1967). For France, there is Jean Hébrard, *Vingt-cinq années d'aviation militaire, 1920–1945,* 2 vols. (Paris: Albin-Michel, 1946), and a recent and incisive article by Robert J. Young, "The Strategic Dream: French Air Doctrine in the Inter-War Period, 1919–1939," *Journal of Contemporary History,* IX, no. 4 (October 1974), 57–76. Interwar developments in America are amply covered in a whole series of monographs sponsored by the U.S. Air Force. Two of the most useful are Frank Robert Futrell, *Ideas, Concepts, Doctrine: A History of Basic Thinking in the United States Air Force, 1907–1964* (Maxwell AFB: Air University, 1971), and Thomas H. Greer, *The Development of Air Doctrine in the Army Air Arm, 1917–1941* (Maxwell AFB: Air University, 1955).

The major air power figures of the 1920s and 1930s have attracted biographers. Lord Trenchard has been ably and sympathetically portrayed in Andrew Boyle, *Trenchard: Man of Vision* (London: William Collins, 1962). Billy Mitchell's life has been written several times, but the most informative work on air power matters is Alfred F. Hurley, *Billy Mitchell: Crusader for Air Power* (New York: Franklin Watts, 1964). There is as yet no satisfactory biography of Douhet or even a comprehensive study of his thought. He is known chiefly through the excerpts from his works published under the title *Command of the Air* (New York: Coward-McCann, 1942). An equally valuable compilation has been made by Antonio Monti, *Giulio Douhet: Scritti inediti* (Florence: Scuola di Guerra Aerea, 1951).

The apocalyptic literature of the era has been examined and conveniently cataloged by I. F. Clarke in *Voices Prophesying War, 1763–1984* (New York: Oxford University Press, 1966). The efforts made in the aftermath of the Great War to limit or prohibit aerial bombing were studied by M. W. Royse in his *Aerial Bombardment and the International Regulation of Warfare* (New York: Henry Vinal, 1928). The story is carried on into World War II by Geoffrey Best in *Humanity in Warfare* (New York: Columbia University Press, 1980) and by D. C. Watt's essay "Restraints on War in the Air Before 1945," in *Restraints on War: Studies in the Limitation of Armed Conflict* (New York: Oxford University Press, 1979), edited by Michael Howard.

The German air offensive against the British Isles in 1940–41 is an oft told story by now, but among the better accounts are the following: Derek Wood and Derek Dempster, *The Narrow Margin: The Battle of Britain and the Rise of Air Power, 1930–1940,* new ed. (London: Arrow Books, 1969); Basil Collier, *The Defence of the United Kingdom* (London: H. M. Stationery Office, 1957); and Theo Weber, *Die Luftschlacht um England (1940/1941)* (Wiesbaden: Flugwelt Verlag, 1956). The ordeal of the city of London is recorded by Constantine Fitzgibbon, *The Winter of the Bombs: The Story of the Blitz of London* (New York: W. W. Norton, 1958). Terence O'Brien in *Civil Defence* (London: H. M. Stationery Office, 1955) covers this aspect of the British resistance, while Richard M. Titmuss treats the stresses and strains on the British population in his *Problems of Social Policy* (London: H. M. Stationery Office, 1950).

The Allied air offensive against Germany—if indeed we may consider it a single offensive—may be studied in a variety of sources, beginning with the memoirs of the men who planned and led the offensive; for example, Gen. H. H. Arnold, *Global Mission* (New York: Harper and Row, 1949), and Sir Arthur Harris, *Bomber Offensive* (New York: Macmillan, 1947). Then there are the "official" histories: Sir Charles Webster and Noble Frankland, *The Strategic Air Offensive Against Germany, 1939–1945,* 4 vols. (London: H. M. Stationery Office, 1961); and Wesley Frank Craven and James Lea Cate, eds., *The Army Air Forces in World War II,* 7 vols. (Chicago: University of Chicago Press, 1948–58). There are many unofficial assessments, such as Anthony Verrier, *The Bomber Offensive,* rev. ed. (London: Pan Books, 1974); Gen. Haywood S. Hansell, Jr., *The Air Plan That Defeated Hitler* (Atlanta, Ga.: Higgins-McArthur/Longino & Porter, 1972); and Max Hastings, *Bomber Command: The Myths and Realities of the Strategic Bombing Offensive, 1939–1945* (New York: Dial Press, 1979). Finally, for those who want to draw their own conclusions from the raw data of history, that data are supplied in two notable compilations. The first is in the various reports of the American bombing survey conducted in both Germany and Japan immediately after the war, a mass that David MacIsaac has called "the Domesday Book of strategic bombing" (the British survey was much more modest). The most important reports, edited by MacIsaac, have been reissued recently as *United States Strategic Bombing Survey,* 10 vols. (New York: Garland, 1976). On the German side, the Bundesministerium für Vertriebene, Flüchtlinge und Kriegsgeschädigten has published its own study of the destruction of Germany: *Dokumente deutscher Kriegsschäden,* 3 vols. (Bonn, 1958–62).

The seesaw battle between Allied bombers and German defenders is ably recounted in Alfred Price, *Battle over the Reich* (London: Ian Allen, 1973), and by Franz Kurowski, *Der Luftkrieg über Deutschland* (Düsseldorf: Econ-Verlag, 1977). Alfred Price has also recounted the high-frequency aspects of the struggle in *Instruments of Darkness: The History of Electronic Warfare* (New York: Scribners, 1978). The German night-fighter effort is the subject of a recent work by Werner Held and Holger Nauroth, *Die deutsche Nachtjagd* (Stuttgart: Motorbuch-Verlag, n.d.). Horst-Adalbert Koch, *Flak: Die Geschichte der deutschen Flakartillerie, 1935–1945* (Bad Nauheim: H. H. Podzun, 1954), deals with antiaircraft defenses, as does Otto Wilhelm von Renz, *Deutsche Flugabwehr in 20 Jahrhundert* (Frankfurt: E. S. Mittler, 1960). Hans Rumpf, *Der hochrote Hahn* (Darmstadt: E. S. Mittler, 1952), describes the work of German fire brigades, while Erich Hampe covered civil defense in *Der zivile Luftschutz im zweiten Weltkrieg* (Frankfurt: Bernard and Graefe, 1963).

Air attacks on individual German cities have been the subjects of a considerable literature in German, with over seventy books and articles listed in Köhler's *Bibliographie.* David Irving, *The Destruction of Dresden* (London: William Kimber, 1963) is probably the best-known work of this type in English, but there are a number of others. Thomas M. Coffey has studied one of the U.S. Army Air Forces' most difficult missions in *Decision over Schweinfurt: The U.S. 8th Air Force Battle for Daylight Bombing* (New York: David McKay, 1977), and Ralph Barker has told the story of the great raid on Cologne: *The Thousand Plan: The Story of the First Thousand Bomber Raid on Cologne* (London: Chatto and Windus, 1965). Martin Middlebrook has described one of Bomber Command's least successful raids in *The Nuremburg*

Raid, 30–31 March 1944 (London: Allen Lane, 1973), and one of its most spectacular successes in *The Battle of Hamburg: Allied Bomber Forces Against a German City in 1943* (New York: Scribners, 1981). Finally, Berlin's fate in the bombing war is related in Werner Girbig, . . . *Im Anflug auf die Reichshauptstadt* (Stuttgart: Motorbuch-Verlag, 1970).

While Germany was the chief object of the Allied bombing raids, other countries also knew destruction from the air. The bombing of Italian cities figures in two works by Giorgio Bonacina: *Obiettivo Italia: I bombardamenti aerei delle città italiane dal 1940 al 1945* (Milan: Mursia, 1970), and *Le bombe dell'Apocalisse* (Milan: Fratelli Fabbri, 1973). Belgium's Commissariat General à la Protection Aérienne Passive has published *La Belgique sous les bombes, 1940–1945* (Brussels, 1948), and Johann Ulrich has chronicled the Austrian experience in *Luftkrieg über Österreich 1939–1945* (Vienna: Österreichischer Bundesverlag, 1967).

The air war against Japan has attracted few historians, and most of the documentation comes from the American side. Craven and Cate's *Army Air Forces* covers the Pacific war in volumes 4 and 5. William Boyd Sinclair has treated the B-29 and its role in *The Big Brothers: The Story of the B-29s* (San Antonio: Naylor, n.d.), and Wilbur H. Morison has chosen essentially the same theme in *Point of No Return* (New York: Playboy Paperbacks, 1980). The terrible fire raid on the Japanese capital in March 1945 is vividly recounted in Martin Caidin, *A Torch to the Enemy: The Fire Raid on Tokyo* (New York: Ballantine Books, 1960). On the Japanese side, most of the literature consists of survivors' narratives, but considerable information can be gleaned from the reports on Japan in the *U.S. Strategic Bombing Survey* previously cited. The organization and functioning of the Japanese air-defense system is described in *Defense of the Homeland and End of the War*, a compilation of studies prepared by Japanese officers after the war and published as volume 12 of *War in Asia and the Pacific*, edited by Donald S. Detwiler and Charles B. Burdick, 15 vols. (New York: Garland, 1980).

Shortly after the end of the war, a number of studies appeared— authored by Americans for the most part—seeking to sum up the effects of strategic bombing, both in its physical destructiveness and in the psychological stress it placed on those subjected to it. Horatio Bond prepared a comprehensive study on *Fire and the Air War* (Boston: National Fire Protection Association, 1946). Hilton P. Goss studied *Civilian Morale Under Aerial Bombardment, 1914–1939* (Maxwell AFB: Air University, 1952); Fred Iklé described *The Social Effects of Bombing* (Maxwell AFB: Air Research and Development Command, 1953); and Irving L. Janis offered a psychologist's analysis of *Air War and Emotional Stress: Psychological Studies of Bombing and Civilian Defense* (New York: McGraw-Hill, 1951).

But inevitably studies of the efficacy of strategic bombing gave rise to moral questions, producing a debate that continues to this day. It was probably J. M. Spaight who began the debate with his *Bombing Vindicated* (London: Geoffrey Bles, 1944), a reply to the few wartime critics. F. J. P. Veale took up the gauntlet after the war with his *Advance to Barbarism* (London: Thomson and Smith, 1948). Both J. F. C. Fuller and B. H. Liddell Hart were critical of strategic bombing in their postwar writings. P. M. S. Blackett subjected it to a searching reappraisal in his *Military and Political Consequences of Atomic Energy* (London: Turnstile Press, 1949), and so did Sir Gerald Dickens in *Bombing and Strategy: The Fallacy of Total War* (London: Sampson Low, Marston, 1947). In the United States, Stefan T. Possony cast the strategic bomber in the role of guarantor of peace and security in *Strategic Air Power: The Pattern of Dynamic Security* (Washington, D.C.: Infantry Journal Press, 1949), while Bernard Brodie took a much more nuanced view in his *Strategy in the Missile Age* (Princeton, N.J.: Princeton University Press, 1959). Not suprisingly, German treatments of the strategic bombing campaigns have been critical, such as Hans Rumpf, *The Bombing of Germany* (London: White Lion, 1963). And in Italy, Douhet's doctrines and their moral implications have been questioned by Raffaele Giacomelli in *Il terrorismo aerea nella teoria e nella realta* (Rome: Associazione Italiana d'Aerotecnica, 1945), and more recently by Gen. Amedeo Mecozzi in *Guerra agli inermi ed aviazione d'assalto* (Rome: Libreria all'Orologio, 1965).

INDEX